# KILLER WITH A BADGE

# KILLER WITH A BADGE

Chuck Hustmyre

BERKLEY BOOKS, NEW YORK

**THE BERKLEY PUBLISHING GROUP**
**Published by the Penguin Group**
**Penguin Group (USA) Inc.**
**375 Hudson Street, New York, New York 10014, USA**
Penguin Group (Canada), 10 Alcorn Avenue, Toronto, Ontario M4V 3B2, Canada
(a division of Pearson Penguin Canada Inc.)
Penguin Books Ltd., 80 Strand, London WC2R 0RL, England
Penguin Group Ireland, 25 St. Stephen's Green, Dublin 2, Ireland (a division of Penguin Books Ltd.)
Penguin Group (Australia), 250 Camberwell Road, Camberwell, Victoria 3124, Australia
(a division of Pearson Australia Group Pty. Ltd.)
Penguin Books India Pvt. Ltd., 11 Community Centre, Panchsheel Park, New Delhi—110 017, India
Penguin Group (NZ), Cnr. Airborne and Rosedale Roads, Albany, Auckland 1310, New Zealand
(a division of Pearson New Zealand Ltd.)
Penguin Books (South Africa) (Pty.) Ltd., 24 Sturdee Avenue, Rosebank, Johannesburg 2196, South Africa

Penguin Books Ltd., Registered Offices: 80 Strand, London WC2R 0RL, England

KILLER WITH A BADGE

A Berkley Book / published by arrangement with the author

PRINTING HISTORY
Berkley mass-market edition / November 2004


Cover design by Judith Murello
Book design by Kristin del Rosario


For information address: The Berkley Publishing Group,
a division of Penguin Group (USA) Inc.,
375 Hudson Street, New York, New York 10014.

ISBN: 0-425-19994-0

BERKLEY®
Berkley Books are published by The Berkley Publishing Group,
a division of Penguin Group (USA) Inc.,
375 Hudson Street, New York, New York 10014.
BERKLEY is a registered trademark of Penguin Group (USA) Inc.
The "B" design is a trademark belonging to Penguin Group (USA) Inc.

PRINTED IN THE UNITED STATES OF AMERICA

10 9 8 7 6 5 4 3 2 1

# ACKNOWLEDGMENTS

I would like to thank everyone who helped me with this project, especially my editor, Tom Colgan, and my agent, Jim Cypher, both of whom have read and reread, edited and re-edited this book without complaint and have always been around to answer any question of mine, no matter what the hour or how dumb the question.

I would also like to express my profound sympathy to the Vu and Williams families. It has been an honor to get to know, at least in some tiny part, Ha, Cuong, and Ronnie.

In researching this case there were four people without whose help I could not have written this book. To them I owe a huge debt. They are Eddie Rantz, Glen Woods, Mary Williams, and Baton Rouge attorney and all-around-get-things-done-guy Joe Long. The first round is always on me at Lafitte's Blacksmith Shop.

# AUTHOR'S NOTE

Following the murders at the Kim Anh restaurant, the New Orleans Police Department, under the leadership of Chief Richard Pennington, completely overhauled their recruiting, screening, selection, and officer performance evaluation programs. They have also aggressively weeded out the unfit officers who slipped in during the bad old days.

Today, the NOPD is a different department from what it was in the early 1990s. Like all police departments, there are still problems, but under Chief Pennington and his successor, Chief Eddie Compass, the department has tackled its problems head-on.

I was very proud to work with many great New Orleans cops during my law enforcement career and would not hesitate to go through a door with any one of them.

Chuck Hustmyre
Special Agent, ATF (retired)

# ONE

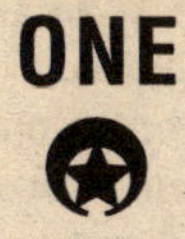

**New Orleans—Saturday, March 4, 1995, 1:55 A.M.**

**Just** moments after the sound of the last gunshot fades away, twenty-three-year-old Chau Vu huddles close to the floor of the walk-in cooler inside her family's Vietnamese restaurant. Shivering in the darkness, she wraps her thin arms around her chest to try to keep warm and prays for the police to arrive.

After what seems like an eternity, Chau (pronounced Chow) sees car headlights in the parking lot. She steps onto a metal rack to get a better vantage point and peers through the glass cooler doors. A police car glides past the front of the restaurant, but Chau is afraid to move. She is terrified that Antoinette Frank might be in that police car.

Narcotics detectives Wayne Farve and Reginald Jacques are working an off-duty security detail just a couple of miles from the Kim Anh restaurant. They are earning extra pay by patrolling a set of apartment buildings on Michoud Boulevard near the sprawling NASA complex.

In 1995, New Orleans has the lowest paid police department of any comparable-sized city in the country. Almost all New Orleans police officers have to work off-duty security details just to earn enough money to survive.

The two narcotics detectives are in Jacques's unmarked car, a two-door, white Pontiac Grand Prix. At 1:55 A.M., they are headed to a twenty-four-hour gas station for a shot of caffeine when their radios crackle with the call of a 34-S (a shooting). The dispatcher says that a Vietnamese male has been shot on Bullard Avenue near Chef Menteur Highway.

Farve turns to his partner. "You want to check it out?"

Jacques nods. "It's right around the corner."

Farve glances at the digital clock in the dash. "What I want to know is why the fuck people are out shooting each other at this time of night."

They roll toward Bullard.

Less than a minute later, the dispatcher comes back on the air and advises that she is upgrading the call to a 108 (police officer needs help). "Be advised that a police officer is supposed to have been shot and is down on the scene," she says. "The location is the four thousand block of Bullard."

Jacques punches the accelerator to the floor. A blue Dashmaster police light is wedged between the dashboard and the windshield, but with almost no traffic on the road, he doesn't bother to turn it on. At night the blue glare ricocheting off the windshield is more trouble than the light is worth.

"Where on Bullard did she say?" Jacques asks.

"Somewhere in the four thousand block."

"That Vietnamese restaurant is the only place it could be. Everything else is closed."

"A policeman works a detail there," Farve says.

"Oh, shit."

The Kim Anh restaurant, at 4952 Bullard Avenue, is a

three-thousand-square-foot, single-story building with brick sidewalls, a glass front, and a blue tin roof. Tucked away in the left front corner of the building is a small convenience store, where the Vus sell soda, beer, snacks, and a few grocery items. Along the back wall of the store are several glass doors, behind which are racks of shelves for soft drinks and other items that have to be stored cold. Just behind the racks is a walk-in cooler, which can be accessed through two doors: one in the convenience store and one in the kitchen.

The Kim Anh is located in eastern New Orleans—an area called New Orleans East—and is in the police department's 7th District. Several 7th District officers take turns working an off-duty security detail at the restaurant.

As they head west on Chef Menteur, Detectives Farve and Jacques rocket past a dark vehicle with its emergency flashers going. Jacques turns onto Bullard. Because of the grass median, he has to pass the restaurant, then whip his Grand Prix through a tight U-turn before pulling into the parking lot. Jacques stops his car at the left front corner of the building. Only rookies pull up to the front door at a shooting. Farve has been a New Orleans police officer for fifteen years. Jacques has spent the last six years in narcotics. They know what they're doing.

Three minutes after the first call came out, Farve keys his radio. "25–52," he says, giving his radio call sign, "put me on the scene with 25–53." Jacques is 25–53. The two off-duty detectives are the first police officers to arrive.

The scene is quiet, too quiet. It's eerie, almost unnerving. Farve and Jacques have been to a lot of shootings. There is usually plenty going on. People scattering, bloody victims lying on the ground, someone running around with a gun—that's the norm, so it surprises the two detectives that absolutely nothing is going on at the Kim Anh restaurant. The parking lot is deserted, and a sinister silence hangs over the entire place. Whatever is going on is happening inside.

There isn't any question as to what Farve and Jacques are going to do. Waiting for backup is not an option. Although the information is sketchy—no details as to the number of shooters or where they were—the two detectives know one of their brothers is probably down inside the restaurant. Every cop carries a radio, even for off-duty security details. Since the officer who is in trouble hasn't come on the air and given any additional information about the situation, there is a very good chance he is badly hurt.

Farve and Jacques have to cover both the front and the back of the restaurant.

"I got the front," Farve says.

Jacques nods and starts circling around the left side of the building toward the back.

Farve draws his gun and cuts across the open space between their unmarked narcotics car and the building. He hugs the windowed front wall and starts sliding along its length toward the front door.

From her hiding place inside the cooler, Chau Vu sees a second car slide into the parking lot. It's smaller than the first car and doesn't look anything like a police car, but unlike the marked patrol car she just saw, this one pulls to a stop in the parking lot. It sits off to one side of the building, but its headlights remain angled toward the front door. Two men climb out. Because the glare from the car headlights partially obscures them, Chau can't tell if they are wearing police uniforms. Both men carry guns—and radios. Now Chau knows for sure. These are real policemen, and they are here to save her.

She throws open the cooler door on the convenience store side of the building, then bolts through the store toward the dining room. As she runs past the small L-shaped bar that sits between the store and the restaurant, she glances down and once again sees, wedged behind the bar where he fell, the bloody body of a uniformed New Orleans policeman. It is twenty-five-year-old Ronnie Williams.

At the edge of her field of vision, Chau detects movement inside the dining room. Terrified, she looks up. Antoinette Frank, a twenty-four-year-old, off-duty New Orleans police officer, stands in the shadows of the dining room. She has been waiting for Chau to emerge from her hiding place. She has a .38-caliber revolver tucked into the waistband of her jeans.

Yvonne Farve picks up the 108 call on her radio. Yvonne is Wayne Farve's wife and a detective with eighteen years on the job. She is assigned to the fugitive unit and is also working an off-duty security detail. She is in her uniform, driving an unmarked police car—a four-door Ford Crown Victoria—and patrolling an upscale neighborhood. Even though the Farves have this Friday night off, they have to work two separate details to earn enough money to pay their bills.

When Yvonne Farve hears that the location of the call is a restaurant on Bullard near Chef Menteur, she knows immediately it is the Kim Anh and that a policeman regularly works a detail there. She flips on the blue police light mounted to the dashboard and makes the scene in just a couple of minutes. Because she came down Bullard from the north, the opposite direction from her husband, she is able to turn straight into the parking lot without having to pass it and make a U-turn.

She is the second unit on the scene. The car her husband is in is parked at the left front corner of the building, so she pulls her Ford to a stop on the right front corner to cover the opposite side. A marked patrol car sits backed into the shadows outside an insurance company office next to the restaurant, but it doesn't look to Yvonne as if it is there in response to the call.

Police officers responding to an emergency call—especially a 108—don't take the time to back their cars into parking spaces. The patrol car at the insurance building is dark and silent. Yvonne hears sirens close by. Other units are on the way.

Detective Wayne Farve is only a few yards away from the front entrance, a double set of glass doors, when he hears the sound of squealing tires. He glances over his right shoulder as another car rolls into the parking lot. There's a blue strobe light popping on the dashboard. It is his wife's unmarked police car.

Farve sees movement inside the dining room. As the front door bangs open, he tenses and jerks his gun up into a combat position. A young Vietnamese woman charges through the door and runs into the parking lot. A second later, a young black woman darts through the door. She's only a dozen feet behind the Vietnamese girl. It almost looks like she's chasing her.

The second woman looks familiar. Farve recognizes her. He doesn't know her name but knows she's a police officer assigned to the 7th District. He angles away from the building and grabs her arm. "Where are they?" he says.

"They're in the back," the policewoman says. "Three of them wearing ski masks."

"Where's the police officer?" Farve demands.

The policewoman looks terrified. She glances at Chau, then at Farve. "By the bar," she tells him.

"Is he hurt?"

She nods.

Across the parking lot, Farve sees his wife step out of her police car. The Vietnamese girl runs toward her. He knows Yvonne will get control of her and find out what happened. He turns again toward the door. According to what the female police officer just told him, there is a wounded cop inside the building and three masked gunmen. Jacques has the back and isn't going to let anyone get out. Yvonne has the front. Farve takes a deep breath and rushes inside.

Chau knows she has to get away from Antoinette Frank. The farther away she gets, the better. In the parking lot, Chau passes the first policeman and runs toward the car he and his partner drove up in. The headlights are still on. Both doors are open. But when she reaches the car, she finds it empty. There's no one there to help her.

She spots a second car in the parking lot. It's big and white and looks like a police car. A blue light flashes behind the windshield. A woman jumps out of the driver's seat. She is wearing a police uniform. Chau runs toward the second car and dives into Yvonne Farve's arms.

As Farve sees her husband disappear inside the restaurant, she hugs the hysterical Vietnamese girl tightly. "Just calm down," she says. "Just calm down and tell me what happened."

Seconds later, Frank runs up to Yvonne Farve and Chau. "Chau, Chau, what happened with your brother and sister?" she asks.

Chau turns her tear-streaked face away from Yvonne Farve for just a moment and says, "You were there. You know everything. Why are you asking me that question?"

Frank eases closer to Chau. "Don't worry, I'll take care of you," she whispers.

But the frightened Vietnamese girl edges away. "Antoinette, why my brother and sister get killed . . . and Ronnie?"

"I don't know," Frank mumbles. Her eyes dart back and forth between Yvonne Farve and Chau Vu; then she backs away. In the initial chaos at the crime scene, no one notices as Frank slips back inside the restaurant.

# TWO

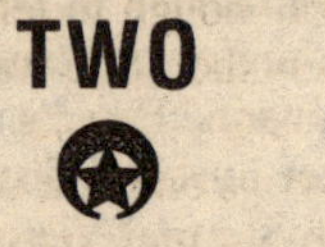

**The** first thing Wayne Farve sees when he charges through the door and into the dining room is Ronnie Williams's body wedged behind the bar. Tactically, Farve knows he's in a bad spot. His next decision is a toss-up: go to the aid of the downed officer, or continue to look for and try to neutralize the threat from the armed suspects who might still lurk inside the restaurant. There is no clear-cut right answer.

Wayne Farve makes his decision. He runs to the fallen officer. Williams is facedown behind the L-shaped bar, and Farve can see that the damage to the back of the officer's head and neck is tremendous. Brain matter has oozed out onto the floor. Holding his gun in one hand, Farve reaches down with his other hand and presses two fingers against the side of Williams's bloody neck, hoping to find a pulse. He feels nothing.

Farve jerks his radio from his gunbelt. "25-52, I'm at the 108, at the restaurant. I need EMS, code three. I've got an officer down—he's been shot."

In the parking lot, other police units begin arriving. Chau

struggles to tell Yvonne Farve what has happened, but she is so upset she keeps switching back and forth between English and Vietnamese. Yvonne strokes her hair and soothes her as best she can. In the policewoman's comforting embrace, Chau relaxes enough to tell Yvonne that her brother and sister have been shot. She wants someone to check on them.

Yvonne Farve keeps one arm draped over Chau's slender shoulders and leads her back into the restaurant. As soon as they cross the threshold into the dining room, Yvonne sees her husband. He's on his knees, bending over the body of a policeman. The black woman, the one who came running out after the Vietnamese girl, is standing behind him.

Wayne Farve hears the door behind him swing open. When he spins around, he sees Yvonne and the Vietnamese girl walking in. He also sees the female police officer standing right behind him, peering over his shoulder. He didn't even hear her come in.

As soon as Antoinette sees Yvonne and Chau walk in, she runs into the kitchen.

Yvonne Farve gets her first look at the officer on the floor. He's in uniform. He's obviously been working a detail, usually a safe way to make extra money. Rarely on a detail did you ever have to make an arrest. The mere presence of a cop in uniform was almost always enough to deter anyone from starting trouble. Now this officer was facedown on the dirty floor behind the bar, his head and upper body swimming in a pool of blood.

Yvonne Farve creeps over to her husband. Chau clings to her side. "How is he?" Yvonne asks.

Wayne Farve just shakes his head.

Chau pleads with the two officers to please check on her brother and sister. "They are in the kitchen."

The two Farves lead Chau into the back.

As Yvonne crosses into the kitchen, the young black woman, whom she thinks is a witness, is already there. The woman tries to run past Farve toward the dining room. Yvonne grabs her arm and pulls her to a stop. "Where are you going?"

"I'm a twenty-six, I'm a twenty-six," the woman says, giving Farve the New Orleans code for a police officer. It strikes Yvonne as a bit unnerving to have this plainclothes female officer running around the crime scene, popping up everywhere, and it certainly isn't by-the-book procedure for securing a crime scene, but there are just too many victims to check on and there is the very real possibility that the perpetrators might still be in the building, so Yvonne doesn't give much thought to the woman. She'll have to deal with her later. As soon as Farve lets her go, the woman dashes back into the dining room.

"She appeared trapped," Yvonne Farve later recalled.

In the kitchen, the cramped space beside the stove is a slaughterhouse. Chau's seventeen-year-old brother, Cuong, lies on his left side, his sandaled feet just brushing his sister's arm and head. A puddle of blood from his bullet-riddled body has spread four feet across the floor and mingles with the blood of his sister. Ha Vu, Chau's twenty-four-year-old big sister, is still crouched on her knees. She wears a pink blouse and white pants. Her porcelain face presses against the tiles of the floor, barely peeking out from beneath her thick mop of black hair. Her hands rest beside her head. There is slightly less blood around her body. She died more quickly than her brother.

"Both of them had their hands together," Wayne Farve said later. "It was like they'd been praying when they died."

Yvonne lets go of Chau and kneels down on the bloody floor. She checks Cuong and Ha for signs of life but finds none.

With the final confirmation that her brother and sister are dead, Chau again slips into hysteria. "She just grabbed on to me," Yvonne Farve said. "So I held her."

There are no masked gunmen.

Wayne Farve steps back into the dining area and radios his partner to come to the front. Then he calls headquarters and tells them he has a "triple 30." A signal 30 is New Orleans police code for a homicide. He asks the command desk to make the proper notifications: supervisors, homicide detectives, and the coroner.

Yvonne Farve guides Chau to the back of the dining room and sits her down at one of the tables. Frank hovers nearby. As Yvonne tries to soothe the frightened girl, Frank leans closer to Chau. "Where did you hide?" she asks. "Where were you at?"

Chau doesn't answer. She doesn't want to tell Antoinette where she had hidden. She's afraid that one day Frank will come back. She's afraid that one day she'll have to hide again. From Chau's perspective, it is a distinct possibility. It has only been five years since she came from Vietnam, and in her native country no one trusts the government, especially the police. Here, in the dining room of her family's restaurant, among several police officers, stands one of the two people who have just murdered her brother, her sister, and a fellow policeman, yet Antoinette Frank is still free. No one has even spoken to Antoinette about what she has done. Chau is terrified, she is confused, she is heartbroken.

What Chau doesn't yet understand is that the other police officers are there to help her. They want to find the person who killed Ha and Cuong Vu, and they desperately want to find the person who gunned down Officer Ronnie Williams. It just doesn't occur to them that that person could be one of their own.

When Reginald Jacques comes through the front door, he takes one look at Ronnie Williams lying on the floor behind the bar and rushes toward the fallen officer. "Let's get him out, let's get him out," he shouts.

Farve understands. Jacques wants to shove the officer's body into his car and head across town to Charity Hospital.

Police officers don't wait for ambulances for wounded comrades. They throw them into the backseat of the nearest police car and race to the emergency room. One advantage to living in one of the most violent cities in America is that Charity Hospital, the hospital that caters to the poor and the uninsured, has one of the best trauma units in the country. Charity's emergency room staff is used to treating gunshot victims. They do it every day.

As Jacques bends toward Williams, Farve lays a hand on his partner's shoulder. "There's nothing we can do for him. He's gone."

Farve stares at the policeman's body. Two days. That's how long it has been since Wayne Farve met Ronnie Williams. Wednesday night Farve and Jacques had been working their usual detail when a 7th district unit kicked in a chase just off of Chef Highway. The detectives rolled to back up the patrolman. When they arrived in the area, they found Ronnie Williams and another 7th district officer named Stanley Morlier chasing a suspect on foot. By the time Farve and Jacques caught up to the two patrolmen, the suspect had jumped into a canal to try to get away. Williams stood at the edge of the water, shouting at the crook who was slogging toward the far side. "You better get your ass out of there and not make me come in and get you." But words alone weren't enough to make the suspect turn around, so Williams dove in after him and dragged him back.

Now that same patrolman, who had shown such tenacity to a couple of veteran detectives, lay dead on the floor.

When Farve asks Antoinette Frank for a better description of the shooters, she repeats the same story from earlier: She saw three black males wearing ski masks running from the restaurant. The sole detail Frank adds is that the suspects jumped into a dark-colored car and fled down Bullard. Farve keys his radio and advises the command desk of the description of the phantom gunmen and the suspect vehicle. He also tells the dispatcher that he and Jacques saw a dark sedan, possibly a Toyota Camry, headed west on Chef with its hazard lights flashing. The dispatcher relays Farve's information citywide.

**Responding** to the 108 call on Bullard, Officer Ernest Bringier, a 7th District patrolman working a one-man car, spots a dark sedan with its emergency flashers on headed west on Chef Highway.

Bringier is assigned to the 3rd platoon, working the night watch—10:35 P.M. to 7 A.M. It is Bringier's platoon that relieved the second watch, including Officers Ronald Williams and Antoinette Frank.

Bringier is headed east when he sees the car. He has heard the description the dispatcher put out about a possible suspect vehicle, a small dark car with flashing hazard lights.

By the time Bringier spins his police car around and advises the dispatcher that he has spotted a vehicle that might be connected to the shooting, the sedan is already starting to pull toward the shoulder. Bringier flicks on his police lights and pulls up behind the car. When he gets closer, he sees that the car is a Nissan Stanza with what appears to be one male occupant. Bringier keys his radio again and calls out the car's description and license plate number to the dispatcher. He also gives his location.

As a second police car glides to a stop behind him to back him up, Bringier gets on his public address system and calls to the driver of the Nissan to step out of his car. The driver is a black male, six feet, two inches tall and weighs somewhere around 250 pounds. He has no gold teeth. Radio traffic from the command desk, based on a 911 call from one of the victims, mentioned something about a short black male with a lot of gold teeth.

Bringier and the other officer approach the driver. The

man doesn't appear nervous. Instead, he is calm and cooperative. Bringier asks for his driver's license and runs his name through the dispatcher. The man has no warrants and a clean record.

The two officers explain the situation. They tell the man that they are looking for suspects in the shooting of a police officer and that his car matches the description of a vehicle seen in the area of the shooting and at the time of the shooting.

The man raises his hands. "You want to search me, search my car, that's fine with me. I don't want no trouble, Officer."

Bringier barely manages to conceal his disappointment as he searches the man's car and finds nothing—no guns, no ski masks, no money.

He thanks the man for his cooperation; then the two officers climb back into their patrol cars and continue to cruise the area, looking for three men in a dark car.

**Renee** Braddy is watching TV when her boyfriend, Rogers LaCaze, bursts through the front door. They share an apartment at 6801 Cindy Place, number 211. The apartment is just five minutes from the Kim Anh restaurant. LaCaze makes so much noise Renee is afraid he'll wake the baby. She can tell something is wrong with him. LaCaze doesn't talk, just walks straight into the kitchen, picks up the phone, and dials a number. After listening to the handset for a second, he punches in more numbers, then hangs up. He is paging someone. Whatever is wrong probably has to do with Antoinette Frank. Since LaCaze got shot in November of last year, he and Frank have been spending an awful lot of time together.

LaCaze paces around the apartment for a couple of minutes. Then his cell phone rings. As he answers it, he walks down the hall toward the bedroom.

It's LaCaze's brother, Michael, calling. "What's up?" Michael says.

"I need you to come pick me up," Rogers tells him.

"Why?"

"Something got fucked up. Me and Antoinette did something, and it got all fucked up."

"What'd you do?"

"I can't talk about it on the phone. I need you to come pick me up."

"All right," Michael says.

Five minutes later, Rogers LaCaze stands outside his apartment building waiting for his brother. He lurks in a shadow cast by a streetlight. As he waits, he tries calling Antoinette Frank's cell phone several times but doesn't get an answer.

His brother's gray Cutlass Supreme rolls around the corner.

Rogers steps out to the street as his brother eases to a stop against the curb. He climbs into the passenger seat. "I need to stay at your apartment tonight. Maybe for a couple of days."

Michael LaCaze steers toward the interstate. "Why, what happened?"

"Something went down on Bullard. Involving that restaurant where Antoinette and those other cops work that detail."

"What went down?"

"It's a Vietnamese restaurant. They were supposed to have a lot of money in there." Rogers tells his brother that he and Frank planned to rob the restaurant. She worked there. She knew the ins and outs, knew the people who worked there, including the cop working the detail. "He always be fucking her over. Those Vietnamese do whatever he say, so Antoinette doesn't get to make any money working that detail."

"What the fuck did you do?"

"She went to the door first and got their attention. I went

in behind her and shot the cop. She was supposed to take care of all the others, but somebody got away and hid. It was the girl who runs the place. She saw us."

"Where's Antoinette?" Michael asks.

"She dropped me off by Renee's, then went to the Seventh District to play it off."

"How is she gonna play it off?"

"Act like she was a witness or something. She's going to tell them some dudes in ski masks did it."

"What's she going to say about you?"

"She better not say anything about me," Rogers says.

**The** New Orleans Police Homicide Division is inside the Detective Bureau, on the third floor of police headquarters at 715 South Broad Street. Homicide detectives are the elite of the elite. They pride themselves on their tailored suits, their unflappable composure, and their iron stomachs. A detective, no matter how good his or her sleuthing skills, who squirms at the sight of blood or who barfs after catching a whiff of a rotting corpse on a hot summer day gets bumped quickly to another division. The detective will be following up on bicycle thefts, or investigating assaults on meter maids, because a detective who can't stomach the sight of death in all its grisly forms isn't going to make it in Homicide.

For the Homicide Division, whose business is death, business is good—very good. The week ending Saturday, March 4, 1995 has been a busy one. Before the murders at the Kim Anh, the toll of death and destruction for the week stands at eighteen people murdered and nine wounded.

Sergeant Eddie Rantz commands one of the three shifts, or platoons, in the Homicide Division. The 3rd platoon has come on at 11:00 Friday night and is scheduled to work until 7:00 Saturday morning. Three hours into their shift, most of the 3rd platoon homicide detectives are in the office doing paperwork or following up leads with phone calls. It's not easy to get in touch with normal witnesses—people with jobs, kids, and a regular life—at two o'clock in the morning.

"We were sitting around waiting for somebody to die," Sergeant Rantz said.

They didn't have long to wait.

Just before 2 A.M., the bell rings—a homicide cop's phrase for a murder call. The command desk advises Sergeant Rantz about a shooting in New Orleans East. "I didn't think it was any big deal," Rantz said. He has worked more than a thousand homicides and doesn't get excited very easily. "I was waiting for the command desk to give us more details. If the victim didn't die, then it wasn't going to be our call."

A few minutes later, the command desk calls back. The dispatcher advises Rantz that the shooting in the East was at a restaurant and that it involved a police officer. Rantz stands up and slips into his suit coat and straightens his tie. Across the cramped office space he spots veteran homicide detective Marco Demma hammering away at a typewriter. "Marco," he shouts.

The detective looks up.

Rantz nods toward the door. "Come take a ride."

"What's up?"

"We got a twenty-six involved in a shooting."

Demma stands and shrugs on his jacket.

New Orleans Police Department policy requires that a homicide supervisor, a sergeant or above, handle all police officer–involved shootings. The department defines "police officer–involved" as any shooting in which a police officer either shoots someone or is shot, regardless of whether or not it results in death.

Rantz has just hit the interstate heading east when the dispatcher calls on the Homicide Division's private radio channel. She tells him that an officer has been shot at the restaurant. Rantz shoves his Kojak light onto the dash and steps harder on the gas pedal.

As Rantz's unmarked police car crests the High Rise, the Interstate 10 bridge that arcs high enough over the Inner Harbor Canal to allow cargo ships to pass underneath, the command desk calls again. The dispatcher notifies him that a police officer and two civilians are dead on the scene.

Rantz tells the dispatcher to order every detective who is working to respond to the scene. It is going to be a long night.

# THREE

**Rogers** LaCaze's brother lives in an apartment in the small town of Gretna, on the west bank of the Mississippi River, at 636 Farmington Place, number 100. Michael LaCaze, two years older than his brother, is no stranger to violence, which is one of the reasons he lives on the ground floor of his apartment building. He was shot in the back in 1994. The bullet that tore through his spine left him paralyzed from the waist down. At the time of the Kim Anh murders, Michael is on probation following a 1992 conviction for illegally carrying a firearm.

Michael's fuel gauge shows empty as he parks in front of his apartment just after 2:00 A.M. He has a girlfriend who works back across the river. He's supposed to pick her up at around three o'clock. Confined to a wheelchair, it's a hassle for Michael to get out of his car to pump gas.

Inside the apartment, Rogers is nervous. He paces the floor. He tries a few more times to reach Frank on her cell phone but gets no answer. What is she doing, what has she told the police, what do they know about him?—these questions and others flood through LaCaze's mind. His brother's small apartment seems almost like a prison cell. The walls squeeze tighter. Rogers is going stir-crazy. He volunteers to go put some gas in his brother's car.

Just down the street, two blocks from Michael's apartment, is an all-night Chevron gas station. Rogers hops into his brother's Cutlass Supreme and drives to the gas station.

The Chevron has eight pumps. He coasts to a stop beside pump number two. Standing at the pump, LaCaze fishes through his pockets and pulls out a leather wallet. It isn't his wallet. It belongs to the cop he shot—the dead cop. LaCaze flips open the wallet and digs out a Chevron credit card. At 2:29 A.M., Rogers LaCaze shoves Officer Ronald Williams's Chevron card into the credit card slot in pump number two. The card reader feeds the data it pulls from the magnetic strip on the back of the card into a central computer. The LED screen built into the face of the pump flashes the word "AUTHORIZING . . ." LaCaze waits.

Because Officer Ronald Williams is a decent, tax-paying citizen with a job and good credit history, and because the central computer is unaware that at that very moment paramedics on the other side of the city are struggling to load his bloody corpse into an ambulance and rush him to Charity Hospital in a futile attempt to save his life, the computer takes only a few seconds to authorize the purchase of gas with Williams's card.

Inside the Chevron gas station, late-night cashier John Ross walks toward the back of the store when he hears the printer under the cash register start spitting out receipt tape. When someone uses a credit card at any one of the eight pumps, the computer system records the transaction by first printing a transaction authorization number.

When Ross hears the printer, he steps back to the register and looks outside at the pump area. He sees a guy he's known for at least a few months standing beside pump number two. The guy is pumping gas into the gray Cutlass. There are no other customers. Ross recognizes the man and the car. He doesn't know the man's name, but he knows both him and his brother as regular customers and has talked to them both on several occasions. Referring to Michael LaCaze, Ross later said, "I pumped gas for him at the station once. He came one day and he couldn't get out of the car."

When Ross sees who is at the pump, he is surprised. He's never seen the guy with a credit card before. The gas station attendant thumbs the button on the intercom. "When did you get a credit card?" he jokes.

LaCaze looks toward the store. He just smiles and shrugs his shoulders. After pumping $15.29 worth of gas into the car, he slides behind the wheel and drives back to his brother's apartment.

**In** the dining room of the Kim Anh restaurant, Detective Yvonne Farve huddles with Chau at a back table. When the detective asks her what happened, Chau tells her that a short black man with gold teeth came into the restaurant twice that night. The second time he came in was when they started shooting everybody.

"Do you know his name?" Farve asks.

Chau shakes her head.

Yvonne Farve has heard the off-duty female police officer, the one wandering around the restaurant, mention three men in ski masks. "Who was he with?" she asks Chau.

Chau hesitates, then nods at Frank, who stands just a few feet away. "He came in with Antoinette."

Farve turns and looks at the police officer. Her jaw drops.

Yvonne Farve pulls Chau out of the chair she has been

sitting in and moves her to a different table, farther away from Frank. She understands exactly what the frightened young woman is saying. Officer Antoinette Frank isn't a witness. She is one of the killers.

**By** the time Chau tells Yvonne Farve what happened, the restaurant is swarming with police officers. Someone says that the new police chief is on the way to the scene. Superintendent Richard Pennington was sworn in just five months before, after being hired away from his post as assistant chief of the Washington, D.C., Metro Police. The new mayor of New Orleans, Marc Morial, scoured the country looking for someone who could curb the skyrocketing crime rate and bring honor, integrity, and a much-needed morale boost to a police department rocked by a number of sensational scandals during the past several years.

The entire Vice Squad had been disbanded and several of its members either fired or sent to prison for corruption. The Internal Affairs Division, the cops who police the police, had also been disbanded for incompetence. The FBI had taken over the NOPD's internal investigations. Then in April 1994, Officer Weldon Williams was arrested for dragging Mitchell Ceasar and another man into a field and shooting them with his 9 mm duty weapon. Ceasar died; the other man lived.

In December 1994, the FBI announced the arrest of ten New Orleans cops on federal drug trafficking charges. The feds also arrested veteran officer Len Davis for murder. Then in early 1995, just before the Kim Anh murders, the Justice Department announced that New Orleans had the previous year's highest per capita homicide rate and had earned the dubious distinction of being the murder capital of the nation.

Although the number one designation for murder stung the mayor and other city officials, New Orleans's reputation for murder was nothing new. In his 1952 book, *Ready to Hang: Seven Famous New Orleans Murders* (Harper & Brothers, NY), Robert Tallant recorded the observations of a visitor to New Orleans from New England, who wrote to his wife in 1849, "The corpse of a murdered man can lie in a New Orleans street for three days without the citizens paying it the slightest notice. Only the odor of decomposition stirs them into action."

**While** he waits for Homicide to arrive, Wayne Farve does what he can to contain the crime scene. All of the 7th District patrol cops who are on duty respond to the Kim Anh crime scene, but most of them are so upset that they are almost useless. "Everybody who worked with Ronnie was screwed up in the head," Farve said.

Frank is no help either, but Farve notices something different about her reaction. "She looked like a caged fucking rat," he said later. Frank paces the restaurant, looking for a way out. At one point, she rushes into the kitchen but finds Wayne there. "You have to get back up front and stay there," he tells her. "You can't leave."

In the dining room, Frank tries to slip out the front door, but Yvonne blocks her path. The detective tells Frank to sit down, that she has to wait for Homicide to get there. Frank slumps into a chair across the room from Yvonne and Chau.

Yvonne catches Wayne's eye and nods for him to come closer. She doesn't want to leave Chau alone. When Wayne gets to her, Yvonne shoots a glance at Frank, then pushes her lips close to her husband's ear and whispers, "This little girl says that bitch killed all these people."

**The** reason three off-duty detectives arrived at the scene before any of the working patrol cars from the 7th District is that Bullard Avenue sits on the far eastern edge of the city. Although the city limits stretch some ten miles past Bullard and reach out into Lake Pontchartrain, Bullard Avenue, with few exceptions, is the last outpost of civilization. From there to the parish line—because of its strong Catholic roots Louisiana is divided into parishes instead of counties—there are probably more alligators than people.

Most New Orleans East residents live on the western side of the 7th District, so most of the police calls are there. The East, as it is often referred to, is a strange mix of mansions and federally subsidized Section 8 housing. During the 1960s and '70s, those who had money moved to the East to get away from those who didn't. They also moved there to escape the crime and urban decay that plagued the rest of New Orleans. Separated from the rest of the city by the Inner Harbor Canal, a wide shipping channel that cuts between the Mississippi River and Lake Pontchartrain, and upon which drift oceangoing cargo ships, New Orleans East residents built sprawling subdivisions and palatial homes. They felt separate and safe—at least for a while.

Eventually the interstate and public transportation reached out to the East and made it more accessible. That accessibility brought with it the crime and decay from which the original settlers had been trying to escape in the first place.

By the mid-1990s, the East was still considered a decent place to live—more decent at least than downtown. It was home to many of the New Orleans Saints football players, although most of them lived on the eastern side of the district, in the gated subdivisions off of Bullard Avenue. But for the 7th District cops, the action was on the western side of the district. They spent all of their time, like the rest of the severely understaffed New Orleans Police Department, jumping from call to call, just trying to keep a lid on things. They were miles from the grisly murder scene at the Kim Anh restaurant.

Homicide detectives Eddie Rantz and Marco Demma reach the scene about forty-five minutes after the shootings.

The first thing Sergeant Rantz likes to do when he arrives on a crime scene is to take a walk. He wanders around and tries to get a feel for the place. At first glance, the crime scene at the Vietnamese restaurant doesn't look that complicated. The restaurant is housed in a stand-alone building, not much bigger than a good-sized house, and from what he's heard, the actual crime scene is pretty much contained inside the building.

Rantz circles the restaurant, searching the ground, studying the bits of trash lying around, looking at the walls, the windows, and at the cars in the parking lot. You can tell a lot by the position of the police cars: who got there first and how much of a hurry they were in. The two unmarked cars were obviously first on the scene. They took commanding positions within the small parking lot, each with a good angle on the building, positions that provided a clear line of sight, cover, and a superior field of fire if armed suspects rushed out of the restaurant.

The other police cars, the patrol units from the 7th District, arriving after the two unmarked cars, hadn't had as much choice in their positioning, but had nevertheless been placed in decent tactical locations so that the officers could see as much of the building as possible and be in a position to block the suspects' escape. But then there is that one car, that one 7th District car. It seems out of place.

Rantz stares at the marked police car backed into a parking space at the State Farm Insurance office next door. It sits hidden in the darkness, just outside the circles of light cast by the street lamps and the lights from the restaurant parking lot. Whoever drove that car did not park there for any tactical purpose. From where the car sits, the driver would have had to crank his or her neck past the shoulder just to see the front of the restaurant. The only reason

Rantz can figure that the driver parked there was so that the car couldn't be seen from inside the restaurant. But why would a police officer, responding to the scene of a shooting with an officer down, want to hide? Why take the time to back into a parking space?

When he reaches the back door of the restaurant, which is really located on the side, along the south wall of the building, Rantz pokes around by the trash cans, looking for discarded clothing, wallets, purses, anything an armed robber might toss away while leaving the scene of the crime. Rantz's experience, combined with the late hour, the isolated location, and the violence, tells him that this case is going to be about an armed robbery—an armed robbery gone bad.

# FOUR

**Sergeant** Eddie Rantz knows a thing our two about armed robberies. By 1995, he's been a detective for nearly twenty years, and a large part of his career has been spent chasing down armed robbers. Before transferring to Homicide, Rantz served as assistant commander of the Armed Robbery Division and as commander of the Bank Robbery Squad.

According to Rantz, armed robbers are more aggressive than most criminals. "They live closer to the edge," he said, "and are willing to take bigger chances." He said that one of the biggest attractions of armed robbery is that it is an all-cash business. There's no middleman taking a cut of the proceeds, no fence the robber has to sell his plunder to at cut-rate prices. As soon as it's over, the robber gets to start spending the cash.

It takes a certain type of personality to stick a gun in someone's face and demand money. Armed robbery is not a crime of passion like most murders, it's not a sneaky crime like burglary, and it doesn't require good math skills like drug dealing. "Most armed robbers aren't smart enough to deal dope," Rantz said.

But what they lack in passion, sneakiness, and mathematical capacity, they make up for in raw violence. Sometimes, even when an armed robber gets what he wants, he will still take his crime a step further—dead witnesses don't testify.

Rantz also knows a thing or two about violence. During his career as a New Orleans police officer he was in thirteen shootings and killed six people in the line of duty.

"I was with Eddie on his first kill," said legendary New Orleans homicide detective Joe Waguespack, Sr.

Late one day in the early 1970s, Rantz, then a rookie policeman working uniform patrol in a one-man car, was dispatched to investigate a "shots fired" call in Gert Town, a rough neighborhood off South Carrollton Avenue, on the uptown side of Canal Street.

Thirty years later, sitting behind his desk in a high-rise office overlooking downtown New Orleans, retired detective Eddie Rantz, now a practicing attorney, said, "In that neighborhood they always had shots going off, so I didn't think much of it."

When the call came out over the police radio, detectives Joe Waguespack and Billy Roth happened to be in the area. It had been a long day for the detectives, who were just ending their tour of duty. Waguespack knew Rantz was in a one-man car, and he didn't hear any other cars responding to assist.

Waguespack was driving. He turned to his partner. "We got to go back up that one-man car on this shooting call."

Roth shook his head. "We're almost to the station."

Waguespack shrugged and spun the steering wheel.

The complainant lived in the neighborhood and said an older black male had been wandering around the neighborhood most of the day firing a shotgun.

The complainant had given an address where the man

with the gun lived. It was a rundown shotgun-style house, elevated off the ground two or three feet and set on brick columns. New Orleans–style shotgun houses are shaped like a shoebox. They have a narrow front and long sides.

Rantz parked his cruiser next door and approached the house. It had a raised porch that spanned the narrow front. The front door was on the right-hand side of the porch, and a picture window was on the left. When Rantz climbed the steps onto the porch, he found the wooden front door standing open and the screen door closed. Because of the bright sunlight outside, he couldn't see into the dark house. There was also no safe place to stand on the porch. If he stood to the left of the door, he'd have his back to the big picture window, but to the right of the door was barely a foot of space between it and the porch railing.

Rantz chose the right-hand side. He turned sideways and squeezed himself into the tight space between the door and the railing. With his face pressed against the screen, he peered into the tiny front room. Sitting in a chair, opposite the door, was a black man in his late fifties. Rantz knocked on the frame of the screen door.

Inside, the man stared through the screen. "Who is it?"

"It's the police," Rantz said. "Open up."

The man dropped his hand beside the chair. "The police? Fuck the police." He came up with a double-barreled shotgun.

Rantz pressed tighter into the tiny space and drew his revolver.

The man inside the house pointed the gun at Rantz and cut loose with a blast that shredded the screen door.

Detectives Waguespack and Roth rolled up just as the man's first shot ripped across the porch and out into the street.

Eddie Rantz, pinned between the edge of the door and the porch railing, poked his .38 around the door frame and fired back.

The detectives sprang out of their car and ran toward the house. Waguespack jumped onto the porch while Roth skirted around the side to cover the back. Faced with two armed cops at the front door, a lot of criminals will beat a hasty retreat through the back door. Unless they're crazy.

As Waguespack compressed his bulky frame into the couple of inches of space between the door and window, Rantz reloaded his six-shooter.

"What you got?" Waguespack asked. He noticed that the rookie patrolman seemed to be handling himself like a veteran.

Rantz snapped the cylinder closed on his revolver. "Nut with a gun. Neighbors said he's been shooting up the street all day."

"How many?"

"Just one, far as I know."

The detective turned toward the screen door and shouted, "Mister, you need to come out with your hands up."

A second blast tore through the door.

"He's only got two shots in that thing," Rantz said.

Waguespack tightened his grip on his pistol. "Let's go."

Rantz threw open what was left of the screen door, and the two policemen rushed inside.

The man still sat in his chair, the shotgun broken open on his lap. He shoved the last of two shells into the breech. As he snapped the barrels closed, Rantz and Waguespack opened fire. The man died in his chair, his hands wrapped around the shotgun.

"We caught the guy while he was reloading," Waguespack said. "We did what we had to do, and we dragged him out."

**At** the Kim Anh restaurant, while Sergeant Rantz strolls around outside, soaking up details of the crime scene, Detective Marco Demma goes about the work of securing the scene and preserving the evidence. Demma has been a homicide detective for fifteen years and knows exactly what he has to do. He posts uniformed officers outside, at both the front and back doors, and instructs them to keep anyone out who does not absolutely have to be inside the restaurant. He tells a couple of other district cops to circle the whole outside area with crime scene tape. Then he starts a general survey of the inside of the restaurant so he can get an idea of what he is looking at and what evidence he needs to collect.

No crime scene is ever perfectly preserved, and the Kim Anh is certainly no exception. The first officers on the scene had to go inside the restaurant to check on the victims and to search for the perpetrators. When the EMS wagons arrived, the paramedics—who could not care less about trampling all over a crime scene—rushed inside to try to save the victims.

By the time Rantz and Demma arrived, Officer Ronnie Williams's body was already gone. Despite the massive, and instantly fatal, wounds, the police officers and detectives on the scene told the paramedics to take him to Charity Hospital. No matter how bad Ronnie Williams's wounds looked, or whether or not the medics were convinced he was already dead, the cops on the scene wanted an emergency room doctor to try to save him.

In treating Ronnie Williams on the scene and in hauling him out of the restaurant, the EMS crew had made a mess of the crime scene. Demma sees a thick smear of blood along the floor where they pulled Williams's body out from behind the bar to get more room to treat him. On the floor in front of the bar lies the pen from Williams's shirt pocket. His leather gun belt rests on top of the bar. There are bloody footprints all over the place.

Spent 9 mm shell casings litter the floor. In the wall behind the bar, roughly midway between the floor and the ceiling, Demma spots two bullet holes very close to each other. One of them has penetrated the wall and gone into the kitchen.

Tiptoeing around the scene, Demma sees a blue shirt button lying on the floor in the doorway between the dining room and the kitchen. It is from Williams's uniform shirt. How it got there, whether a bullet tore it off, or an enthusiastic medic pulled it loose, the detective has no idea.

Demma threads his way into the kitchen. He stares at the carnage that lies on the floor. This is about as bad as it gets, he thinks. A murdered policeman and two young lives stolen, one of them just a kid, really. The same thought rattles around inside Demma's head as was running through Rantz's—a robbery gone bad. Or good, depending on how you looked at it. As detectives, Rantz and Demma know they have to find witnesses, but from the perpetrator's standpoint, the systematic execution of the witnesses can mean a clean getaway.

Demma sees more 9 mm shell casings, along with bullet fragments, spread out on the kitchen floor and countertops.

When Eddie Rantz walks through the front door, he sees several police officers milling around inside the dining room. Crime scene techs are breaking out their collection gear. At a table in the back sits Detective Yvonne Farve with a young Vietnamese female. The girl is hysterical, crying, hugging Yvonne, and speaking nothing but Vietnamese. There is another woman in the restaurant, a young black woman. She sits alone at a table across the room from Detective Farve and the Vietnamese girl.

Rantz doesn't need all of his sleuthing skills to figure out that the girl Yvonne Farve is talking to is probably connected to the restaurant. As for the other woman—the black lady in the leather jacket sitting all by herself—he can't figure her out. He asks one of the uniform cops who she is. The officer tells him that she's a witness to the murders. She's also a cop.

In police work, it's important to interview witnesses as

soon as possible after a crime, before their memories get cluttered up with bits of information they pick up from other sources. In the emotional chaos and confusion swirling around the Kim Anh restaurant, Rantz thinks the information the uniform cop just gave him is good news. One of his witnesses is a police officer. She may be able to provide vital evidence, perhaps a direct link between the crime and the criminals.

In almost every instance, a trained police officer is a better witness than an untrained civilian. Police officers know about firearms; they know what key factors go into a suspect's description: height, weight, complexion, build, hair color, and clothing description. They know how to describe vehicles; they are used to looking at license plates.

After twenty years of detective work, Rantz knows that some cases are solved just because of pure, dumb luck. Here he is, just arrived on the scene of a triple homicide, including a murdered cop, and he stumbles upon a witness who is also a police officer. How lucky can you get? He walks toward her.

As Demma steps out of the kitchen, Yvonne Farve catches his eye and waves him over to the table where she is sitting with Chau Vu. Farve has been keeping an eye on Frank. For the last several minutes, Frank has been staring daggers at Chau.

At the table, Yvonne Farve nods toward Chau and tells the homicide detective, "She's got something I think you should hear right away."

**Just** after Frank and LaCaze's bloody rampage, Quoc Vu, Chau's eighteen-year-old brother, who'd been hiding inside the cooler with his sister, fled to a nearby friend's house to find help. After a frantic call to 911, he stands inside his friend's kitchen, staring out the window. He's looking toward the restaurant, worrying about his sister.

His friend's family huddles around him. Quoc wants to go back, but they won't let him, not until they are sure help has arrived.

Just before two-thirty in the morning, Quoc can see the area of the restaurant awash with flashing blue and red lights. He pleads with his friend's father to let him go back. The man agrees but says that he will drive Quoc to the restaurant. The whole family piles into a van and heads for the Kim Anh.

When they arrive, they find the parking lot nearly full. Police cars, detective cars, and ambulances—all are jammed together in front of the restaurant. Quoc's friend's father eases to a stop outside the jumble of vehicles. Quoc opens the sliding side door of the van. When a policeman walks over and asks what they are doing, Quoc tells him the restaurant belongs to his family and that he was here during the shooting. The police officer escorts Quoc into the restaurant. Shuffling toward the horrifying scene, Quoc's body shakes as he cries for his dead brother and sister.

# FIVE

**As** Chau tells her story to Detective Marco Demma, she keeps switching back and forth from English to Vietnamese. Demma knows she is telling him something about the other woman in the restaurant, the one sitting with Sergeant Rantz, but it is impossible for him to understand everything she is saying. She starts to tell her story in English, switches to Vietnamese, then starts crying. Yvonne Farve never leaves the girl's side and comforts her whenever she breaks down.

Across the dining room, Sergeant Rantz is talking to Antoinette Frank. Although there is no language barrier, Rantz has his own difficulties with Frank's story. The problem isn't that he doesn't understand her rapid-fire delivery; the problem is that her story just doesn't make sense. When Frank finishes, Rantz cants his head to one side. He looks the off-duty policewoman dead in the eye and says, "Can you do me a favor? Can you slow it down just a little bit and tell me that again?"

Frank takes a deep breath and starts over. "Me and my

nephew came here to get something to eat before we went to the show over at the—"

"What do you mean?" Rantz asks. "What show?"

"The movie theater at the Plaza. They got a midnight movie plays there on weekends."

"You and your nephew were going to a movie?"

Frank nods. "But once we got there—over to the Plaza—it was kinda late and he didn't feel like going. He was tired and I was tired, so we decided to get something to eat and go home."

"Whose home?"

"Mine."

"Your nephew lives with you?" Rantz asks.

Frank shakes her head. "He stays on Cindy Place with his girlfriend, but we were going to go to my house to eat."

"Okay."

"I called Chau and asked her to have her momma fix us something—"

"Who's Chau?"

Officer Frank points across the dining room. "She works here. Her family owns the restaurant."

Rantz nods.

"She say her momma was already gone, but she would see if her sister could fix us something to eat. I held on while she went and asked her sister. When Chau came back on the line, she told me her sister couldn't fix us hamburgers, but that she could fix us some steak and fries. I said that's fine and told her we'd be there in a few minutes."

"The shooting happened after you and your nephew got here the second time?"

"Yeah . . . Well not, not really. Really it was like the third time, but my nephew wasn't with me."

"I don't understand," Rantz says. "You came back a third time?"

"Yeah."

"Why?"

"Well, what had happened was . . . we came back to eat, but my nephew didn't want to eat the food here. He wanted to get it to go, so that's what we did, but by the time we got to my house, we realized we'd forgot to get drinks. So I came back—"

"Where's your house?"

"On Michigan Street. 7524 Michigan."

"Where's that?" he asks.

"Off Bullard, on the other side of the interstate."

"So you came back here to get drinks instead of stopping at a store closer to your house?"

"My house is like five minutes from here."

"Where was your nephew when the shooting happened?"

"He stayed at my house."

"You came back by yourself?"

Frank nods.

"To get drinks?"

Again, she nods.

"So what happened?"

Frank takes another deep breath. "I walked into the back, into the kitchen, to talk to Chau. You know, thank her and her sister for fixing us some food. All of a sudden, I hear all these gunshots going off behind me."

"Behind you where?"

"In the dining room," Frank says. "I know Ronnie was—"

"Are you talking about Officer Williams?"

Nodding, she says, "Yeah, Ronnie Williams."

"Did you know him?"

"Yeah. We were both on the second platoon."

"At the Seventh District?"

Frank nods again. "Right."

"What did you do when you heard the shots?"

"I was just kind of freaked out, frantic-like."

"Did you just stand there?" Rantz presses. "You're a police officer. Did you take any action?"

"I just . . . I didn't know what was happening, so I just . . . I just tried to get everybody out the back door."

Rantz just looks at her.

"So that's what I did," Frank continues. "I gathered everybody up who was in the kitchen, and I told them to calm down . . . just calm down. Everything was going to be all right. I was going to get them out, so then I pushed the back door open and got them outside."

Rantz thinks about his stroll around the crime scene, about the back door standing open with the screen door closed. He thinks about something else, too. "You opened the back door?"

"To get everybody out."

"How many people did you get out through the back door?"

Frank shakes her head. "I went out first, so I couldn't exactly see who came out after me."

"What'd you do when you got outside?"

"I got in my car and drove to the Seventh District."

"What about the people you led out?"

"They stayed there."

"You left them here?" Rantz says.

Frank's head bobs. "I went to get help."

"Did you have your radio with you?"

"No."

"What about a gun?"

"No," Frank says.

"What happened then?"

"I drove like crazy to the Seventh. When I got there, my car conked out on me. I ran inside and told the desk officer there'd been a shooting. I told him I thought Ronnie had got shot. Then I took a police car and hurried back here to see if I could help."

"Did you bring a gun with you?"

"No."

"Do you have a weapon on you now?"
"No," Frank repeats.
"Where is your gun and your police radio?"
"At home," she says.
"Where's your car right now?"
"At the station. I told you, it conked out on me when I went to get help, so I left it there."
"What kind of car is it?"
"Oh, it's old," Frank says. "It's a Ford Torino."
"What color is it?"
"Kind of like a reddish color."
"What about your nephew? Is he still at your house?"
Frank shrugs. "I don't know."
"What's his name?"
"Rogers."
Rantz pulls a notebook out of the inside pocket of his suit jacket. "Roger what?"
"Roger*sss*," she says, emphasizing the last consonant. "With an 'S' at the end. His name is Rogers LaCaze."
Sergeant Rantz jots down the name, making sure to include the "S." He looks up at her. "And you think he's still at your house?"
Frank shrugs again.
Rantz stands up. "Wait here," he tells her.
There is a lot about the officer's story that bothers him, especially the part about her hustling the survivors out the back door. Then there is the part about her leaving them behind while she drove to the 7th District station. She knew there was a uniformed policeman in the dining room and that shots had been fired inside the restaurant, yet she didn't even bother to go up front to check on him? It didn't make sense. None of it.
Rantz is sure there is a lot Frank isn't telling him. His gut instinct says she's involved somehow. He pulls Marco Demma aside and confides his suspicions to the veteran

homicide detective, but he cautions Demma to keep the information to himself. This is a volatile situation, and he needs everyone to focus on his or her job.

Rantz then sits down at the table with Demma, Yvonne Farve, and Chau Vu. Yvonne has managed to calm the Vietnamese girl down enough so that she can tell her story to the homicide detectives in English.

Rantz's face tightens as he listens to Chau.

When Chau finishes, a uniformed cop walks over to Rantz and tells him there is another witness outside he might want to talk to.

"Who is it?" Rantz asks.

The officer can't pronounce the young man's name, but says he is a member of the family who owns the restaurant and he was inside during the shootings.

Rantz follows the officer outside.

Quoc Vu stands in the parking lot, still shaking with fear. He is still two months away from graduating high school. He came to the United States nearly fifteen years ago with his father. Mr. Vu, who had served in the South Vietnamese Navy during that country's unsuccessful struggle against North Vietnam, wanted his family to escape the violence and poverty of the communist regime, but he couldn't get everyone out at once. In 1979, just after his four-year-old son, Huy, died in a tragic car accident, Mr. Vu and three-year-old Quoc fled their homeland and headed for the United States.

It took eleven years of backbreaking work before Mr. Vu managed to scrape together enough money to bring the rest of his family to their new home in New Orleans. Meanwhile, while his father worked and saved, little Quoc adjusted well to the transition. He learned the language and pastimes of his adopted home country. When his brother arrived from Vietnam, Quoc taught him to play football.

After their reunion in the United States, all six Vus had to live for a while in a single room and had to share one bathroom, but at least they were together. By 1993, things seemed to be looking up. Mr. and Mrs. Vu had managed to save enough money to pay off most of their debts and to buy the Kim Anh restaurant in New Orleans East. Quoc and his brother were in high school, and the Vu girls were in college. To Mr. Vu, it seemed as if almost all of his prayers had been answered.

In clear English, Quoc Vu tells Rantz what happened inside his family's restaurant that night. When Quoc finishes, Rantz knows exactly what he is going to have to do—question a fellow police officer as a suspect in a multiple homicide. The thought of it turns his stomach.

"I wanted to vomit," Rantz said later.

# SIX

**More** people arrive at the crime scene every minute. Cops, press, brass from headquarters—all crowd into the parking lot. Rantz scans the faces and sees the newly sworn-in superintendent of police standing nearby. *Great. Just great,* he thinks. *The new chief is here, and I'm in charge of a triple 30 that's turning out to be a fucking FUBAR—Fucked Up Beyond All Recognition.*

Rantz notices that to the chief's credit, he is staying outside and letting the detectives handle the case. Sometimes chiefs, because they are in charge, like to lumber around crime scenes, giving orders and messing things up. Although he is a recent transplant to New Orleans, the new police chief has been a cop for a long time.

In 1968, after a tour in Vietnam with the U.S. Air Force, Richard Pennington joined the Metropolitan Police Department in Washington, D.C. While working the streets, he managed to find enough time to earn a bachelor's degree from American University and a master's from D.C. University. During his twenty-six-year career with Metro,

Pennington worked in almost every aspect of local law enforcement, including a stint as a robbery detective and as commander of the Homicide Division. He retired as an assistant chief in 1994 to accept the job as police superintendent in New Orleans, where he took command of a department teetering on the edge of self-destruction.

Eddie Rantz walks back into the dining room of the Kim Anh. The inside of the restaurant is barely ordered chaos. Crime lab techs crawl around collecting evidence while a police photographer snaps pictures to document the condition of the scene. Marco Demma is trying to orchestrate the madness. Yvonne Farve and Chau Vu are gone.

Rantz drops into a metal-framed, cushioned chair across the table from Antoinette Frank. As he stares at the off-duty 7th District police officer, Sergeant Rantz doesn't see a fellow cop, he doesn't see a victim, he doesn't see a witness. He sees a murder suspect.

"Your story is just not adding up," he tells her.

"What do you mean?" Frank asks.

"You said you were trying to save people's lives, right?"

Frank nods.

"So when the shooting started, you led some of the employees out through the back door, right?"

Again, she bobs her head. "Like I already told you, I was frantic. I didn't know what was going on, and I didn't have a gun or a radio. I just did what I thought was best and tried to keep everybody calm and get them out of the restaurant."

"But you knew Officer Williams was up front, where the shots were coming from?"

"Yeah."

"So you knew that just a few feet away from you there was a fellow police officer involved in some kind of shooting incident?"

"But I didn't have—"

Rantz raises his hand to shut her up. "When we talked

just a few minutes ago, you said you came back to the restaurant alone to get drinks for you and your . . ."

"My nephew."

"Your nephew, right. What's his name again?"

"Rogers LaCaze."

"But you said you were alone. You'd left him at your house. On Michigan Street. Is that right?"

Frank's eyes dart away. She doesn't answer.

After talking to Chau and Quoc, Rantz knows that the gunshots started seconds after Frank let herself into the restaurant. He knows that Frank was inside the restaurant with the man she'd told everyone was her nephew and that they were searching for something—probably money. "If Rogersss," Rantz drags the "S" out to make sure Frank hears it, "was at your house on Michigan, then who was it who came into the restaurant with you?"

Frank's eyes snap back and lock on Rantz's. "He didn't come in with me!"

"Who didn't come in with you?"

"Rogers."

"When did he come in?"

She shakes her head. "I don't know. All I know is I came inside to get something to—"

"Where was he when you came into the restaurant?"

Frank takes a deep breath. When she finally speaks, her voice is low, barely above a whisper. "In the car."

"So he wasn't at your house?"

"I don't know what he was doing. All I know is I didn't want him to come inside."

"Why?"

"Because," Frank says, "he'd been talking about robbing the place. When I heard those gunshots, all I could think about was getting everybody out."

"So you took whoever you could find and got them the hell out of here. Is that right?"

"I was just so panicked I didn't know what else to do," Frank says.

"Let me ask you one more thing . . . After you got everybody out through the door, how did you lock it again?"

Frank opens her mouth, but no words come out, nothing but "Ah, ah, ah . . ."

"When I got here the screen door was still locked," Rantz says. "It was locked from the inside."

Rantz sees nothing from Frank but the startled stare of a frightened animal caught in headlights.

"Unless you're a magician," Rantz continues, his voice edged in sarcasm, "the door had to have been unlocked when you led everybody out to safety. So what I want to know is, how did you lock it back after you got out?"

Frank doesn't have an answer.

Outside in the parking lot, Rantz finds the new superintendent of police. "Chief, I'm about to book this motherfucker with three counts of first-degree murder." He says it matter-of-factly. He isn't asking the chief's permission. He is simply telling the man what is about to happen.

A flash of anguish crosses Chief Pennington's face as he looks at Rantz. The police department he came to overhaul is in worse shape than he could have ever imagined. Pennington has been on the job less than six months and already a federal grand jury has indicted ten of his police officers for conspiracy and drug trafficking.

Among the ten who are under indictment is Officer Len Davis. In addition to drug trafficking violations, Davis has also been charged with the murder of Kim Groves, a thirty-two-year-old mother of three. Groves filed a brutality complaint against Officer Davis on October 12, 1994—the day before Pennington was sworn in as superintendent—for pistol-whipping the teenage son of a neighbor. The next day, October 13, the day of the new chief's swearing-in ceremony at City Hall, Officer Davis made a telephone call to his friend, Paul "Cool" Hardy, and ordered him to kill Groves.

Hardy was notorious in the area of New Orleans called the lower 9th Ward. He was a dope dealer and killer, who operated with Davis's protection and who had already beaten one murder charge. On October 13, Davis cruised the streets around Kim Groves's house until he spotted her. He called Hardy from his cell phone and told the killer where Groves was and what she was wearing. When Hardy got to Groves's lower 9th Ward neighborhood he found her strolling down the sidewalk. He walked up behind her and shot her in the back of the head with a 9 mm pistol.

What Davis and Hardy didn't know at the time was that the FBI was listening to and recording their telephone conversations. Kim Groves' murder happened too quickly for the FBI to prevent it. Fortunately, they had no trouble proving Davis ordered the killing and that Hardy carried it out.

Despite the pain and embarrassment of yet another police officer going to jail, the chief just nods his head at Sergeant Rantz and says, "Come by my office when you get through."

As he walks back toward the restaurant, Rantz grabs hold of a passing homicide detective. "That black female in there," Rantz nods toward the front door, "her name's Antoinette Frank. She's a patrol officer at the Seventh District. She says she left her personal car at the district station. I want you to go find it and have it towed to headquarters. Put it in the basement outside CE and P [Central Evidence and Property]."

The detective nods. "Okay, Eddie, but why? What are we looking for?"

"Evidence."

In the dining room, Rantz catches Demma's eye and nods toward Frank, who still sits quietly at the table. The two detectives approach the off-duty officer and ask her to stand up.

It is 3:53 A.M.

Demma takes hold of one of Frank's arms. "Are you armed?" he asks as he pats the outside of her black leather jacket.

Frank shakes her head.

Rantz grabs Frank's other arm as Demma reaches his free hand toward her waist.

"What's this?" Demma says, his tone enough to alert Rantz to possible danger.

Both detectives tighten their grip. Demma reaches under the bottom edge of Frank's shirt and pulls out a two-inch Smith & Wesson .38-caliber revolver.

"You're under arrest," Rantz tells her.

"What for?" Frank asks.

Eddie Rantz nods toward the kitchen, then glances at the bar where Ronnie Williams died. "For murdering all these people."

Frank doesn't answer. Her face is blank as Rantz pushes her wrists together behind her back and clamps a pair of handcuffs down on them.

# SEVEN

**In** a neatly printed, handwritten letter addressed "To Whom It May Concern," Antoinette Frank wrote, "I have a strong desire to become a police officer for the City of New Orleans. I have been interested in law enforcement since the age of fifteen . . ."

Antoinette Renee Frank was born on April 30, 1971, in Opelousas, Louisiana, a small town of twenty thousand people in the western part of the state. She is the daughter of Adam and Mary Ann Frank. She has an older brother, Adam Jr., born in 1970.

Although only about a hundred miles northwest of New Orleans, Opelousas is as different from New Orleans as night is from day. New Orleans has a big-city feel. It is a twenty-four-hour town, whose vibrations can be felt any time of the day or night, seven days a week. Bars don't close in New Orleans—ever.

New Orleans is the party capital of the world. It is also one of the most devoutly Catholic cities in the United States. The citizens reconcile this seeming contradiction in typical New Orleans fashion. They throw the biggest party on the planet. They call it Mardi Gras.

Mardi Gras means "Fat Tuesday." Following the Catholic calendar, Mardi Gras Day is always celebrated the day before Ash Wednesday, the day that begins the forty days of Lent, a time of sacrifice for Catholics. If Ash Wednesday is about sacrifice and denial, then Fat Tuesday is about indulgence and excess. In New Orleans, Mardi Gras is a two-week orgy of revelry, eating, drinking, and sex—then more drinking.

During the two-week buildup, vehicle traffic is blocked off at night and parades roll through the streets. Business in the city and surrounding parishes slows during the fourteen-day celebration and finally grinds to a complete halt on Mardi Gras Day. Except for the bars, everything shuts down. According to the U.S. Postal Service motto, "Neither snow, nor rain, nor heat, nor gloom of night stays these couriers from the swift completion of their appointed rounds," but even the post office closes for Mardi Gras. The streets are jammed with drunken carousers. No one cares about the mail on Fat Tuesday.

Opelousas, on the other hand, is a city that has maintained its small-town feel. It's quiet, peaceful, and compared to New Orleans, almost crime-free.

The French founded Opelousas in 1720 as a midway stopping point for merchants traveling between Natchitoches—Louisiana's oldest permanent settlement—and New Orleans. Named after the Opelousa Indians, Opelousas is the state's third oldest city. It sits in the heart of Acadiana, known as "Cajun Country," where French is sometimes still spoken.

For one year during the Civil War, Opelousas served as the capital of Louisiana when the state was part of the Confederacy. Union troops invaded and captured the city, but lost it to Confederate forces, then managed to recapture and hold it for the duration of the war. During Reconstruction, Opelousas was the site of several bloody riots.

Internationally renowned Cajun chefs Tony Chachere and Paul Prudhomme hail from Opelousas, as did Jim Bowie, famous knife maker and hero of the Alamo. Opelousas bills itself as the "Zydeco music capital of the world."

According to Antoinette Frank's mother, Mary Ann, the family left the quiet country lanes of Opelousas and headed for the mean streets of New Orleans in 1975 after her husband enlisted in the Army. When Adam Sr. finished his military hitch, he joined his wife and kids in New Orleans, where the Frank family continued to expand. Adam Sr. and Mary Ann had two more sons.

In New Orleans, Antoinette went to Albert Bell Junior High, then moved on to John McDonogh Senior High School. She also joined New Orleans Police Department Explorer Post number 560. The police explorers were an NOPD-sponsored youth organization geared toward teens who were interested in careers in law enforcement. Upon joining Explorer Post 560, Frank was issued NOPD explorer badge number 183.

Frank spent two years as a member of the Explorers and developed a real hunger for police work, but in 1987, the budding crime fighter had to leave her Explorer Post and her ambitions behind. Her dad took the family back to Opelousas, where he had accepted a job with the telephone company.

The Franks moved into a small wood-framed house at 828 Market Street, just a few blocks from the police station and the courthouse. The house was in a rundown residential section of town with a smattering of businesses strewn up and down the street. In a neighborhood with little entertainment value, Frank probably spent some of her spare time hanging out at the Star Drive-In and Burger Stand. The Star is a tin-roofed building with a brick facade that sits across Market Street and three doors down from the Franks' house. Block lettering along the top of the facade reads,

"FRIED CHICKEN." Directly under that are the words "AMUSEMENT CENTER." The Star is a triple value—burger stand, chicken stand, and game room.

Antoinette enrolled as a junior at Opelousas High School and almost immediately started looking around for something to do that could further her ambitions of becoming a police officer. She managed to convince the Opelousas police chief to let her do volunteer work at the office; she also signed up with the Opelousas Junior Police, a youth organization very similar to the NOPD Explorers.

The Junior Police was great, but Frank also needed a real job, one that paid, so she went to work for Wal-Mart in June 1988. Wal-Mart fired her just six months later.

A neighbor, who still lives across from the Franks' old house on Market Street, says she remembers clearly a very strange encounter she had with the Frank family in the late 1980s.

The neighbor, who didn't want her name used, says she was inside her house doing a little cleaning when she heard a knock on the door. She opened the door to find Antoinette Frank and her father standing there.

"Can we borrow some money?" Antoinette asked. Her father loomed behind her, silent.

"Excuse me?" the neighbor said.

"I said, can we borrow some money? We just need a few dollars."

It was such an unusual request coming from a stranger, and such an unusual situation, a high school girl and her father standing mute behind her. They weren't selling cookies or raffle tickets or magazine subscriptions or collecting for a senior trip; they were just asking for money. The presence of the father almost made it feel like intimidation. It seemed so strange that it took a moment for the neighbor to gather her thoughts. When she did, she realized the two were making her nervous. "I don't keep money in my house," she said and closed the door as quickly as good manners would allow.

Although Antoinette Frank missed twenty-nine days of school during her senior year, she still managed to graduate with her high school class in May 1989. But almost as soon as she was out the door, the faculty and staff of her alma mater forgot about her. They didn't forget her on purpose. She hadn't been a troublemaker or a badass. They simply forgot her because she was such a nonentity.

"I don't remember her at all," says Dawn Hurst, who was Frank's homeroom English teacher. "She didn't make any impression on me, good or bad."

Frank wasn't a member of any school clubs, nor did she participate in any after-school activities. She doesn't even show up in the Opelousas High School yearbooks in either of the two years in which she was a student there. It was almost as if she didn't exist.

In Opelousas, Frank kept to herself and maintained a low profile; it was definitely not where she wanted to be. She'd tasted life in the big city, and in the two years since she'd been exiled back to small-town Louisiana, Frank hadn't forgotten the flavor of New Orleans, nor had she forgotten her life's ambition: to wear the star-and-crescent badge of the NOPD.

Antoinette's brother Adam Jr., older by just thirteen months, was starting out on a path that seemed totally different from that of his quiet, unassuming sister, but in the end, it turned out to be eerily similar. Adam had frequent run-ins with the police and racked up arrests for burglary, armed robbery, battery on police officers, and two counts of attempted manslaughter.

St. Landry Parish Sheriff Howard Zerangue, who used to be chief of police in Opelousas, remembers Adam Jr. "He was pretty rough," the sheriff says.

During the summer of 1989, right after graduating from high school, Frank again struck out for the New Orleans, this time by herself. Despite her having been fired from the Wal-Mart in Opelousas, the Wal-Mart in New Orleans East had no problem giving Frank a second chance. They hired her as a sales clerk. Helen Corley, a Wal-Mart personnel clerk, later told an NOPD investigator that Frank's job performance was "excellent in the categories of work, character, dependability, attendance, and cooperation."

Frank rented a house at 7932 Sheephead Street in New Orleans East. Set up with an income and a place to live, she was eager to get back to working toward her goal of becoming a New Orleans police officer, but she had to wait. At eighteen years old, she just wasn't old enough.

According to neighbors, and by all other accounts, Antoinette Frank lived a quiet life on Sheephead Street. Although she was a very attractive young woman, no one remembers her ever having a boyfriend. As she'd done in her hometown, Frank kept to herself, working at Wal-Mart and counting down the days until she could apply to the police department.

The day she turned twenty—the minimum age for applying to become a New Orleans police officer—Frank was ready. With application in hand, she launched an all-out assault on the police department and the city, demonstrating a single-minded determination that some later said bordered on obsession, to become a cop.

To her application, Frank attached a handwritten note in which she tried to explain why she wanted to become a police officer. In the note, she claimed that she'd been preparing for a law enforcement career for most of her life and that she'd joined the NOPD Explorers and performed office work for the Opelousas Police Department in order to gain valuable experience and to familiarize herself with police work. She concluded the note by writing, "I perceive myself to be a strong young woman with guts and who is willing to endure any obstacles to become the best law enforcement officer I can be."

As a police applicant, the mousy girl from Opelousas High, whom none of her teachers could remember, started to show a relentless dimension to her personality that no one had seen before. It was an aggressiveness that would stay with her, supporting her through the difficult barriers that lay ahead in the application process, and would last through her police academy training, where some of Frank's instructors couldn't say enough good things about her. But later, on the street, as a working police officer, that high level of assertiveness would vanish like early morning fog on the river, and Frank would revert back to the meek little mouse she had been before, that is, until it was time to plan the assassination of a fellow police officer and a couple of helpless victims.

While the department processed Frank's application, she managed to convince someone at police headquarters to give her a job doing volunteer work. Frank worked as a clerk—not a police officer as she later claimed—in the records room, the Office of Public Affairs, and in the Narcotics Division, but unlike her time at Opelousas High, all three of those offices, as well as the entire police department, would have a reason to remember Antoinette Frank.

# EIGHT

**Ronnie** Williams grew up in an upper middle-class neighborhood in New Orleans East. His parents took him and his younger brother, Shawn, on a lot of family vacations. They cruised to Hawaii, they skied, they had fun together as a family. Ronnie also worked hard. His dad owned a tractor, and Ronnie made money by cutting lots in and around his neighborhood. Neighbors frequently spotted him cruising down the street on the tractor, a ball cap cocked back on his head.

Ronnie was in his sophomore year at Brother Martin Catholic High School when he spotted a cute brunette moving into the house across the street. When he found out she was just a freshman, he blew her off. He didn't have time to fool with a freshman, even a cute one.

Ronnie Williams loved to work on cars. He had a gift when it came to things mechanical. He was also pretty good with electronics. His grandmother tells a story about an old busted television she'd had tucked away inside her house for years. Ronnie was just ten when he decided to take it apart. She watched him huddle over the old TV's innards, moving wires around, going in and out with different tools. Still, he was just a boy; he was just playing around. But when he put it back together, it worked.

In high school, Ronnie bought a black Mustang. He poured hundreds of hours of love into that car, fixing it, polishing it, souping up the engine. He customized a huge pair of wooden boxes for his stereo speakers and filled up the backseat with them. His four-seater became a two-seater but he had a hell of a sound system. Sometimes late at night he'd cruise up and down Marconi Drive next to City Park or roll along Michoud Boulevard out in the East with his music blaring through the open windows.

The summer after he graduated, Ronnie took some friends to a neighborhood party. He ran into Mary Buras, the girl from across the street, the freshman he hadn't had time for a couple of years before. Mary wasn't a freshman anymore. She was going into her senior year, and boy how she had grown up. Someone had found time for her because she was with a date.

Ronnie started giving her a little grief, teasing her, pretending he was trying to piss her off. Anything to try to get her mind off her date. He kept his eye on her all night, waiting for an opportunity to catch a couple of minutes alone with her. Finally, he saw her heading into the bathroom. When she came out he was standing outside the door, waiting for her, a big goofy grin on his face. She tried to step past him but he kissed her.

"That was it," Mary says. "I dumped the guy I was dating and started dating Ronnie." Before she knew what had happened, Mary Buras was in love with the kid from across the street.

They went to parties together, hung out in the French Quarter, listened to music, shot pool, watched friends drag race down Marconi Drive. Mary even dragged Ronnie to a few dances. He hated to dance and would only even try it if it was a slow song. "He had no rhythm," Mary says. But boy did he love to work on cars. "He always had grease under his fingernails," Mary remembers, "but I never cared about that." She loved to watch Ronnie work on his Mustang and sometimes played the part of his assistant, handing him tools like a surgical nurse.

Ronnie's size, his aggressive attitude, and his sharp sense of humor sometimes put him at odds with other young men his age. He was not the kind who would back down. "Ronnie was the strongest guy I know," Mary says. "I don't think he ever lost a fight." A couple of times he came by Mary's house to see her dad, a doctor, for a quick patch job.

The couple got married in 1989. They had a son, Christopher, that same year. Ronnie took a construction job and did other odd jobs to earn extra money. He worked hard because he wanted the best for his new family. Every night, he came home filthy and exhausted. He took college classes whenever he could.

After Ronnie met a New Orleans police officer, it wasn't long before he knew what he wanted to do. He joined the police department in 1991 and after graduating from the police academy was assigned to the 7th District. Mary Williams says that her husband loved the camaraderie that came with the job, and he loved the friends he made there, friends like Bobby O'Brien and Clay Clement. Mary liked that he was a police officer. "I thought he was hot in his uniform," she says.

Lt. C. J. Roebuck was one of Ronnie's field training officers. "He was a good kid," Roebuck says. "He would back you up."

A rookie cop can't get a higher compliment from a seasoned veteran than an acknowledgment that he can be trusted to back up another cop.

Lt. Frank Van Dalen, Ronnie's platoon commander, says, "Everybody liked Ronnie Williams. He was always joking around."

Sgt. Dave Slicho, Ronnie's squad sergeant, shares that opinion. "I looked forward to him working because he was always in a good mood. It's contagious."

Christopher loved his dad being a cop. Sometimes Ronnie would drive his son around the block in his police car. In the driveway, he'd let the boy turn on the lights and toot the siren.

Ronnie and Mary bought a house. Since Ronnie was on the three-to-eleven shift, he didn't get home until almost midnight, so that' s when the couple would start their home improvement projects. "We were both night owls," Mary explains. "It is kind of crazy now to think of how we built a dog run, put in doors, and fixed floors at two in the morning. I remember holding flashlights more times than I can count."

Once they'd fixed up their house, Ronnie and Mary starting throwing parties for their friends. From his secret, twelve-ingredient salads to boiled crawfish, Ronnie did all the cooking. "He liked the crawfish to be spicy enough to make your eyes water," Mary says.

When Mary got pregnant again, Ronnie started working the security detail at the Kim Anh restaurant to earn extra money for his growing family. But no matter how hard he worked or how tired he was, Ronnie never lost his sense of humor, nor did he stop pulling pranks. One night, Mary and Chris were in the den watching television. Ronnie was in the back taking a shower. Suddenly, Ronnie called out from the bathroom, "Hey, you guys, come here, quick!"

Mary and Chris dashed into the bathroom, thinking something bad had happened. Ronnie pulled back the top half of the plastic curtain and swiveled the showerhead down toward his son and blasted him with the water. Chris and his mom fled the bathroom screaming and laughing with water dripping from their heads.

* * *

**The** first step in Antoinette Frank's application process to become a New Orleans police officer was a written Civil Service test. According to Opelousas High School principal Raymond Cassimere, during her two years at Opelousas High, Frank took four English classes and three math classes; she also took history, biology, chemistry, and Spanish. Frank had been a pretty good student, and she sailed right through the Civil Service test.

Following the written test, the police department gave Frank a polygraph exam and a physical agility test. Once again, she passed with flying colors. In fact, in one of her letters in support of her application, Frank claimed to have been on her high school's basketball, softball, volleyball, and track teams—although no one remembers her doing any of that, and there are no records of her sports participation. She also wrote in the same letter, "I am presently in the finest physical and mental condition."

But despite her claim, it was Frank's mental state that first caused her application to stumble.

Under hiring procedures in place at the time of Frank's application, the New Orleans Police Department, through the city's Department of Civil Service, required all police applicants to take two standardized psychological evaluations: the MMPI-2 (Minnesota Multiphasic Personality Inventory) and the CPI (California Psychological Inventory), both of which are in multiple choice format. Once the applicant completed both tests, a psychologist under contract to Civil Service evaluated the results and prepared a written report.

In July 1992, Dr. Penelope Dralle, a psychologist with the Louisiana State University Medical School, evaluated Frank's scores for the Department of Civil Service. The results did not bode well for Frank's law enforcement career aspirations.

According to Dr. Dralle's report, she gave Frank the lowest possible score in tolerance, open-mindedness, and impulse control; and the next to lowest possible score in stability, maturity, and probable adjustment to organization. In her report, Dr. Dralle wrote:

*Applicant responded to both tests in such a naively avoidant, denying, and evasive manner that further personality description is questionable other than to suggest excessive over-valuation of her own worth, extreme lack of tolerance and flexibility, excessive use of repression and denial, and a conscious effort to represent herself as above even common problems. In spite of this approach there are suggestions of rebelliousness, problems with authority and regulations, and marked assertiveness.*

Dr. Dralle recommended a psychiatric evaluation, an option under Civil Service rules for applicants who failed the psychological screening. The psychologist also noted in her report that Frank had lied on her police department application by claiming Wal-Mart had transferred her to New Orleans. Dr. Dralle based that conclusion on a report filed by Edwin Ducote, the police officer assigned to conduct Frank's pre-employment background investigation.

Ducote was assigned to the NOPD Applicant Investigation Unit. He had interviewed Frank back in February 1992. As part of Ducote's investigation, he fingerprinted and photographed Frank, verified that she did not have a criminal record, checked with her neighbors, and called her previous employers. It was Ducote, who on March 12, 1992, spoke with Rita Smalley, a personnel clerk at Wal-Mart in Opelousas, and learned that six months after starting at Wal-Mart Frank had been fired for "personality conflicts with other associates" and that she had received an "unsatisfactory" rating on her end-of-employment evaluation. Frank had claimed on her NOPD application and again in her interview with Ducote that Wal-Mart had transferred her from the store in Opelousas to one in New Orleans. Ducote noted this discrepancy in his report of Frank's background investigation, which he had submitted to chief of police Arnesta Taylor on May 22, 1992.

At that time, being caught red-handed lying on a police application apparently wasn't enough of a transgression to merit disqualification. Evidently, in the mid-1990s, honesty was not a requirement for becoming a New Orleans police officer.

On September 1, 1992, Frank sat down for a formal interview with Dr. Philip Scurria, a board-certified psychiatrist and assistant professor of psychiatry at the Louisiana State University Medical Center. The LSU Medical Center had a contract with the police department to evaluate any applicants whom the psychological tests indicated needed further screening. Prior to the interview, Dr. Scurria reviewed Frank's MMPI and CPI test results as well as Dr. Dralle's report. He also read the report of her police background investigation.

Frank showed up for the interview on time and neatly dressed. The interview took about thirty minutes, during which Dr. Scurria noted that Frank seemed very comfortable talking with him and not at all intimidated. "But I had the impression that she was preoccupied with making herself look good," he later said. That behavior, an unnaturally strong desire to make herself look good, was a common theme with Frank. It had been detected on her CPI test results and in Dr. Dralle's evaluation. In CPI lingo, it is called "faking good."

Then there was the name-dropping. "Within the first five or ten minutes of the interview, she mentioned the names of several people in the police department," Dr. Scurria said, "and I wasn't sure exactly what she wanted to impress me with, but I had the feeling that again she was trying to influence me by letting me know that she had lots of connections with the police department."

One way in which Dr. Scurria often judged an applicant's honesty was by asking a question to which he already knew the answer. He had Frank's police background investigation report and knew she'd been fired from the Wal-Mart in Opelousas. "Have you ever had any job-related problems?" he asked.

"Like what?" Frank asked.

"Have you ever been fired from a job?"

"No." Frank didn't bat an eye. "My employer, Wal-Mart, recently transferred me from the store in Opelousas to one here in New Orleans."

Dr. Scurria knew she was lying, so he pressed her. "So you've never been fired or had any other problems at work?"

As Frank shook her head, her body posture shifted from open and honest to closed off. Her voice took on a defensive edge. "No, sir."

In a written report following the interview, Dr. Scurria evaluated Frank on fourteen characteristics relevant to the job of a police officer. He rated her as unacceptable in integrity, forthrightness, non-defensiveness, and willingness to accept responsibility for mistakes. He graded her below average in her ability to follow normal conventions and rules, personal insight and empathy with others, sound judgment and common sense, as well as freedom from psychopathology.

In a hand-written notation on the report, Dr. Scurria wrote that Frank "seemed shallow and superficial." He also reported, "Applicant was not honest."

Dr. Scurria concluded his evaluation by writing, "I do not feel, especially considering her concealment of her work problems, that the applicant is suitable for the job of police officer."

Frank had failed. The screening process had worked. It had established that Antoinette Frank was not qualified to become a New Orleans police officer.

# NINE

**In** a perfect world, the story would have ended there and Antoinette Frank would have been just another NOPD applicant who didn't make it. Not everyone needs to carry a gun and a badge and have the power to throw people in jail. She would have gone on to do something else, and three people would have stayed alive, two little boys would have a father, a wife would still have a husband, two sets of parents would still have their sons and daughter, and others would still have their brothers and sister.

But it's not a perfect world—never has been and never will be—and Antoinette Frank didn't just give up. And in a city obsessed with hiring quotas and manufactured diversity, the police department let her try again. The New Orleans *Times-Picayune* said, "Sheer pushiness may have been Frank's strongest suit."

Starting in mid-September, Frank launched a campaign that would have made most publicists and politicians green with envy.

She dropped in to see state district judge Dennis Waldron

in the criminal courts building at Tulane and Broad, next door to police headquarters. Frank explained to him the problems she was having getting past the police psychological tests. Then she asked the judge for a letter of recommendation to the police department. Waldron hemmed and hawed until Frank whipped out a letter she had written herself and asked him to sign it.

She had written the letter as if it were from the judge. It was typed on a plain sheet of white paper and addressed, "To Whom It May Concern," and although it was full of mistakes and bad grammar, Judge Waldron signed the recommendation letter. Frank took one of the judge's business cards and later photocopied the signed letter with the business card attached to it. The result was an amateur-looking reproduction of the judge's letterhead.

Frank also looked up an old family friend. Attorney George Simno III returned to his office, a converted wood-framed shotgun house on North Carrollton Avenue, late one rainy afternoon and was surprised to find Frank waiting for him on the front porch. It had been at least a couple of years since he'd seen her. After walking through the rain, Frank looked like a drowned rat. A Southern gentleman, Simno invited her inside. After Frank dried off somewhat, the two of them sat down across Simno's desk from each other and caught up.

Simno asked about Frank's father, Adam Frank, Sr., whom he had represented in a civil case some eight years before. Simno and Frank Sr. had become casual friends, seeing each other occasionally over the years. The lawyer knew of Adam's passion for raising pigeons. "Whenever I would run into him," Simno says, "I used to ask him about his pigeons. I didn't raise birds myself, but I was fascinated by the stories he would tell." During the course of their friendship, Simno had also come to know the Frank family.

Antoinette steered the conversation away from small talk. She had not come to discuss her dad or his pigeons.

She was on a mission and came quickly to the point. "Can you write a letter of recommendation for me?"

"Sure," Simno said. "You're trying to get a job?"

Frank nodded.

"Where?"

"The New Orleans Police Department. I'm going to be a police officer."

"That's a very noble occupation," Simno said.

"They're trying to say I'm not qualified."

"Really? Not qualified how?"

"They said I didn't do that well on the psychological part of the testing." Frank looked pained. Simno could tell she was very upset about being rejected.

Because he'd seen Antoinette off and on since she was a young teen, because he knew both of her parents, and because he had never heard of Antoinette getting into any kind of trouble, Simno had no qualms about writing a recommendation letter for her.

He spun around in his chair, fired up his computer, and pecked out a simple, generic letter, recommending to the New Orleans Police Department that they hire Frank as a police officer. Looking back on it years later, though, Simno, a former federal and state prosecutor, says, "That letter came back to haunt me." But at the time he wrote it, on a rainy afternoon in late 1992, the genteel lawyer and Frank family friend, had no idea that Antoinette Frank was capable of cold-blooded murder.

Frank also did some letter writing of her own. She knocked out another "To Whom It May Concern" letter and sent it to the police department. In the letter, she dropped names like crazy and closed by saying, "I have been working hard all of my juvenile and adult life to prepare myself to become a police officer . . . I am a stable and dependable individual; and I deserve a chance to prove my ability to function as a law enforcement officer in the next upcoming police academy."

Another glowing letter of recommendation reached police headquarters, and it also was addressed, "To Whom It May Concern." The letter purported to be from Frank's physician, a Dr. Thomas, although the wording didn't read like something written by a well-educated medical professional; rather, it bore striking similarities to letters Frank had written herself.

Sometime during her campaign to jump-start her application and have it reconsidered, Frank popped in to visit the chief of police. Soon after taking over as police superintendent in 1991, Chief Arnesta Taylor instituted an open door policy. Anyone—police or civilian—could walk into his office and talk to him. The chief later testified that Frank came in looking for a job and asking for his help. "But I told her that I just couldn't help her," he explained, "because I didn't get involved in the day-to-day procedures for hiring new police officers."

But Frank was insistent. She asked the chief to write a letter of recommendation for her. Taylor said that he held firm and refused to get involved with Frank's application to the police department.

Later, after the shootings at the Kim Anh precipitated an exhaustive examination of just how Antoinette Frank became a police officer, investigators discovered a letter of recommendation that appeared to be from Chief Taylor but did not bear his signature. Taylor has since stated under oath that he did not write the letter. He also said that at the time he meet with Frank, he did not know she was having trouble with the psychological portion of the screening process.

Even then–New Orleans mayor Sidney Barthelemy wasn't safe from Antoinette Frank's campaign of persistence and forgery, although he apparently didn't know it at the time. During her application process, Frank turned in a preprinted Civil Service form, called a "PERSONNEL ACTION FORM," to the Department of Civil Service. The document bore the mayor's signature, although according to city officials, such forms were routinely reviewed and signed by the city's chief administrative officer, and according to one official, it would have been "highly, highly unusual" for the mayor to have signed such a routine employment form.

Just after the Kim Anh shootings, Barthelemy, who had left office by that time, told the *Times-Picayune* newspaper that his signature at the bottom of the form "was lifted from somewhere else." The former mayor said that he did not know Frank, had never met her, and had not intervened with the police department on her behalf. He told the newspaper, "I have never signed anything like that. I am not the appointing authority for the police department." He also added that the form is simply used to document an applicant's personal history and would not have been useful as a boost to anyone seeking employment with the city.

In the mid-1990s, the city of New Orleans had an odd loophole in its Civil Service rules. Anyone who had failed the psychological screening portion of their application to become a New Orleans police officer was allowed to scrounge up a second medical opinion on their own. They had to obtain the opinion at their own expense; but if the second opinion was favorable, the rules allowed the Department of Civil Service to reconsider the aspiring police officer's entire application package. In other words, those who had flunked out got a second chance.

Frank found out about the quirky rule and clung to it. She was drowning, and someone had just tossed her a life-jacket.

Dr. Dennis E. Franklin, a psychiatrist whom Antoinette Frank hired, interviewed her on October 9, 1992. His report says that she came in as a referral from Judge Dennis Waldron, something the judge later denied in a sworn deposition.

Following the interview and his own research, Dr. Franklin prepared a five-page, typed, narrative report, which was labeled "PSYCHIATRIC EVALUATION." He sent the report to the Department of Civil Service and to the police department.

In the report, Dr. Franklin said that he discussed with Frank the results of a second MMPI, which she took prior to his interview with her. Franklin, who did not have access to Frank's first MMPI results, noted that, "the results of the MMPI essentially was in the *abnormal* limits." (Emphasis added.) On the copy of Dr. Franklin's report in the police department files, someone used a pen to mark out part of the text and rewrite it by hand so that it reads, "the results of the MMPI essentially *were* in the *normal* limits." (Emphasis added.)

It is unknown whether Dr. Franklin meant what he originally wrote, that Frank's second MMPI results were abnormal, or whether he simply made a typographical error and decided to correct it with a pen. Or, perhaps someone changed his report to suit her own needs.

Also in his report, Dr. Franklin noted that the new MMPI results indicated Frank was "somewhat rigid and attempting to project an overly positive self-image." The results were very similar to her first MMPI. During the interview, Frank told the doctor that she felt she had higher moral values than most people, but that she didn't think they would cause her any problems as a police officer.

Dr. Franklin also noted Antoinette Frank's five-year career at Wal-Mart and her "very good work record" there. He cited as proof, a glowing letter of recommendation that was supposed to have been written by Frank's New Orleans Wal-Mart boss.

At the time of Dr. Franklin's evaluation, the New Orleans Police Department had known for eight months that Frank had lied on her police application about being transferred from the Wal-Mart in Opelousas to the store in New Orleans. They knew that she had in fact been fired in Opelousas for "personality conflicts with other associates" and had been rated "unsatisfactory" at the termination of her employment. Franklin's report makes no mention of Frank having been fired.

On the last page of his report, under the heading "IMPRESSION," Dr. Franklin wrote: "I put heavy weight on the letters of recommendation. I think it is significant that the patient's statements regarding her employment is [sic] substantiated with a very positive recommendation from her employer . . . The letters from family and friends . . . the letter from Arnesta Taylor of the NOPD, all are taken into careful consideration."

The doctor also concluded that the results of Frank's second MMPI—the indications of "rigid adjustment, denial and repression, as well as some obsessional features" and the "unrealistic sense of moral values"—were not necessarily all that accurate. He closed his report by writing, "I feel this applicant could function in a position as a police officer . . . I see no *major* psychopathology." (Emphasis added.)

The lifejacket was snugly in place. Now all Antoinette Frank had to do was drift along.

**After** they received a second opinion from Dr. Franklin, the Department of Civil Service's rules required that one of their own doctors conduct an additional interview and a re-evaluation of Frank. Less than one month after "passing" Dr. Franklin's psychiatric evaluation, and only two months since she completely blew her first psychiatric interview with Dr. Scurria, Frank sat down with Dr. J. Robert Barnes, a psychiatrist working under contract for the Department of Civil Service.

During the interview, Frank impressed Dr. Barnes with her appearance and professional behavior. Later in his report, Dr. Barnes cited Frank's work as a volunteer police officer (which she hadn't done) and her time as a Police

Explorer as the basis for her keen understanding of police work. He also commented on her "well thought out" motivation for wanting to become a police officer.

Dr. Barnes, who had access to Frank's MMPI test results—the same ones examined by Dr. Dralle and Dr. Scurria—reported his interview with Frank on a form called a "PSYCHIATRIC INTERVIEW REPORT," the same form Dr. Scurria had used just two months earlier. One section of the report, entitled "Evaluation of job-related characteristics," lists fourteen categories on which the applicant is graded. There are five possible scores: unacceptable, below average, average, above average, exceptional. In September, Dr. Scurria had rated Frank unacceptable or below average in six of the fourteen categories, average in five of them, above average in only three, and exceptional in none.

However, Dr. Barnes saw things differently. His report rated Frank average or above average in all fourteen categories. In none of them did Dr. Barnes think Frank was unacceptable, below average, or exceptional. He drove down the middle of the road, right between the lines.

In the narrative portion of his report, Dr. Barnes wrote that he had reviewed the previous psychological and psychiatric reports, including Dr. Franklin's evaluation. Dr. Barnes said he also examined Frank's police background investigation, but his report did not mention that Frank had lied to a police investigator and to Dr. Penelope Dralle about being fired from Wal-Mart.

Dr. Barnes's conclusion said, "No problems elicited *in this interview* which would indicate a problem with performance as a police *recruit*." (Emphasis added.)

What Dr. Barnes did not say in the carefully crafted wording of his conclusion was whether anything in the other material he reviewed—the psychological and psychiatric evaluations and the police background report—indicated a potential problem with Antoinette Frank and her performance not just as a police recruit but as a full-fledged police officer. Maybe he thought the police academy would weed her out.

Perhaps if Dr. Barnes had carefully studied the previous doctors' reports and the background investigation, if he had questioned why the police department and the city were still considering hiring someone who had lied to them—both on her application and during an interview—he would have reached a different conclusion.

At the bottom of the "PSYCHIATRIC INTERVIEW REPORT," just above the signature line, is the recommendation section. The psychological tests, the interviews and evaluations, the re-tests, the re-interviews and re-evaluations—they all came down to two choices: "suitable for job" or "not suitable for job."

On November 2, 1992, Dr. Barnes typed triple "X"s on the check line next to "suitable for job" and scrawled his signature at the bottom of the report, thereby setting in motion a chain of events that would end twenty-eight months later in a nightmare of gunfire, blood, and death.

# TEN

**Antoinette** Frank's writing wasn't limited to letters of recommendation, whether forged or genuine. Less than three weeks before the New Orleans Police Department finally hired her, Frank penned a half-baked suicide note addressed to her father.

The morning of January 20, 1993, was cool and crisp by New Orleans standards. The temperature was in the low fifties, with a north wind slicing off the lake.

Frank needed to go downtown to talk to an attorney. She'd done everything else she could think of to get a job with the police department. Maybe an attorney could help. Her dad, Adam Frank, Sr., decided to ride with her.

At about ten o'clock, Frank slid her old Ford Torino Elite into a parking space outside the downtown building where the attorney she was visiting had his office. She went inside while her father waited in the car . . . and waited.

By noon, Antoinette had still not come out of the building, so Adam Frank decided to go in and look for her. He rode the elevator up to the law office and approached the receptionist.

"Can I help you, sir?" the receptionist asked, a helpful smile plastered across her face.

"I'm looking for my daughter. She came in here for an appointment about ten o'clock."

The receptionist glanced down at her appointment book. "What's her name?"

"Antoinette Frank."

The receptionist's finger traced a line of names and stopped at one near the top. She looked up at Adam Frank. "She was here for her appointment, but she's already gone, sir."

"What time did she leave?"

The receptionist shook her left hand to center her watch on her wrist. "She was only here for a few minutes, sir. I'd say she left about ten-fifteen."

Adam Frank took the elevator down to the lobby. On his way out, he passed the building security desk. The guard sat behind it reading the newspaper. Frank trudged back out to Antoinette's car and climbed into the passenger seat. He fidgeted around and listened to the radio.

After what Adam Frank later told police was about an hour, he decided to go back inside the building to see if anyone else had seen his daughter.

He stopped at the security desk. "I'm looking for my daughter," he told the guard. "She came in here a few hours ago for an appointment with an attorney, and I haven't seen her since."

"What's your name?" the guard asked.

"Adam Frank."

The guard reached for something behind the raised front portion of the desk; when he lifted his hand he held an envelope. "She told me to give you this when you came in."

Adam Frank's name was written across the front of the

envelope. He recognized the writing as his daughter's neat, hand-printed lettering. He pulled the envelope from the guard's hand and tore it open. Inside he found a short note written on lined notebook paper. It, too, was printed in Antoinette's handwriting. "I cannot live in this world the way I am, so I will not hold you down with me. I don't know where I will go but I want to be away from as many people as I can. I was doomed since the day I was born. I see that now, I hate myself and my life."

Adam Frank raced back upstairs and spoke with the attorney whom his daughter had seen. The attorney told him that he had met with Antoinette briefly, but had told her that he couldn't help her. Frank went back downstairs and called the police.

When the officers arrived, Frank told them that his daughter was missing and handed them the note. The officers filed a missing persons report and took the letter as evidence.

Antoinette Frank showed up back at home the next day. No one knows if she offered her father an explanation for her strange disappearance.

Apparently, neither the missing persons report nor Frank's suicide note reached any of the people involved in applicant screening, because on February 7, 1993, just two and a half weeks after the bizarre events at the lawyer's office, the New Orleans Police Department decided that Antoinette Frank was physically, morally, and mentally fit enough to don the uniform of a police cadet. They hired her and sent her to the police academy. At long last, Frank's dream had come true.

Several of Frank's academy classmates and some of her instructors said that although she was often quiet, and sometimes goofed off at inappropriate times, she was a good student.

* * *

**On** August 6, 1993, at a graduation ceremony at police headquarters, newly appointed New Orleans police superintendent Joseph Orticke, Jr., administered the oath of office to police cadet Antoinette Frank, who raised her right hand and said, "I, Antoinette Frank, do solemnly swear that I will support the Constitution and the laws of the United States, the constitution and the laws of this state, and the charter and ordinances of this city, and that I will faithfully and impartially discharge and perform all the duties incumbent on me as a police officer according to the best of my ability and understanding, so help me God."

The chief placed badge number 628 into Frank's eager hand. It was the symbol of her appointment to the position of police officer and the culmination of a lifelong pursuit.

Despite the incredible odds, and after having overcome all of the obstacles in her path—being caught lying on her police application, three unsatisfactory scores on psychological evaluations, failing a psychiatric interview, and leaving a halfhearted suicide note—Frank had still managed to muscle her way into the job she'd prepared herself for and strived toward for so long. She had finally made it. She was a New Orleans police officer. Now all she had to do was prove herself where it counted—on the street.

There is a reason why police applicants have to endure so much in order to become police officers. There is a reason why so much time and money goes into the screening of applicants. There is a reason why so much sweat and misery goes into the training of police officers. The reason is that there is simply no other job that bestows upon such a young person so much power.

In the case of Antoinette Frank, the system worked fine. The screening in place at the time clearly identified her as someone better suited to another line of work. Yet the New Orleans Police Department insisted on hiring her anyway.

In the early 1990s, the NOPD was losing far more officers than it could afford to replace. The work hours were long, the pay was lousy, and the residency law required that all police officers live inside the New Orleans city limits, which disqualified a lot of good applicants from the suburbs. During that time, the department was losing an average of more than one hundred officers per year—at least a couple of dozen of them having been arrested—and was hiring fewer than half that. Experienced officers were flocking to other departments where they could at least earn enough money to live on. So in New Orleans, the hiring standards just kept dropping.

In 1994, CBS's Mike Wallace branded New Orleans as "the number one city in the nation for police brutality and corruption."

Mayor Marc Morial, on the job for less than a year at the time of the Kim Anh murders, admitted in a March 20, 1995, story in *TIME* magazine, "I inherited a police department that was a shambles."

With Antoinette Frank's promotion from police cadet to police officer, her salary was bumped up to $1,500 per month, an amount far lower than the national average for officers in comparable-sized police departments.

In the same *TIME* magazine story, Neil Gallagher, FBI special agent in charge, said, "Everybody knows they are grossly underpaid. And still people wonder why there is corruption."

**Frank's** first assignment out of the academy, which turned out to be her only assignment in a somewhat shortened career, was to a uniform patrol platoon at the 7th District. Each of New Orleans's nine police districts has three platoons or shifts. The platoons are commanded by a lieutenant, who has a senior sergeant serving as assistant platoon commander. The platoons are subdivided into two squads each, both led by a sergeant.

The patrol cars are usually manned by two officers, who

share the same days off. One-man units are for officers whose regular partner is on vacation, sick leave, court duty, or special assignment. The platoons are identified by number designation, and each one works a fixed shift. The 1st platoon works 7 A.M. to 3 P.M., 2nd platoon works 3 P.M. to 11 P.M., and the 3rd platoon works 11 P.M. to 7 A.M. A major source of irritation to the officers is that they are required to report for roll call thirty-five minutes before the start of the shift, a seemingly minor thing but one that adds up to eleven extra hours of work per month, eleven hours for which they aren't paid overtime. The lack of overtime money during the early-to-mid 1990s forced a lot of officers to spend as much or more time working off-duty security details as they did working their normal shifts.

Frank was assigned to 2nd platoon, working the second watch, 2:25 P.M. to 11 P.M. Lt. Frank Van Dalen was her platoon commander. Van Dalen put her on Sergeant David Slicho's squad, the same squad as Officer Ronnie Williams. Right from the start, during a time when most rookie cops are out to prove themselves, when many have to be reined in and have their enthusiasm curbed by more seasoned veterans, Frank's work was not exactly awe-inspiring.

"She was too timid," Sergeant Slicho says. "I only saw her at the beginning and end of the shift."

According to a lot of cops at the 7th District, Frank had no idea what police work was about, and she had no idea how to do it. Frank's platoon commander describes her in almost the exact same language as that used by her high school teachers. "Frank was real meek. She was a nonentity," Lieutenant Van Dalen says. "If this [the murders] hadn't happened, we never would have known she was here."

After graduating from the academy, each newly commissioned New Orleans police officer spends four months riding with a field training officer. The FTOs are supposed to show the rookies how to take the knowledge they learned in the controlled environment of the academy and use it in the uncontrolled environment of the street. After just three months, Frank's FTO was ready to send her back to the academy for more training. "She really didn't seem to have a grasp of what she needed to do to be a policeman," one veteran officer said.

In addition to problems on the job, it was also during Frank's time with her FTO that her personal life took a strange turn. Her father vanished.

Just before Frank had entered the academy, she'd moved from her house on Sheephead Street to another rented house at 7524 Michigan Street, also in New Orleans East. Although at the time she moved, Frank couldn't have known what police district she was going to be assigned to, it's very likely—given her past behavior—that she did some heavy-duty finagling while at the academy to boost her odds of getting sent to the district in which she'd recently rented a new house.

On September 26, 1993, at 6 P.M. on one of Frank's regular days off, she strolled into the 7th District station and spun a bizarre tale. She told the desk officer that she needed to file a missing persons report. It seemed her father had disappeared a few days before from the house they shared on Michigan Street, and Frank was starting to get worried. The officer assigned to handle the complaint, James Williams, Jr., radioed the command desk and requested an item number under which he could file the report. Then he sat down with Frank and took a statement from her.

Frank's father, Adam Frank, Sr., was a forty-six-year-old Vietnam veteran. He had worked for the telephone company in Opelousas but had moved back to New Orleans and in with his daughter a year or so earlier. Neighbors had frequently seen him outside painting and fixing up the house. At the time of his disappearance, Adam Frank wasn't working, he had no car, nor did he have a history of unexplained absence.

In her statement to the investigating officer, Frank claimed that she last saw her father three days before, at four-thirty in the afternoon, when she had left the rented house they shared on Michigan Street. She said he'd been wearing black shorts, a white T-shirt, and black combat boots.

She said that when she returned home at about nine o'clock that night, her father was gone. Frank said that about forty-eight hours after her father's disappearance—and a full day before she decided to contact the police—she received a strange telephone call. When she answered the phone, a voice on the line said, "I am gonna get you." Then the caller hung up. Frank didn't mention to the reporting officer if the voice belonged to a man or a woman.

Frank also told Officer Williams that about two months before her father disappeared, he'd mentioned to her that he owed someone money, but she said he hadn't told her whom he owed it to or how much he owed.

Later, Frank mentioned to neighbors that the telephone company had transferred her father out of town. Adam Frank, Sr., has not been seen alive since.

# ELEVEN

**At** the end of her four-month field-training program, and despite the misgivings of her FTO, Frank somehow—just as always—managed to squeak by with a combination of charm and guile.

By January 1994, Frank was a full-fledged police officer. She'd made it through the hiring process, the academy, and the FTO program. All she needed was a partner.

Police partnerships are important. In New Orleans, two-man cars handle the majority of emergency calls for service, such as crimes in progress. One-man cars handle the non-emergency calls, mainly taking reports of crimes that have already happened and working minor traffic accidents. Riding in a car for eight hours a day with someone you don't get along with or don't trust is a recipe for disaster.

Police officers have to make a lot of judgment calls, and partners have to back each other up. They also have to be able to trust each other enough so that if the shit hits the fan, and it's just the two of them surrounded—as they say in New Orleans—by alligators, they'll fight their way out together.

New Orleans is a violent city. The criminals carry guns. The guns are easy to get and legal to carry in a car. In the early-to-mid 1990s, there was a little store just below New Orleans, in neighboring St. Bernard Parish, called Chalmette Jewelry. The store was selling thousands of guns to convicted felons by simply allowing a convict's girlfriend or non-convicted-felon buddy to fill out the paperwork. And they weren't just selling cheap pistols, the typical "Saturday night special." They were selling a lot of Tec-9s and MAK-90s. The MAKs were a Chinese-made, civilian version of the Soviet AK-47 assault rifle. The Bureau of Alcohol, Tobacco and Firearms (ATF) eventually put some of the owners of Chalmette Jewelry in prison, but it didn't do much to stop guns from getting into the hands of criminals in the area.

At the 7th District, Lieutenant Van Dalen tried to find the right partner for Antoinette Frank. He tried a couple of male officers, but that didn't work. She accused them of sexually harassing her. He tried a couple of female officers, but that didn't work either. According to one former 7th District field training officer, "She wouldn't get along with guys, and she wouldn't get along with the girls."

By the spring of 1994, Van Dalen had to do something with Frank. She couldn't get along with a partner, yet she wasn't competent to work alone. Frank had been on the job, including her four months at the academy, for just over a year and had Civil Service protection. She had also, at least on paper, successfully completed her field training.

The lieutenant's options were limited. With her Civil Service protection, firing Frank wouldn't be easy. Then there was the racial component Van Dalen may have considered. In a city in which racial tension is always simmering, Van Dalen, as a white male supervisor, wouldn't have been doing himself or his career any favors by recommending the firing of a newly hired, black female police officer. He also genuinely liked Frank. He thought she was nice; she just didn't need to be a police officer.

Another option was to transfer her, to another platoon or maybe even to another district, but Van Dalen wasn't like that. He was the kind of man who liked to take care of his own problems, not pass them on to someone else.

So if firing Frank was out and transferring Frank was out, that only left one option: Van Dalen had to make her a better police officer. He reached out to Officer Colin Danos (name changed at the officer's request). Danos was one of the district's FTOs, but he didn't have a trainee at the time. He'd also just transferred to the 2nd platoon from the night watch and didn't have a regular partner yet. Danos was a good cop. Although standing just five feet, two inches, he was muscular, with the build of a fireplug. He'd also spent time on the district task force and in narcotics. Task force cops didn't handle calls; they were a hard-charging group of officers, mostly young, mostly male, whose job was to go out, kick ass, and put criminals in jail. Danos had racked up several medals and commendations for bravery.

One day just after roll call, Danos heard the lieutenant was looking for him. "What's up L-T?" he asked as he strolled into the boss's office.

"Close the door," Van Dalen said, then nodded to a chair. "Have a seat."

"Uh-oh. I got another complaint?" Aggressive officers earned two things—commendations and complaints.

"Colin," Van Dalen said, coming straight to the point. "I want you to ride with Frank."

Danos shook his head. "No, L-T. You can't do that to me."

Van Dalen raised his hand. "Just for a little while. I want you to evaluate her and tell me what you think."

"Man, I heard she don't get along with nobody."

"I'm not asking you to marry her, just ride with her."

"What's this about?" Danos said. "You trying to get rid of her or what?"

"No. I think she'll be all right if we just put her with the right person. She's a nice kid. She's just a little bit . . ."

"Scared?"

"Timid," Van Dalen said. "I don't think she learned enough at the academy, so I want you to kind of give her an advanced course in how to be a policeman."

However reluctantly he had accepted it, Danos took his assignment seriously. He and Frank became partners. "I rode with her the whole summer," he says. "She was a little country, a little bit slow. She was not an aggressive person."

When they were working, Danos had to do almost all the driving because Frank didn't like to drive. And when Danos forced her to drive, it sometimes nearly led to disaster. "She almost wrecked the car one time because she was trying to keep from running over a cat," Danos says. "You know if it comes down to wrecking a police car and maybe getting somebody killed or running over a damn cat, you're going to kill that fucking cat."

One night on a shots-fired call, Frank and Danos rolled up on a guy with a gun. Danos bailed out of the car and ran the suspect down on foot. "I grabbed the guy and the gun, handcuffed him, and I turn around and she's just standing there, watching."

Sometime during the summer of 1994, Frank's twenty-four-year-old brother, Adam Frank, Jr., moved into her house at 7524 Michigan Street, the same house from which their father, Adam Frank, Sr., had disappeared the previous fall.

Adam Jr. was big—six feet, five inches tall—and weighed in at about two hundred pounds. He was also a fugitive. He had been convicted of burglary in their hometown of Opelousas and was wanted for probation violation. The police department in Opelousas also had a warrant out for Adam Jr.'s arrest on two counts of attempted manslaughter. Opelousas was too small a town and Adam Jr. was too well known for him to hide there for very long, so he decided to head to New Orleans to lay low for a while.

It was during that long, hot summer of 1994, as the murder rate in New Orleans skyrocketed to new heights, that Danos met Frank's brother for the first time. "Me and her would be riding together," Danos says, "and he'd call her on the phone and tell her he'd cooked some food. So we'd stop by her house, and he'd fix us dinner."

**One** of the 7th District officers, Stanley Morlier, Jr., had a lucrative security detail at the Kim Anh restaurant on Bullard Avenue. During the summer of 1994, he asked a couple of his friends and fellow 7th District officers, Colin Danos and Ronnie Williams, to help him work it. Ronnie and his wife already had one son and another one on the way, so he was only too happy to get the opportunity to find a steady supply of extra income.

The restaurant was owned and operated by the Vu family, a tight-knit and hardworking Catholic Vietnamese family who had immigrated to the United States piecemeal over an eleven-year period beginning in 1979, just four years after their native South Vietnam fell into communist hands.

All six Vus—mom, dad, and the four children (Ha, 24; Chau, 23; Quoc, 18; Cuong, 17)—worked at the restaurant. The Vu children were good kids. None of them had ever been in any kind of trouble. The oldest, Ha, a student at Delgado Community College, and the youngest, Cuong, a junior at Sarah T. Reed High School and a member of the school's football team, both had plans to enter the Catholic clergy. Chau was also in college, and Quoc was in his senior year of high school.

The Vus treated the detail officers like family.

According to Danos, the elder Vus were part of a community financial organization that operated like an informal bank. Vietnamese families pooled their money by paying into the club a certain amount of cash every month. The pool of cash allowed members to take out short-term loans to buy a house or start a business. Mrs. Vu was the club treasurer and held most of the cash. According to Chau Vu, her parents had just borrowed $10,000 from the club to make improvements to the restaurant plumbing and parking lot.

Danos also managed to work his "partner," the skittish Antoinette Frank, into the detail at the Vus' restaurant. The reaction of the Vus to Officer Frank was immediate acceptance. Almost from the start, they took her in and made her feel at home. According to Danos, "The Vus took a real liking to her. I mean they were in love with this girl. They bought her presents for this, presents for that; anything she wanted, anything she needed, they gave her."

The Vu family's generosity, particularly Mrs. Vu's, and their love for Antoinette Frank were reiterated after the shootings in a statement Chau gave to the police. In slightly broken English, she told investigators, "But we think her like family. My mom loves her. I think she like my family. We kiss her . . . we, we like . . ." Although Chau broke down at that point and couldn't finish her thought, it's clear enough. The Vus loved *and trusted* Antoinette Frank.

By the end of the summer, Morlier and Danos picked up a second detail, this one at a bar at Chef Menteur Highway and Michoud Boulevard. Because the bar detail paid better, the two officers let Ronnie Williams take over the Kim Anh, and they left Antoinette Frank to help him.

While Frank had been busy ingratiating herself with the Vus, she'd also been trying to look out for her brother, Adam Jr. With Antoinette's consent, Adam started spending a lot of time hanging out at the Kim Anh. The Vus had a karaoke machine, and on weekend nights, customers took to the small stage set up across the dining room from the bar to belt out their favorite songs. Sometimes Frank would drop her brother off at the restaurant in the afternoon before she went to work and not pick him up until the end of her shift, nearly nine hours later. Sometimes, Adam Jr. stayed until the Kim Anh closed at one o'clock in the morning. "He was just hanging around, mooching free food. He had nothing to do," Stanley Morlier says.

The fact that Adam Jr., a convicted felon and a fugitive wanted for trying to kill two people, a man who had fled to New Orleans to escape law enforcement, spent so much time around policemen said a lot for the faith he had in his sister's ability to shield him.

According to Danos, Adam Jr. was at the restaurant so much that the Vus eventually put him to work as a bar back and an occasional bartender. Danos says that it was while Adam Jr. was working that he got a look at the safe the Vus had built under the bar. Inside that safe is where Mrs. Vu kept the financial club deposits. Danos occasionally saw inside the safe. "There were stacks of money in there, mainly hundred-dollar bills."

**By** September, Officer Colin Danos felt as if he'd done what Lieutenant Van Dalen had asked him to do. He'd ridden with Frank and evaluated her performance. Now all that was left for him to do was report back to Van Dalen, or so he thought.

Danos shut the door as he stepped into the lieutenant's office.

"Well?" Van Dalen asked. "What do you think?"

Danos dropped into a chair in front of his boss's desk. Then he looked at Van Dalen and shrugged. "She might make it if she rides with somebody, but she'll never make it on her own."

"Why do you say that?"

"She's shy, she's timid, she's just afraid."

Van Dalen dragged a hand down over his face. Silence hung between the two men for several seconds. "I want you to keep working with her."

Danos leaned back in the chair, as if he could distance himself from Van Dalen's order. "No way, Lieutenant. You asked me just to evaluate her. I been riding with her all summer."

"I think you've already done her some good. I've seen some improvement."

"Put her with—"

"I need her with you."

"Why?"

"Because I want you to look out for her and keep her out of trouble. If you stay with her, I think she'll make it. If not . . ." He shrugged. "I don't know."

Danos felt the pressure. Another officer's career might be in his hands. If he stayed with Frank, she might get to keep her job; if he quit working with her, she might very well lose it.

"The rank was trying to make up their mind if they were going to keep the girl or not," Danos says. "But you really can't teach somebody how to be a police officer. It's got to be in you, and it was not in her to be a police officer."

Still, Danos agreed to try.

# TWELVE

**Rogers** LaCaze was born in New Orleans on August 13, 1976, the son of Michael LaCaze, Sr., and Alice Chaney. He had an older brother by a couple of years, Michael LaCaze, Jr. Rogers, whose IQ as an adult was tested at 71, wasn't cut out to be a student, so after an undistinguished academic career in New Orleans public schools, considered by many to be some of the worst in the country, he dropped out during tenth grade.

Iona Brown, best friend of LaCaze's mother, has known LaCaze since he was seven years old. "Rogers was a good child," she said. "He never gave me no disrespect." But during LaCaze's teen years, Ms. Brown said she noticed a change in her best friend's son. "He did wrong as a teen," she said. She also noticed that by the time he was fifteen or sixteen, Rogers, who never had a job, was wearing nothing but designer clothes. Brown knew his mother hadn't bought the clothes for him. "He had the street life," she said.

During his teen years, LaCaze fathered at least three children. Renetta Marigany had two sons by him. Renee

Braddy, the woman LaCaze was living with on the night of the Kim Anh murders, had a daughter with him.

At seventeen, LaCaze was arrested for illegal use of a firearm. The charge was later dropped. That same year, his mother kicked him and his brother out of her house. Alice Chaney's bedrock Christian beliefs didn't tolerate sons being disrespectful to their mother. Nor did her faith allow her to tolerate drugs, so when she found drug paraphernalia in her sons' rooms, she called the police. She thought the shock of it—the police coming to her house—might straighten her boys out. It didn't, so she kicked them both out of her house.

In 1994, the police arrested Michael LaCaze for carrying a gun. When he got out of jail, someone shot him, paralyzing him from the waist down and condemning him to a wheelchair for the rest of his life.

After his mom gave him the boot, Rogers moved in with Renee Braddy. "Rogers sold dope," Alice Chaney says. "That was his crime."

By the time he turned eighteen, Rogers LaCaze was a street thug. "I was a drug dealer," he admits. He was also not above setting up a friend for a little armed robbery.

Twenty-one-year-old Derrick Jefferson probably considered Rogers LaCaze a friend. They had attended Abramson High School together until LaCaze dropped out.

On Sunday, November 13, 1994, Jefferson saw LaCaze and another man at the Plaza shopping mall in New Orleans. A few hours later, Jefferson got a call asking him to meet LaCaze at a house in New Orleans East.

Although in later testimony Jefferson was steadfast in his denial that the meeting that night was a drug deal, he did admit to selling cocaine to LaCaze on previous occasions.

Whatever the real reason for the meeting, Jefferson, who was unemployed, had at least $600 cash in his pocket. He also had a gun.

When he drove up to the house where he was to meet

LaCaze, he found his old high school buddy standing outside with the same guy he'd seen him with earlier at the mall. As Jefferson rolled to a stop, both LaCaze and the other man strolled up to the driver's side window of his car. They stood side by side. After Jefferson cranked down the window, LaCaze's companion shoved a gun in Jefferson's face. LaCaze said, "Let me get what you got. Give me what's in your pocket."

Jefferson was stunned. He looked from one to the other. He hadn't been expecting this.

"I said give it up," LaCaze shouted at him. The muzzle of the gun was just a foot away from Jefferson's head. He dug into his pocket and handed LaCaze a wad of money.

The man with the gun started shooting.

Jefferson later said, "I had a gun in my car, so I started shooting back."

In the hail of gunfire, Jefferson was hit four times. One bullet ripped into his arm, two hit his right leg, and one tore into his left leg. When Jefferson started shooting back, LaCaze and the guy with the gun ran for their lives. Jefferson dragged his wounded arm up high enough to shift his car into gear and punched the accelerator. He drove straight to his mom's house.

A couple of months later, Jefferson and LaCaze spotted each other driving on the street. LaCaze signaled for Jefferson to pull over. Jefferson did.

The two men stood on the side of the road, facing each other for the first time since the shooting. "Bro, I just wanted to let you know I ain't had nothing to do with what happened with you getting shot," LaCaze said. "That was all that other dude's idea. I didn't even know he had that gun."

"You're the one who said you wanted what was in my pocket," Jefferson said.

"I was just trying to do what that other dude wanted so nobody got hurt."

"I got shot four motherfucking times," Jefferson said.

"Bro, I'm telling you, I feel bad about that, but you could see I ain't had no gun. If I was trying to rob you, don't you think I would've had a gun?"

"We'll see what happens."

"If you're trying to put a charge on somebody, please don't put it on me because I ain't did nothing to you. That dude's crazy, and in fact, I was trying to save you from gettin' hurt."

Jefferson watched LaCaze climb back into his car and drive away. After that, Jefferson just went home.

**Although** they didn't actually meet on the night of November 25, 1994, it was the first time the paths of Rogers LaCaze and Antoinette Frank crossed.

Officer Colin Danos had taken a night off, and Antoinette Frank was working a one-man car. Just before 10 P.M., a 34-S (shooting) call came out. Frank was one of several units that responded to the scene at 13565 Chef Menteur Highway, apartment 75, the home of Rogers LaCaze and Renee Braddy. When Frank arrived, she found twenty-year-old Nemiah Miller lying on the grass in the courtyard in front of the door to LaCaze's ground-floor apartment. Miller had been shot full of holes but was still alive. His hysterical girlfriend, Tara Decux, knelt on the ground beside him.

Decux told Officer Frank that a neighbor had already carted off the second victim, Rogers LaCaze, who had also been shot, to a nearby hospital.

Frank got on the radio and told the dispatcher she needed an EMS unit to respond to the location, code three. Lights and siren.

When Frank's assistant platoon commander, Geraldine Prudhomme, rolled up to the scene, her experience told her that Miller was probably not going to make it, so she asked the command desk to notify Homicide.

At 10:10 P.M., the desk officer at the Criminal Investigation Bureau called the Homicide Division and told them that the 7th District had requested their assistance in a double shooting. There were two victims, both with multiple gunshot wounds.

When the EMS truck arrived, the medics loaded Miller into the back and took him to Methodist Hospital. Methodist was closer than Charity, but the trauma unit wasn't as good.

Homicide detectives don't always wait for their clients to die before they get involved in the case. In a serious shooting—one in which the victim hasn't been pronounced dead yet, but is likely to die—homicide cops will often get called in to handle the crime scene work and initial interviews. They gather the evidence and collect witness statements, then wait for at least one of the victims to bleed out. If that happens, then it's a murder case. If it doesn't, then Homicide turns the case over to somebody else.

As detectives arrived on the scene of the Rogers LaCaze and Nemiah Miller shooting, they began to piece together what had happened.

According to Renee Braddy and Tara Decux, they and their boyfriends, LaCaze and Miller, had just been hanging out at the apartment that night. At about nine o'clock, a friend of theirs, nineteen-year-old Damon Scott, who went by the nickname "Freaky D," knocked on the door. Scott strolled into the apartment wearing a dark blue jogging suit and flashing four gold teeth across the top of his mouth. He said he needed to talk to LaCaze and Miller.

LaCaze, Miller, and Scott huddled together in the apartment for nearly half an hour. No one who was there will say exactly what they talked about, but LaCaze's mother thinks she knows.

"It was behind a dope deal," Ms. Chaney says. "Rogers and Nemiah had just scored."

After the three young men finished their business, Scott walked to the front door as if he were leaving. LaCaze and

Miller went with him. Decux told police it was then, while Scott stood at the door, that he pulled out a pistol and started shooting.

Braddy said she heard several gunshots, then heard Scott shout at either LaCaze or Miller, "Bitch, don't run." Braddy said she dove to the floor as more shots went off.

As soon as Scott started firing, LaCaze and Miller turned and ran. One bullet hit LaCaze in the back. Another struck the left side of his face, a through-and-through wound that blasted out his right cheek. But LaCaze kept on his feet and kept moving. Miller wasn't so lucky. He took two bullets in the chest and one in his right arm, then caught another one in the spine as he ran across the courtyard. He collapsed twenty-five feet from the apartment door, paralyzed from the waist down.

Seconds after the crash of the gunshots ripped through the air, apartment manager Jack Lindell saw a man run past him toward the back of the building. The man was carrying a gun and bleeding heavily. Since only two men had been shot and one of them, Miller, lay paralyzed in the courtyard, the man Lindell saw had to have been Rogers LaCaze. Lindell saw the man toss the gun into some bushes then stagger back toward the front of the building.

Caesar Martinez, from apartment 44, was standing outside talking to some neighbors when the shooting started. He heard about six gunshots; then he saw LaCaze run past, wounded and trailing blood. LaCaze crouched at the back of the apartment building for a few minutes. Then he crept back toward the front and told Martinez that he had been shot and asked him to call the police.

Yvonne Miller (no relation to Nemiah) lived in apartment 74, next door to Braddy and LaCaze. She was lounging on her bed watching television when she heard the shots. She screamed to her kids to get down on the floor. When the shooting stopped, she jumped out of bed and peeked through the window. Nemiah Miller was on the ground in the courtyard. As Yvonne Miller threw on a robe so that she could go outside to find out if she could help, she saw two bullet holes in the living room wall of her apartment. On the floor lay the two spent bullets.

Anthony Spencer was in apartment 72, on the second floor, when he heard the shots. He stepped outside to see what was going on. Peering over the balcony, he saw Nemiah Miller lying on the grass below him. Spencer shouted to a neighbor to call the police and then ran downstairs. LaCaze staggered into the courtyard, carrying a set of keys. He handed the keys to Spencer and asked him to drive him to the hospital. Then he led Spencer to Nemiah Miller's Chevy S-10 pickup truck. Spencer stuffed the wounded man into the passenger seat and took off for Lakeland Hospital.

As they worked the crime scene, detectives followed a blood trail from apartment 75 to the back of the building, where apartment manager Lindell had seen one of the wounded men—almost certainly Rogers LaCaze—toss away a gun. Near the end of the blood trail, detectives found an H&R model 733, .32-caliber revolver.

Inside LaCaze's apartment, detectives also found a .38-caliber Colt Detective Special and a Glock 9 mm pistol.

Neither of the victims had a job. Both young men wore gangster clothing and had expensive shoes. They had gold jewelry and gold teeth. It didn't take the detectives long to decide that they were dealing with a drug-related shooting.

Nemiah Miller didn't make it. He died a week later, and the case officially became a homicide investigation.

According to a couple of veteran 7th District officers, word on the street has always been that LaCaze and Miller and maybe Damon Scott got into an argument, one that escalated into a shoot-out, and that LaCaze is the one who actually killed Miller. The officers say that whether or not Damon Scott, aka "Freaky D," was really there is anyone's guess. The District Attorney's Office later declined to prosecute Scott.

As the district officer assigned to handle the call, it was Frank's responsibility to conduct the preliminary investigation and write the initial report. As part of her investigation, she put together a photo lineup that included a picture of Damon "Freaky D" Scott. A couple of days after the shooting, Frank went to Lakeland Hospital to see the surviving victim.

As Frank walked into the hospital room, she saw LaCaze lying in bed with tubes sticking out of his arms and nose. Wires from electronic sensors taped to his body ran to a cart stacked with beeping monitors. Officer Frank introduced herself. For some reason, a reason that no one has since been able to adequately explain, the twenty-four-year-old policewoman formed an instant bond with the eighteen-year-old drug dealer and thug.

If Frank was looking for someone to form a relationship with, someone whom she could push around and dominate, she couldn't have found a person better suited to those needs than Rogers LaCaze. It may have been a simple case of opposites attract. In addition to the difference in age, Frank and LaCaze stood in polar opposition in other respects. With an IQ far below average, standing just five feet, two inches tall, and weighing 135 pounds, LaCaze was considerably smaller and less intelligent than Frank, who was five feet, nine inches tall and weighed close to 150 pounds. Then there were their different lines of work—Frank was a cop, LaCaze was a criminal.

"I want to show you some pictures," Frank told LaCaze. "Tell me if you see the person who shot you."

She held the photos up so LaCaze could see them. Even in his weakened condition, he had no trouble picking out the photograph of the man whom he claimed had shot him and his friend, Nemiah Miller. LaCaze raised his hand and pointed to the picture of Damon Scott. "He's the one."

"Are you sure?" Frank asked.

LaCaze looked into her eyes and nodded. "I'm sure."

With the identification made, there was enough evidence to obtain a murder warrant for Damon "Freaky D" Scott, and with Homicide handling the investigation, Frank's role in the case was at an end. But Frank wasn't finished with Rogers LaCaze yet, not by a long shot.

**When** LaCaze was discharged from the hospital, he went to stay at his mother's house. Even though she had kicked both Rogers and Michael out of her house almost a year before, and even though both of them had been shot since she tossed them out, Alice Chaney took Rogers back in. Although calling the police on him that time hadn't worked, she held out hope that Rogers's most recent, and by far most serious, brush with death would be enough to make him change his ways and straighten out his life.

After lying around his mom's house for two or three days, LaCaze had a surprise visitor. He knew about Nemiah's death and had been waiting for the police to show up to ask him more questions, but he thought it would be detectives from downtown who would come calling, not a young, rookie female patrol officer from the 7th District.

According to LaCaze, Frank told him that he needed to stay out of New Orleans East. "She came to tell me that I needed to stay by my momma's house," he later says. Certain people, Frank warned, were out to get him, including some of her fellow 7th District police officers.

Frank became a frequent visitor to Alice Chaney's home, always with dire warnings and showing much concern for LaCaze's safety. She repeatedly cautioned LaCaze and his mother that New Orleans East was too dangerous for LaCaze to return to. Although she was vague on the details, Frank assured LaCaze that there were drug dealers and police officers looking for him, and that he should stay out of the East altogether.

LaCaze appreciated Frank's attention and concern, but didn't think her warnings were for real. He knew she wasn't married and didn't have a boyfriend. "I kind of figured that she had started liking me," he says, "and she was just making up something to be around me."

Frank offered to help LaCaze. According to statements later made by both LaCaze and his mother, Frank bragged about the connections she had as a police officer and told LaCaze that she could get him a job whenever he wanted one. She also offered to help him get a driver's license—with a 71 IQ, LaCaze was having a tough time trying to pass the written portion of the test—and told him that she could get him back into school so that he could earn his GED. LaCaze claims that the shooting changed his life. "I was out of the game," he says. "In the game, they got a rule there's no such thing as out of the game, but I was out of the game."

Even after LaCaze left his mother's house and moved into a new place on North Tonti Street with his girlfriend, Renee Braddy, the mother of one of his three children, Frank continued to visit him. She would pick him up and drive him out to the suburbs, towns like Metairie and Kenner, to look for work. LaCaze didn't find any work out there, but he and Frank spent a lot of time together.

LaCaze and his mother both claim that after LaCaze had sex with Frank she became obsessed with him.

Months later, after the brutal, execution-style murder of three people at the Kim Anh restaurant, LaCaze said he found Frank's continued fascination with him kind of unusual. "Something seemed funny about her," he claims to have told his mother. "I felt that she was stalking me because everywhere I went, she was there."

LaCaze's apprehension about being stalked didn't seem to bother him enough to stop him from wearing the clothes Frank bought him, or to turn down the pager and cell phone she got for him, or to prevent him from jumping behind the wheel of the brand-new Cadillac she rented for him during the weeks of his recovery.

As LaCaze sat on the witness stand, on trial for his life, he was asked, "Did you look up to Ms. Frank?"

LaCaze answered, "Yes, sir, I did." He explained that he looked up to Frank because she was a police officer. He also told the state prosecutor that he had harbored a dream since the age of five—to be a New Orleans police officer.

# THIRTEEN

A fight broke out one night at the Kim Anh. Some young Vietnamese men sitting at a table started swinging at each other. No one is sure exactly why they started fighting, but according to several sources familiar with the Kim Anh and its clientele, it was very unusual for there to be any trouble.

Adam Frank, Jr., who'd been hanging around the restaurant, mooching so much free food that the Vus had to put him to work, waded into the brawl to break it up. Although at six feet, five inches, he towered over them, one of the Vietnamese combatants managed to land a punch on Adam Frank's face that busted his mouth open. It was a serious enough cut that after the fight was over, Adam Jr. went to the emergency room to have it stitched up.

The next day, both Franks—Antoinette and Adam Jr.—asked the Vus about covering the cost of Adam's hospital visit. The Vus said they would think about it, but later, when Chau asked Ronnie what he thought, the policeman said, "If he wants to play like he's the police and try to break up fights, let him pay for it himself."

"I rode with the girl for eight months," Officer Colin Danos says, talking about Antoinette Frank, "and we developed a little bit of a friendship. I probably know things about her that nobody else does."

The front seat of a patrol car is a tight space, tighter even than a regular car, because unlike the family sedan, the front seat of a police car is packed with equipment—radios, siren control head, clipboards, a shotgun, a laptop computer terminal—and eight hours a day is a long time to spend in such cramped quarters. Because there's not much else to do besides talk, partners get to know a lot about each other. They get to know each other's eating habits, bathroom schedules, and a lot about each other's personal lives. Sometimes too much.

One night in December 1994, Danos and Frank stopped by Prime Time Video on Chef Menteur Highway. The next day was an RDO—a regular day off—for both officers, so Danos rented a couple of movies for him and his wife to watch.

In the parking lot, Danos opened the back door of the patrol car and dropped the two videos into his black nylon duffel bag resting on the backseat. Then he slid behind the wheel and eased the cruiser into traffic.

"I've got a boyfriend," Frank said.

Danos was surprised. One night in the intimate confines of the front seat of a patrol car, twenty-three-year-old Frank had confessed to Danos that she was still a virgin. Danos knew Frank had been looking for a boyfriend, but didn't know she had been dating anyone. He didn't think it was a policeman. "She didn't trust police officers," he says, "so she never dated cops." In fact, although Frank was a very attractive young woman, in the time he'd known her, Danos hadn't ever known her to date anyone, or even to talk about people she'd dated in the past.

"Who is he?" Danos asked.

"A guy I met."

"Who?" Danos didn't understand her reluctance.

"His name is Rogers."

"He got a last name?"

"LaCaze."

"Rogers LaCaze." An image flashed through Danos's mind, an image of a guy with gold teeth. A little trouble-maker. "Does he have a brother named Michael?"

Frank shrugged. "I think so."

"You talking about that guy who got shot?"

"Yeah."

"I don't think that's a good idea."

"Why not?" Frank's voice was defensive.

"Because the guy is a criminal," Danos said, "him and his brother. I know that whole family from having to deal with them." Danos had known the LaCaze brothers for a couple of years. He'd stopped them a few times and was pretty sure he had arrested them at least once. In his opinion, they were nothing but thugs. "I think you need to find another boyfriend," he told his partner.

"I like Rogers," Frank said. "He's sweet."

"Then you better be careful," Danos warned.

**One** night, just a few months before the murders, Chau Vu was in the restaurant dining room and walked past Adam Frank, Jr., who, as usual, was propped up at the bar drinking free booze. Adam reached out a long arm and laid a hand on Chau's shoulder. When she turned toward him, he said, "How about a good-night kiss," then puckered his lips. Chau pulled away from him easily enough, and Frank didn't pursue it, but it left Chau a little shaken.

"Adam Frank was real big," Officer Colin Danos says, "and a lot of the Vietnamese people were afraid of him."

Chau loved Antoinette but didn't really care for her brother. Two days later, the incident was still bothering her, so she decided to mention it to Ronnie Williams and Stanley Morlier.

"What?" Williams said, furious after hearing the story. He'd never liked Antoinette's brother and had been hinting to her for a while that he didn't need to hang around the Kim Anh so much.

Within a couple of nights, Williams and Morlier caught up with Antoinette Frank and Colin Danos on a call.

Ronnie Williams pulled Frank aside. "Your brother's got to go."

"What?"

"I've been trying to tell you in a nice way, Antoinette, that he's been hanging around the restaurant too much. The Vus have been feeding him, giving him free drinks, and now this thing with Chau."

"What thing with Chau?" Frank wanted to know.

Williams repeated what Chau had told him.

"That's bullshit!" Frank said.

Stanley Morlier nodded. "I heard it, too."

"Your brother can't be there. He can't come around to the restaurant anymore," Williams said.

Frank spun on her heel and stormed to her patrol car. This time, she jumped in behind the wheel. "Come on," she shouted at Danos. "Let's get the fuck outta here." She rolled down the window as she sped off. "Fuck you," she yelled to Williams and Morlier.

Years later, Morlier recalls, "That's what set her off. That was the bomb right there. She went ballistic and left in a red frenzy."

Just minutes after she left Williams and Morlier in a cloud of road dust, Frank braked hard in the Kim Anh parking lot. She found her brother inside. "Let's get the hell out of here. Come on, fuck these people if they don't want you here." Everyone at the restaurant just stared as Frank practically dragged her brother through the front door. No one tried to stop her.

For the next couple of weeks, Frank ignored Williams and Morlier. She wouldn't speak to them at work, and she didn't work the restaurant detail. "It didn't matter to us," Morlier says. "We didn't need her. We were giving her work because we felt sorry for her."

Then Williams and Morlier ran into Frank and Danos on a call. Frank marched up to Morlier and said, "Ronnie shouldn't have fucked me over. I'm going to get him."

"What are you talking about?" Morlier asked.

"You can tell Ronnie, if he messes with my brother, he's messing with my family, and that means he's messing with me." Frank's eyes took on a maniacal glaze. "And I'll take him out."

Although Ronnie Williams and Stanley Morlier didn't see any more of Adam Jr., another 7th District officer was seeing him on a semi-regular basis. A female officer, who, according to some sources, was kind of halfway dating Adam Jr., started to get a little suspicious of him. Maybe it was her police instincts, but something about the way the guy acted didn't sit right with her.

On the night of December 27, the officer ran Frank's name through the police department computer system to see if he had a criminal record. The system also automatically checks names against the database of wanted persons entered into the FBI's National Crime Information Center (NCIC).

Seconds after punching in Adam Frank, Jr.'s name and date of birth, the officer got a hit. The top of the computer screen flashed the words "WANTED PERSON."

NCIC is a vast system, and hundreds of law enforcement agencies have the ability to enter wanted subjects into its database. An initial hit on a name is just the preliminary step in the process of arresting a fugitive. The first thing that law enforcement officers have to do after a computer hit is verify that the person they are investigating is the same person for whom the warrant was issued. Most of the time, NCIC has enough information, such as numerical identifiers, physical description, and details on marks, scars, and tattoos, that the officers can confirm the match.

The second thing they have to do is confirm with the originating agency, called the ORI in NCIC-speak, that the warrant is still valid. Sometimes the person has already been arrested, but the warrant remains listed in the computer system.

A third step that applies mostly to interstate arrest warrants is to confirm with the prosecutor in the jurisdiction where the warrant was issued that he or she is willing to extradite the fugitive. Often, extradition in minor, nonviolent felonies just isn't worth it to the prosecutor. Extradition often involves lengthy legal proceedings, and the prosecutor usually has to foot the bill for an extradition team to travel to the jurisdiction where the fugitive was caught and to drag him or her back.

In the case of Adam Frank, Jr., extradition wasn't an issue because he was an intrastate fugitive. He was wanted in Opelousas for one count of probation violation from his previous burglary conviction and two counts of attempted manslaughter. The warrants were still good, and Frank was definitely the right guy.

The officer printed a copy of the fugitive bulletin and showed it to another 7th District officer, James Pollard. Pollard took the printout and said he was going to call Frank and talk to her about it. The officer who'd run the computer check didn't want to discuss the subject of Frank's brother at the station, so she waited until after work and then called Sergeant Geraldine Prudhomme at home. She told the sergeant what she'd found out.

That night, Officer Pollard drove to Frank's house on Michigan Street and handed her the printout.

Two days later, Capt. John Landry, commander of the 7th District, called Lieutenant Van Dalen at home and asked him to come in early.

"We've got a problem," Captain Landry said as Van Dalen stepped into his office. After Landry explained the situation, the two of them decided to confront Frank after roll call. They needed to find out if she knew her brother was a fugitive and if she knew where he was. Landry and Van Dalen realized there was a very real possibility, depending on what Antoinette Frank had to say, that she could be charged criminally with something akin to harboring a fugitive, and under Louisiana law, possibly even as an accessory after the fact to the two attempted manslaughters.

Just before the 2:25 P.M. roll call, Frank called in sick.

Captain Landry sent two sergeants, one from the warrant squad and one from the 7th District, to Frank's house on Michigan Street to look for her brother. When Frank answered the door, the sergeants asked her if her brother was home.

"No," she said. "He's not here."

"Is he staying here?" one of the sergeants said.

Frank shook her head. "He was staying with me for a while but not anymore. What's this about, anyway?"

After they told Frank why they were there, she claimed that she had no idea her brother was wanted. "He left yesterday," she said. "I don't think he's coming back."

"Where'd he go?"

Frank shrugged. "He went to stay with a friend of his, probably a girlfriend, in Metairie somewhere."

They asked if she was sure her brother wasn't inside the house somewhere, maybe even without her knowledge—the cops giving her a way out. No, she assured them, he wasn't inside.

The two sergeants, in an incredible move that demonstrated just how little trust they had in fellow police officer Antoinette Frank, searched the house anyway. Adam Jr. and his belongings were gone.

The sergeants explained to Frank that if her brother showed up back at her house, or if she heard from him or learned of his whereabouts, she was to call the 7th District station immediately. Brother or no brother, Adam Frank, Jr., was a wanted man, a fugitive from justice; and Antoinette Frank, as a sworn police officer, had a duty to turn him in.

Adam Frank didn't have a car, and Antoinette's partner, Colin Danos, thinks he knows what happened. "Her brother gathered his belongings, and he was gone within an hour. I don't know if she brought him to the airport . . . I don't know where the hell she brought him, but she brought him somewhere."

Danos says that from that point forward, the 7th District rank kept an eye on Frank; they wanted to find out if her brother was coming back. Captain Landry reported the incident to Internal Affairs, but the department didn't take any action against Frank. According to Felix Loicano, who was the commander of the Internal Affairs Division at the time and who later ran the Public Integrity Division, Frank did not become the subject of any internal investigations. Apparently, no one was too keen to learn why a fugitive was living with a police officer, or why Frank had threatened to "take out" Ronnie Williams.

As Frank's relationship with LaCaze grew, her grip on reality seemed to slip, and there was much more bizarre behavior to come before her final act of madness.

# FOURTEEN

On the night of January 30, 1995, fifty-five-year-old Melford Wilson, Jr., eased his van into the driveway of the abandoned house next door to his own home on Lake Forest Boulevard in New Orleans East. He parked his van there every night after work. The place had been empty for a while, and he figured there was no sense in letting all that good driveway go to waste. His wife had a car, his sons had cars, his sons' friends had cars; it sometimes seemed like his driveway and yard were nothing but a parking lot. Another reason he liked to park at the vacant house next door was that he never got blocked in.

Mr. Wilson climbed out of his van and stretched. He'd been working all day and was ready to relax; he was also ready for some supper. As he cut between the yards and headed toward his front door, he noticed a chill in the air. The temperature had already dropped from the day's high of about fifty-five degrees down into the upper forties. Mr. Wilson stood in his driveway for a few seconds, enjoying the cool night breeze. Then he saw two young men approaching. He turned toward the door. They rushed up on him, and suddenly one of them had a gun. The gun was pointed right at Mr. Wilson's head.

"Give it up, old man," the one with the gun said.

"What?" Wilson stammered.

The punk with the gun twisted his hand in the air, turning the pistol on its side. "Give me all your money."

"I . . . uh . . . don't have money on me." Wilson did have a little bit of cash on him, but he'd worked hard for it, and he sure wasn't going to give it to these punks.

The one with the gun wore orange pants. He glared at Mr. Wilson. "I don't have nothing to live for, so I'll kill you if you don't give it up right now, old man."

Mr. Wilson edged toward the door and rang the doorbell, hoping one of his sons would come out and scare these punks off.

Orange Pants shoved the gun closer to Mr. Wilson's face. "Ring it again, I'll kill you, you motherfucker."

Stubbornly, Melford Wilson rang the doorbell again, and this time he knocked on the door, too. The next thing he saw was a blinding flash that exploded in front of his eyes. The world started to spin, and Wilson felt himself falling. In desperation, he reached a hand out and caught hold of the doorknob. He turned it as he fell.

Mr. Wilson's twenty-six-year-old son, Melford Wilson III, was in the living room playing a video football game with his fifteen-year-old brother when he heard the doorbell chime.

His little brother looked at him. "You gonna get that?"

Melford was just about to score a touchdown and win the game. "Just a sec," he said. "Soon as I whip your butt."

Melford worked the joystick. On the screen, his running back shucked and jived his way toward the goal line. *Just a few more seconds.* The doorbell rang again. This time a knock followed right after it.

"Man, this always happens right when I'm about to score.

If it ain't the phone, it's somebody coming over." Melford let his video controller drop to the floor as he stood up. He was two steps from the door when it flew open and his father collapsed across the threshold. There was blood streaming from a wound just above his left eye.

"Oh, my God!" Melford shouted as he dropped down beside his father and cradled his head. "Dad, what happened?"

Mr. Wilson was still conscious, and even though his voice was weak, he could still talk. "A guy just tried to rob me, and he shot me."

"He shot you!" Melford looked at the jagged gash in his father's forehead.

Melford's little brother was on his feet. He was calm for a teenager, and Melford knew he could take care of calling 911 and looking after their father. Melford was going to catch the son of a bitch who'd just shot his dad while he was standing at his own front door.

Melford stepped outside. Down the street, a couple of blocks away, he saw a guy running away. Melford's car, a 1985 Oldsmobile Delta 88, was at the end of the driveway. As he ran down the driveway, he fished his keys out of his pocket. He jumped behind the wheel of the Olds, cranked up the motor, and screeched out of the driveway.

The Wilson house was on a boulevard, and the robber had run away against traffic. There were cars coming, so Melford couldn't go straight after him. For a few precious seconds, he had to go the opposite direction from the robber; then he whipped his car through a tight U-turn and jammed the accelerator to the floor.

The robber bounded down the sidewalk wearing a pair of long, bright orange pants. As he ran, he must have heard the roar of the big Oldsmobile engine, because he glanced back over his shoulder, and for just a second, Melford saw his face and saw the fear plastered across it. Good, he thought, the son of a bitch better be afraid. But Melford didn't have a gun. He wasn't trained to apprehend armed robbers. He was just a young man pissed off that someone had shot his father.

When Orange Pants ducked into the sprawling Oakbrook apartment complex, Melford knew he had to ditch his car. There were too many places for the guy to hide inside the complex. He would have to search for him on foot. Melford pulled to a stop in the parking lot and sprang out of his car. Up ahead, he saw the guy in the orange pants duck around a corner. Melford ran after him. When he made the corner, Melford pulled up short. Two security guards who had been patrolling the complex on foot had the guy wrapped up in their arms. Orange Pants had turned the corner and run right into them.

"He shot my father," Melford shouted and lunged for the would-be robber. It took both security officers to keep Melford from tearing the little punk's head off.

Antoinette Frank and Colin Danos picked up the call of a 34-S (a shooting) on Lake Forest Boulevard. The dispatcher said the victim was at his house, but the victim's adult son had taken off in pursuit of one of the suspects.

While they headed to the Wilsons' house, Frank and Danos got word from the dispatcher that the victim's son and a couple of security guards were holding a suspect at the Oakbrook apartments. The officers went to the Oakbrook and met with Melford and the security guards. A few minutes later, they stuffed the suspect into the back of their patrol car and relocated to the Wilson house.

Mrs. Wilson had arrived home a few minutes after her son roared off toward the Oakbrook apartments. She walked into her house to find her husband on the floor, bleeding from a gunshot wound to the head. She and her other son half-carried and half-dragged her husband into the master bedroom; then she snatched some towels from the bathroom, soaked them in water, and pressed them against his head. Just minutes later—although they seemed to drag by like hours—the police and an ambulance arrived.

Melford III made it back to the house at about the same time as the police. He ran into the master bedroom and hovered over the shoulders of the medics as they slapped bandages on his father's forehead and shot him up with an IV. The younger Melford managed to slip in a question to his father. "What was the guy wearing, Dad?"

Incredibly, Mr. Wilson was still conscious. So far the medics had not discovered any penetration of the skull. "Orange pants," he mumbled.

Melford pumped his fist in the air. "We got him."

"Out of the way," a medic shouted as he rolled a gurney into the room. Within minutes, the medic crew strapped Mr. Wilson in, and they, along with Mrs. Wilson, roared off toward Charity Hospital.

The young man whom Melford had run down and whom the security guards had grabbed sat handcuffed in the back of Frank and Danos's patrol car parked in the street in front of the Wilson house.

"I've never handled a 34-S by myself," Frank said. "You mind if I write it up?"

Danos shrugged. "That's fine with me. I'll go get the victim's info." He stepped out of the car, leaving Frank alone with the suspected armed robber. Danos didn't realize it at the time, but Frank was lying. She had handled the 34-S call after the shooting of Nemiah Miller and Rogers LaCaze. Why she chose to lie to Danos on the Wilson 34-S call, no one knows.

Standard procedure would have been for Frank to write down the suspect's name, date of birth, and address; and to call that information in to the dispatcher, who would advise Frank of the suspect's criminal record and whether or not he was wanted. Frank had been out of the academy and on the street for almost a year and a half, and Colin Danos had every reason to believe that she was going to follow procedures.

Danos took brief statements from both of Mr. Wilson's sons. After hearing the details, and since no gun or other physical evidence had been found in the suspect's possession, Danos decided that in order to verify if the guy they had in custody was one of the armed robbers, he and Frank needed to transport him to Charity Hospital and find out if Mr. Wilson could make a positive identification.

In the emergency room at Charity, Melford Wilson, Jr., was a bloody mess. Doctors X-rayed his head and were able to determine that the bullet had glanced off of his forehead and had not penetrated his skull. It had, however, left an ugly wound and had robbed him of his sight in one eye.

When Frank and Danos walked in with the suspect in tow, doctors were still treating Mr. Wilson. The officers had to wait for more than an hour before they could get in to see him.

Long-established legal precedent, set by U.S. Supreme Court cases such as *Terry v. Ohio,* allows police officers to detain a suspect in a nonconsensual situation for only a short amount of time without placing the person under arrest. As a veteran officer, Danos knew the legal ice on which the potential case against their suspect rested was thin.

They hadn't caught the second suspect, and the one they had in custody had only been seen running away from a shooting, a perfectly reasonable reaction for anyone—perpetrator or bystander. There was no physical evidence because the suspects hadn't taken anything from Mr. Wilson. The guy didn't have a gun on him when the security guards grabbed him. And there was only one witness, who was now on pain medication, shaken up, and half-blind. To make the case, they needed an identification, and they needed it fast, or else they were going to have to cut this guy loose.

Danos hadn't asked Frank about the suspect's criminal

record or if he was wanted. Every time he thought about it, something else came up. Besides, if the guy was wanted or had a history of armed robberies, Danos was sure Frank would have mentioned it to him. Even if they had to cut the guy loose tonight, they could always go back and swear out an arrest warrant as soon as they got more evidence. New Orleans wasn't really that big of a city, and Danos knew that as long as you had a guy's name, had a picture of him, and knew where his momma stayed, you could find him.

When Frank and Danos finally got in to see Mr. Wilson, his head and face were bandaged, and the vision in his good eye was blurred by painkillers. The two officers dragged the shackled suspect and his orange pants to the side of Mr. Wilson's bed, but they didn't get the reaction they were looking for. Mr. Wilson wasn't sure if it was the same man or not.

"They said they brought the suspect to Charity so my father could identify him, but I don't see how they expected him to recognize the guy," Melford Wilson III says, "the way my father was all bloodied up, his head was bandaged, and only able to see out of one eye."

In the end, Frank and Danos had to drive the suspect back to Lake Forest Boulevard and let him go. Later that night, as their shift ended, Danos took a look at Frank's report of the incident. Something was missing. There wasn't anything about the suspect. "Where's the guy's information?" Danos asked.

"I thought you got it," Frank said.

Danos was stunned. "I was inside the house with the victim's family. You were the one with the suspect. Didn't you at least get his name and run a check on him?"

Frank just shook her head.

Danos ended up having to rewrite the report before they turned it in. Later, the Wilsons filed a complaint with the Public Integrity Division about the shoddy police work. Although Danos was later cleared of any wrongdoing, no one was ever able to identify the suspect whom Frank let slip away.

To this day, Melford Wilson III is positive he chased down one of the men who shot his father. "My dad said one of them was a guy wearing orange pants, and I caught a guy running away wearing orange pants."

Whether Frank's actions were merely gross incompetence or something more sinister, only she and perhaps Rogers LaCaze know for sure. Most of the officers who knew Frank agree that as a police officer, she was a complete failure. Lieutenant Van Dalen, commander of the 7th District's 2nd Platoon, and Antoinette Frank and Ronnie Williams's boss, says Frank was a lousy cop. "She never showed me anything out on the street."

But even Frank, as incompetent as she was, must have known that it was important to write down the name of a person suspected as having just committed attempted armed robbery and attempted murder.

One possible explanation why Frank chose not to record the suspect's name is that the crime may have been connected to Rogers LaCaze. LaCaze had been involved in shootings and armed robbery before; and as investigators later discovered, at the time of the Wilson shooting, Frank and LaCaze were already involved in a close relationship. Perhaps Frank didn't record the name because she feared that if detectives later interviewed the suspect to try to prove his involvement in the attempted robbery of Mr. Wilson, a link to LaCaze and maybe even to Frank herself could be exposed.

Two months after his father's shooting, Melford saw Frank and LaCaze on television as they were paraded to lockup following their arrests, and he wondered if one of the two men who tried to rob his dad—and who permanently cost his father his sight in one eye—might have been Rogers LaCaze. "It was dark, so I didn't get a good look at the guy I chased, and I didn't see the other guy at all," Melford says, "so we just never pursued it."

Just three days after the murders at the Kim Anh, the *Times-Picayune* learned from some 7th District officers that they believed that Frank and LaCaze "were partners in crime, peddling drugs and terrorizing the eastern New Orleans underworld by robbing the drug dealers who operate there."

Danos, who knew Rogers LaCaze, says he's sure the guy he and Frank picked up wasn't LaCaze, but he says that he has no idea about the other guy. It could have been LaCaze.

**After** the Melford Wilson fiasco, Officer Colin Danos had had enough of Antoinette Frank. Within days of Frank's failure to even record the name of the armed robbery and shooting suspect, Danos jumped at the opportunity to transfer out of the 7th District.

Newly appointed lieutenant Edwin Compass was out recruiting for his new command. He'd been put in charge of the COPS unit, an acronym for the Community Oriented Policing Squad. To stem the tide of blood flowing through the streets of New Orleans, a city whose own lifeblood is pumped by the cardiac contractions of tourism, the new police superintendent, Richard Pennington, was forming a new unit of hard-charging aggressive cops to work exclusively in the nine housing projects spread across the city. Danos put in for the assignment, and Lieutenant Compass picked the hard-hitting young officer right away.

"I wanted to work in the projects to get the experience," Danos says. "We had a lot of guns and a lot of drugs in the projects." He also liked the twelve-hour shifts and the four hours per day of overtime. It meant he could cut down on working off-duty security details.

As soon as Antoinette Frank heard where Danos was going, she approached Lieutenant Compass about joining the new unit, too. Compass, who didn't know Frank, asked Danos about her. "He asked me my honest opinion of her," Danos says, "and anybody who asks me something, I'm going to tell them the truth." Danos told the new lieutenant the same thing that he'd told Lieutenant Van Dalen, that Frank was just not aggressive enough. Given more time, and as long as she worked with an experienced partner, she might make it on the job; but he said that in his opinion, Frank couldn't make it in a proactive unit like COPS, nor did he think she could survive working in the projects. "It might have been because of what I told him that he didn't pick her," Danos says, "but I had to tell the man the truth."

Danos admits there was another reason for his brutal honesty. "I knew for a fact," he says, "if she would have went into the project unit, guess who she would have wanted to ride with? Me. And I didn't want to ride with her anymore. I didn't want to ride with her when I did ride with her."

So Danos transferred into the COPS unit and left Frank to fend for herself, and it wasn't long before one of his observations about Frank would prove to be eerily accurate. He had stressed to the rank several times that Frank couldn't make it on her own, that her only chance was to have a partner, someone to ride with her. What no one knew at the time Danos transferred out of the district was that Frank already had someone to ride with. It was just that her new partner wasn't a police officer. He was a criminal.

# FIFTEEN

**Rogers** LaCaze said he always wanted to be a cop. With Antoinette Frank, he got the chance—sort of.

Six days after she bungled the capture of Mr. Wilson's assailant, Frank was again caught up in an armed robbery investigation. This one also involved gunfire, and again one of the suspects managed to slip away from her. Later, an internal investigation proved that the men whom Frank had identified as suspects were actually the victims, and that it was she and Rogers LaCaze who were the real perpetrators.

Saturday night, February 4, 1995, exactly one month before the Kim Anh murders, twenty-one-year-old Anthony Wallis and his twenty-one-year-old cousin, John Stevens, met up at a party at a house off Bullard Avenue, in New Orleans East. The two cousins had arrived in separate cars, but Stevens had since lent his car to a friend named James. James had driven Stevens's car to the nearby Green Tree apartments on Lake Forest Boulevard to check on another friend.

Around ten o'clock, Stevens noticed that James hadn't made it back to the party. He started to get worried about his car. James wasn't a very good driver. Everybody knew that. Stevens asked his cousin if he would drive him to the apartment so he could find out what was taking James so long. James had better not have wrecked his car.

On their way out the door, someone starting chatting with Wallis, so Stevens stepped outside to wait for him. Outside, Stevens ran into Rogers LaCaze and his wheelchair-bound brother. They were with another man Stevens didn't recognize, and were also leaving the party. According to Stevens, "We passed a few words." They argued. Stevens didn't think much of it, and when Wallis caught up to him, the two of them piled into Wallis's white Pontiac Bonneville for the short ride to the Green Tree apartments to look for James and the missing car.

As he drove away from the party, Anthony Wallis found himself behind LaCaze's four-door, blue Cadillac. LaCaze just sat there. He wouldn't move. After a minute or so, Wallis eased around him, and as he passed the Caddy, Stevens noticed LaCaze talking on a cell phone. Stevens and LaCaze glared at each other as Wallis's Pontiac rolled past.

When Wallis and Stevens made it to Green Tree, James had already left and headed back to the party, but they ran into another friend in the parking lot, a guy named Chris.

Stevens rolled down the passenger window. "What's up?"

"Where y'all going?" Chris asked.

"We been at a party," Wallis shouted through the open window.

"Where?"

Wallis shrugged. "It's off Bullard. I don't know the exact address."

"You going back?"

"Yeah," Stevens cut in. "I got to get my car 'fore James wrecks it."

Chris nodded. "He don't even know how to drive a car."

The news made Stevens even more nervous about his car.

"You want to go to the party?" Wallis asked.

"Sure," Chris said.

"Just follow me."

Wallis and Stevens took off westbound on Lake Forest, with Chris following just a few cars behind.

At about ten-fifteen, Wallis caught the red light at Read Boulevard. While he waited for it to change, he noticed a marked NOPD car headed east on Lake Forest. Although Wallis didn't have a criminal record, he wasn't the most legal driver in the city. No license, no insurance, no vehicle registration papers—all of which made him wary of police cruisers.

When Wallis pulled away from the light, he noticed the police car had made a U-turn and was behind him. As soon as he got clear of the intersection, the top of the police car lit up like a Christmas tree, and the siren yelped. "Shit," Wallis said.

"What?" Stevens asked.

"Po-lice is pulling us over."

"Why? We ain't did nothing wrong." Stevens had only had one brush with the law before, a misdemeanor charge of carrying a concealed weapon, to which he had pleaded guilty and received probation. "It's probably just a ticket."

Antoinette Frank was driving the police car. With Danos gone, and no one else eager to take his place as her partner, Frank was riding in a one-man car, or at least that's what she was supposed to be doing. But on this Saturday night she had someone with her. Riding shotgun in her patrol car was Rogers LaCaze. LaCaze cradled a Tec-9 9 mm pistol in his hands. The gun was designed to look like a small machine gun, and LaCaze was carrying it with thirteen rounds in the magazine, although it had the capacity to hold more. The gun had been stolen three years before during a burglary of the home of a man named Fayard Lambert, who lived across the river in the small town of Gretna, the town in which Rogers LaCaze's brother, Michael, also lived.

The intersection at which Wallis found himself being pulled over was crowded and well lit. The two boulevards had eight lanes each and were divided by wide, grassy medians. On the northwest corner of the intersection sat the remnants of the huge, but deteriorating, Plaza shopping mall. Across Read Boulevard from the mall rose the Plaza Tower, a high-rise building that had once been a bustling office complex, but by 1995 had fallen, like the rest of New Orleans East, on hard times. Across Lake Forest from the mall stood a six-story hospital.

Jerome Montgomery, a friend from the neighborhood and distant cousin of Wallis and Stevens, also happened to be stopped at the intersection. He recognized Wallis's Pontiac as the police car pulled it over, so he whipped his car into the Plaza Tower parking lot to see if his friend was going to get off with just a ticket or if he was going to jail.

Frank keyed the squad car's public address system. "Turn your car off," she ordered Wallis, "and toss your keys out the window."

Wallis did as the officer said.

The P.A. blared again. "Driver, put your hands through the window and open the door with your left hand from outside." Frank was using textbook-style procedures for a felony car stop—except that she didn't have any backup and had an armed civilian riding with her. In her report, Frank later claimed that she tried several times to get on the air to radio the dispatcher about the stop, but at that exact moment most of the other officers on Frank's watch were in a high-speed vehicle chase and the suspect had just fired at the pursuing officers. They could have used her help.

One of the officers involved in the pursuit and shooting

says, "We were out getting shot at, and she was fucking around with that bullshit."

But Frank was in her own world, one in which she and Rogers LaCaze were the stars.

After Wallis stepped out of his car, Frank told him to walk to the back of his Pontiac and put his hands on the trunk. Wallis did just as the police officer told him. Frank then ordered Stevens out of the car in much the same way, and within a few seconds, she had him leaning against the trunk also. Frank had positioned the two of them so their backs were to her patrol car.

Frank got out of her car and approached the two men. While Frank talked to Wallis, John Stevens heard a car door close behind him. He turned and was shocked to see Rogers LaCaze stepping out of the police car, the same man with whom he'd "passed a few words" not more than a half hour before at the party.

"Turn back around," Frank warned.

Stevens faced forward, but not before he saw something even more shocking than LaCaze climbing out the front seat of a police car. "The next thing I know," Stevens later said, "he upped a semiautomatic weapon and was trying to cock it."

Wallis turned just in time to see LaCaze jack a 9 mm round into the chamber of the Tec-9. An adrenaline surge hit Anthony Wallis the likes of which he'd probably never experienced before. He pushed off the trunk of his Pontiac and lunged straight at LaCaze.

Stevens stood dumbfounded for a few seconds. Frank grabbed his shirt, but he broke away and ran to his cousin's side. As the three of them—LaCaze, Wallis, Stevens—wrestled for control of the gun, Frank managed to get on the radio and kick in a 108 (officer needs help, life in danger).

When Jerome Montgomery, who'd spotted his friends getting pulled over, saw LaCaze with the gun, he rolled across Read Boulevard and slipped into the mall parking lot. Chris, who'd been following Wallis to the party, also pulled into the parking lot.

The Tec-9 went off with a bang. No one claims to have fired it intentionally, but with three pairs of hands fighting for control of the same trigger, it was bound to happen. "I jumped back up 'cause I thought I was shot," Stevens said. It turned out he wasn't shot. The bullet whizzed off without striking anybody, but when John Stevens stepped back from the fray for a second, he saw someone he recognized sitting in a car in the mall parking lot. Even in court, Stevens wouldn't say whom he had seen, but it had to be either Chris or Jerome, although Jerome denied repeatedly that it was he. Whomever John Stevens saw, the person threw open the car door and shouted, "Come on, jump in the car! Come on, come on, come on!" Stevens ran and dove into the car. Later, Stevens testified, "He [the friend] brought me back to Green Tree by my aunt."

Seconds after the shot went off, Irvin Briant, Jr., a hulking man who had worked for sixteen years as an Orleans Parish sheriff's deputy, was leaving the First National Bank of Commerce drive-up ATM, located in the southeast corner of the mall parking lot. After he heard the shot, Briant glanced to his right. On Lake Forest, right at the edge of the parking lot, he spotted a New Orleans police car on a traffic stop. The female officer was alone and looked as if she was in trouble. "Officer Frank was fighting two black males on the side of the road," Briant said later. At least that was his perception at the time. He could see they were struggling over a gun. Briant didn't think about it; he just reacted. He raced his car across the parking lot to help the officer.

After the gun fired, LaCaze's hands slipped off the Tec-9 pistol, and it dropped to the ground. Wallis reached down and snatched it up, not sure what he was supposed to do with it, but positive he didn't want LaCaze to get it back.

When Irvin Briant jumped out of his car, he saw a gun in Wallis's hands. "Drop the gun," he boomed.

Wallis looked up at the sound of the commanding voice. The big man looked like a cop. Wallis tossed the gun into the grass.

Former deputy sheriff Irvin Briant rushed Wallis and slammed him against the hood of Frank's police car. LaCaze ran up to Briant, so Briant grabbed him, too, and pinned him to the hood. "I didn't know whether or not he was coming to attack me or what," Briant later testified. "I just grabbed him."

Frank pointed to LaCaze. "He's with me. He's the victim." Then she jabbed a finger at Wallis. "He's the 10-15 [prisoner]. He's the suspect."

Briant let go of LaCaze; then he peeled Wallis off the hood of the police car and walked him back to his own car, which he had left running with the door open behind the 7th District car. As he pushed Wallis facedown across the hood of his own car, Briant asked Frank for a set of handcuffs. She tossed him the only set she had on her belt, and the ex-deputy bent Wallis's arms behind his back and cuffed him.

By that time, other police units had arrived on the scene, and one of the officers stuffed Wallis into the backseat of a patrol car. Briant followed Frank to the station, but no one seemed interested in taking a statement from him, so he went home.

A month later, Briant saw Frank and LaCaze again, this time on the television news. He called the D.A.'s office and told them what had happened at the intersection of Lake Forest and Read.

**Antoinette** Frank's version of what happened at Lake Forest and Read was a little different.

At the end of her shift, Frank filed a report under NOPD

item number B-7148-95. The *Times-Picayune* newspaper later referred to Frank's report as "largely fiction," but the report showed just how active Frank's imagination was.

According to Frank's official account of the incident, she was patrolling the area of Bullard Avenue and Lake Forest Boulevard when she "observed an unknown black male standing on the sidewalk in front of the Rainbow Bowling Alley . . . waving and screaming for help." The unknown man was none other than Rogers LaCaze, for whom Frank had rented two cars and had bought a cell phone, a pager, and a bunch of clothes.

Frank claimed that LaCaze, to whom she referred throughout her seven-page report as "the victim," told her that two men had just robbed him at gunpoint and had stolen a twenty-inch gold chain valued at about $300. The victim advised her that as the two armed bandits fled toward their car, he gave chase and "snatched his gold chain from the perpetrator." Frank's report identified that perpetrator as the person she later arrested, Anthony Wallis. The report said that the two suspects then fled west on Lake Forest Boulevard in a white Pontiac Bonneville.

According to Frank's report, the victim hopped into her police car and they went roaring off down Lake Forest in search of the bad guys, whom they managed to catch up with "about one-half mile away from the location of the occurrence."

Frank said that she stopped the vehicle, the white Bonneville driven by Wallis, and ordered the two robbery suspects out of the car. Working without backup because of the high-speed chase and shootout in the 7th District, Frank searched the two suspects, and as she did so, she said that the victim climbed out of her police car and approached the suspects' vehicle in order to positively identify them. Her report went on to say that as soon as Wallis spotted the victim, he shouted, "Bitch, so you called the police. I'm not bitching out to the police." The statement doesn't seem to make sense, but for some reason, Frank decided to quote Wallis's outburst in her report.

It was at that point, according to Frank's narrative, that the passenger (Stevens) reached into the open passenger-side window of the Bonneville and whipped out a Tec-9 pistol. As Stevens came up with the gun, the victim grabbed Stevens's arm and forced the muzzle of the gun toward the ground. Wallis then rushed at Frank and shoved her closer to Stevens and LaCaze. Stevens handed the gun to Wallis, who clutched it in a two-handed grip and pointed it at Frank. Frank said she knocked the muzzle down just before Wallis fired it. LaCaze jumped into the fray again and helped her subdue Wallis while Stevens fled on foot. Then Irvin Briant, the ex-deputy, arrived on the scene and helped Frank handcuff Wallis.

Frank booked Anthony Wallis for armed robbery, attempted murder of a police officer, and resisting arrest. Her report ends with the note, "Because of the confusion of that day, the wanted vehicle was removed by unknown subject or subjects."

Frank had somehow managed to lose Wallis's white Pontiac Bonneville.

At the 7th District station, Officer Stanley Morlier, who'd just been in the chase and shootout, spotted Frank dragging Wallis into the station in handcuffs with LaCaze trailing behind her. The officer recognized LaCaze right away and wanted to know why he was in the station. "She was claiming he was a victim of some kind of cockamamie shit."

But Morlier knew LaCaze. He had arrested the little thug less than a month before.

Back on January 9, LaCaze had called the police after the house where he was staying had been shot up in a drive-by shooting. Morlier handled the call, and during the course of the crime scene investigation, he had grown suspicious of LaCaze—most good cops can spot a career criminal from a mile away—so he ran LaCaze's name and date of birth through the dispatcher. A few minutes later, the dispatcher called back and advised Morlier that there was an outstanding warrant for LaCaze's arrest. It turned out that he was wanted for aggravated battery in connection with the shooting of Derrick Jefferson.

Seeing Frank and LaCaze together at the station and hearing her brag about her armed robbery case just pissed Morlier off. He says, "We're chasing this guy in this pickup truck, and he's shooting all kinds of shit at us—this was a serious shootout we were having with this pickup truck—and here she comes with LaCaze and this other guy in handcuffs, talking about how she made this big arrest. And if you knew her, she wasn't capable of doing that."

Frank managed to obtain an arrest warrant for John Stevens, charging him with the same crimes as Anthony Wallis. Stevens turned himself in a couple of days later.

Both men spent more than a month in jail. Finally, three days after the murders at the Kim Anh restaurant, the D.A.'s office dismissed the charges against Wallis and Stevens. At the time of their release, a spokeswoman for the district attorney said, "There was no credibility on the part of the arresting officer or the alleged victim."

# SIXTEEN

**People** who knew her said Antoinette Frank was strange. "She had a lot of weird shit to her," Stanley Morlier says.

At the 7th District station where Frank worked, there were usually a couple of state prison inmates, prisoners on trustee status, doing odd jobs around the station like cutting the grass and cleaning up. The trustees were housed at a prison facility just south of New Orleans called Jackson Barracks. The facility is only a few miles from the 7th District station. Most mornings, an officer from the day watch would drive over and pick the trustees up. Then in the evening, someone from the second watch would drop them off.

During Frank's time at the 7th, she used to spend a lot of time with one inmate in particular, a trustee named Lloyd. Like both LaCaze and Frank's partner, Colin Danos, Lloyd was short, only a couple inches over five feet. "He was a little bitty guy," Morlier says. "He could have been LaCaze's brother." Apparently, Frank could only get along with men who were considerably smaller than her.

Frank used to go out and pick up food for Lloyd and

bring it back to the station. Prisoners don't carry money, so Frank paid for it herself. Frequently, the two of them—the cop and the inmate—would sit outside and eat together. "It wasn't normal," Morlier says.

One day, things were running behind, and it wasn't until the second watch that one of the ranking officers at the district had time to send someone to pick up a trustee. Morlier was clear, with no calls for service backed up, so he got the job. When he got to Jackson Barracks, he found Lloyd waiting for him, holding a paper sack in his hands. Morlier popped open the trunk of his patrol car, but before he let the trustee put the bag down inside, he searched it to make sure Lloyd wasn't carrying anything he wasn't supposed to.

What Morlier found inside the bag was an expensive-looking, hand-carved jewelry box with Antoinette Frank's picture mounted on the lid. "What the hell is this shit?" Morlier said.

"I made it," Lloyd said. "It's for Antoinette."

"What you got going on with Antoinette?"

"Nothing. We're friends is all, just friends."

Morlier put the bag in the trunk. "You better watch yourself. You're going to get yourself in some trouble messing with her."

**Mary** Williams gave birth to the newest Williams boy, Patrick Austin Williams, on February 23, 1995. The parents couldn't have been happier or prouder.

"When I had my second son, Patrick," Mary Williams recalls, "things were so good between Ronnie and me, and we were just very happy with Chris and our friends and our future."

Their future together would last for only nine more days.

* * *

**On** the afternoon of March 2, 1995, officers Reginald Cryer and Darryl Watson were working a two-man patrol car in the 7th District. They were on the 2nd platoon with Antoinette Frank and Ronald Williams.

Cryer had just five months on the job and had recently transferred from the 2nd District, which was uptown and had been his first assignment out of the academy.

Watson didn't have much more experience than his partner. He had been with the department a little more than a year, and was the senior officer, but he had only been assigned to the 7th District for about nine months.

"702," Officer Watson's radio crackled. It was the dispatcher calling for Cryer and Watson's patrol unit. A code-two call was about to come out.

Watson keyed his mike. "702," he said, letting the dispatcher know that he had heard her and was ready to take the call.

"Signal 20-I, Chef Menteur Highway and Downman Road." A 20-I was a car accident with injuries. It was a code-two because someone was hurt. The officers needed to get to the scene quickly to determine the extent of the injuries and request EMS if needed.

"702, ten-four."

They found the wreck within a couple of minutes. Two cars had piled up at Chef and Downman, right in front of a Chevrolet dealership. Watson parked the patrol car behind the accident and left his overhead lights on.

Once the officers checked with the vehicle's occupants, they found out that no one was seriously injured. The drivers had been lucky. The wreck looked worse than it really was. Cryer pulled his radio from his pistol belt and advised the dispatcher of the situation and asked her to send a one-man car to write the accident report.

While Watson and Cryer took preliminary statements from the drivers and got their driver's licenses, car 711 rolled up to the scene. It was the one-man car that was going to handle the traffic accident, except there were two people in the car.

Watson and Cryer knew the driver, Officer Antoinette Frank. Since she was on their platoon, they worked with her every day. But they didn't know the guy riding in the passenger seat. A short black guy in plainclothes. Neither one of them had been in the district long enough to know all the officers assigned to the Seventh, so they both assumed the guy was an off-duty cop or a detective. It was the only explanation that made sense because department regulations didn't allow civilians to ride around in a police car unless it was official business, and if that were the case—if she was in the middle of something else—Frank wouldn't have been dispatched to handle what turned out to be a minor traffic accident. The guy had to be a cop. But he sure didn't look like one.

Frank stopped her car in front of the two vehicles that had collided. She got out and walked over to Watson and Cryer. Her passenger stayed inside the patrol car. Watson handed her the information he and Cryer had collected from the two drivers involved in the accident; then the two officers got into their patrol car and left.

A couple of minutes later, Frank called on the radio and asked Watson and Cryer to come back to the scene for a minute. When they got back, she asked to borrow their ticket book. She had forgotten to get one. As the two officers sat in their car, they saw Frank waving to the guy in the passenger seat of her patrol car. Then she pointed toward the parking lot of the Chevrolet dealer and shouted, "Pull it up over there."

The guy crawled across the front seat and dropped down behind the wheel. He drove her car into the parking lot.

Watson and Cryer looked at each other. *The guy must be a cop,* they thought.

A couple of minutes later, the two officers left again.

Cryer didn't think any more about it until two days later. Saturday, he was watching the news on television. Like every officer in the department, he had heard about the murder of Ronnie Williams and the arrest of Antoinette Frank. The news had hit Cryer hard. He had worked with both of them Friday night.

As Cryer watched the news tape of detectives parading Frank from police headquarters to Central Lockup, something all the cops called "the walk," he got his first look at the man who'd been arrested with her. What he saw stunned him.

That afternoon, just before 3 P.M., at roll call at the 7th District station, Cryer pulled his supervisor aside.

The man he'd seen on television, the man who'd been taking "the walk" with Antoinette Frank, the man accused with her of killing their fellow 2nd platoon officer Ronald Williams and Ha and Cuong Vu, was the same man he and Watson had seen driving Frank's patrol car at the accident scene two days ago. The guy hadn't been a cop after all.

**Mike** Morgani owned Jay & Mike's Body and Fender Shop at 9700 Chef Menteur Highway. Around five o'clock Thursday afternoon, March 2, 1995, he was standing in the yard outside his shop when one of his tow truck drivers hauled in a car that had just been involved in an accident at Chef and Downman. Mike turned toward the shop to grab the paperwork he needed but stopped when he saw a New Orleans police car pull in behind his truck.

When the police car pulled to a stop in the gravel yard, an attractive black woman in a police uniform stepped out. She surveyed the yard before nodding to Mike, then walked over to him. A young man in civilian clothes, who'd been in the car with her, popped out of the front passenger door. As the little man strutted toward him, Mike noticed his gold chains and gold teeth. He looked like a thug.

The police officer extended her hand. "I'm Officer Frank from the Seventh District."

Mike Morgani shook her hand. "Nice to meet you." He nodded toward the car his driver had just towed in. "Did you handle that?" He figured she was there to get more information about the wrecked car.

But instead of talking about the car hanging on the back of the tow truck, Officer Frank introduced him to the man standing beside her. "This is my nephew Rogers. He's looking for a job."

Morgani didn't know what to say. He glanced at the guy. The kid couldn't be more than seventeen or eighteen years old. What could he know about body and fender work? "What kind of job?" Morgani asked. He said it more as a stall, as something to fill the silence hanging between the three of them, than out of any real interest in hiring this kid.

Frank eyed the yard again. A body and fender shop wasn't exactly the neatest place in town. "Maybe he could clean up, be a porter or something."

Morgani cleared his throat. "I don't really have any openings right now, but maybe I could, you know, get back with you on it."

"He'll do anything you want," she said. "You need to give this man a job."

The tow truck driver signaled to Morgani, so he excused himself and scurried to the truck, thankful for the distraction. The driver asked his boss what was going on, and when Morgani told him that the officer was trying to bully him into giving her nephew a job, the driver said he'd seen her and the little guy at the accident scene where he'd hooked up the car. He told Morgani the guy had been driving her squad car around at the scene.

There was a customer waiting inside the office, one for whom Morgani had been trying to obtain a rental car. With a furtive glance, he saw the officer and her thuggish nephew still standing where he'd left them, waiting for him. Morgani headed for his office, mentioning to Frank as he passed her that he had someone waiting for him inside.

When Morgani entered his office, the cop's brash nephew burst through the door behind him. Frank marched in after him.

"I don't have anything right now," Morgani repeated. Both of them eyed him hard. Morgani wanted to get rid of them and take care of his customer. He picked up a scratch pad and tossed it across the desk to Frank's nephew. "Just put your information down on there, and I'll let you know if something comes up."

Rogers LaCaze scrawled his name and telephone number on the pad; then he and Frank left.

Two days later, Mike Morgani saw the officer and her nephew again; this time they were on television being led to Central Lockup in handcuffs.

**Ronnie** Williams had Thursday off. He went fishing with a buddy named Bryan. Ronnie wanted his son Chris to go with him, but Mary wouldn't hear of it. "It's a school day," she told him.

"It's just kindergarten," Ronnie protested.

But Mary would have none of it. No skipping class, she said. School was too important. "You can go fishing again this weekend and take him with you."

At the end of the day, Ronnie came home sunburned and exhausted, but he was looking forward to the weekend fishing trip with his oldest son. The next day, Friday, March 3, he was scheduled to work 3 to 11 P.M. at the 7th District, then from 11:00 until closing for the Vus at the Kim Anh.

# SEVENTEEN

**On** Friday, March 3, 1995, Sandra Duncan and Debbie Rogers's shifts at the sporting goods and automotive counter at the New Orleans East Wal-Mart overlapped each other between the hours of 3 and 5 P.M. Sandra had just come on at 3:00 and was working until close. Debbie had started at 9 A.M. and was looking forward to getting off at 5. It was sometime during that overlap, between three and five o'clock in the afternoon, when a female police officer and a young man approached the counter.

Frank wore her police uniform and had her hair pinned up at the back of her head. LaCaze had his gangster uniform on and had his gold teeth flashing.

"Do you have any nine-millimeter bullets?" LaCaze asked.

Debbie Rogers, who'd worked for Wal-Mart for five years, gave LaCaze a hard look. "You're too young to buy bullets," she said.

"I'm buying them," Frank snapped.

The clerk shrugged. "We have two brands, UMC and

Federal. UMC is $9.99 a box. The Federal is $16.96."

"Give me a box of UMC then," Frank said.

As Debbie Rogers started to stoop down to look under the counter, her coworker, Sandra Duncan, stopped her. "We sold out of the UMC yesterday."

"That's the cheap kind?" Frank asked.

Duncan nodded. "Yes, ma'am." She handled firearms every day and noticed the Smith & Wesson .38 revolver sitting in the officer's holster. Briefly, she wondered why the lady cop wanted 9 mm bullets if she carried a .38.

"You don't have no other kind?" Frank asked.

"We have the Federal," Debbie Rogers said.

"How much is that again?"

"$16.96 for a box."

Frank looked at LaCaze. "Would you pay $16.96 for a box of bullets?"

"Not me," he said.

"All right, let's go," Frank said. They turned around and left without saying a word to either of the clerks.

Later, prosecutor Elizabeth Teel, co-counsel for the state, said during LaCaze's trial, "They didn't want to buy the good stuff to execute these people. They just needed a cheap box of ammo for that."

The next day, Saturday, March 4, 1995, the day after Frank and LaCaze left Wal-Mart empty-handed, Sandra Duncan noticed an employee buzz going around the store when she reported for work at 3 P.M. She'd seen the news about the murders. Duncan had worked for Wal-Mart for a little less than a year. She had not met Frank before and hadn't known that the officer used to work at the same Wal-Mart as she did until she saw it on the news. After Duncan clocked in, someone asked her, "Did you see what happened on TV?"

"Yeah," Duncan said. "She was in here yesterday, she and that guy."

Although she didn't know it, Duncan's curiosity about

Frank asking for 9 mm bullets when she carried a .38 revolver was well justified. The fact that Frank was looking for a box of 9 mm ammo at a time when she later claimed not to have a 9 mm pistol gives some indication of how long she'd been hatching the scheme to rob the Kim Anh restaurant.

In the weeks leading up to the unsuccessful shopping trip for bullets at Wal-Mart, Frank did have a 9 mm pistol, a blue-steel Beretta, model 92. She picked it up from Officer Dave Talley, who worked in the Central Evidence and Property Division (CE&P) in the basement of police headquarters. Talley also ran a detail at Dillard's department store in the Plaza shopping mall in New Orleans East. He sometimes worked the detail with Antoinette Frank and had occasionally seen Frank and LaCaze together at Dillard's.

Frank and Talley met during Frank's brief stint at CE&P when she worked there as a recruit while waiting for her academy class to start.

CE&P is where the New Orleans Police Department stores everything its officers seize, find, or otherwise take into custody. Drugs, cash, jewelry, bicycles, bloody clothes, taped confessions, body fluids, and guns—all find their way into the catacomb of shelves, bins, and lockers that make up the cramped and dusty world of CE&P. It's a slow-paced world of forms and filing, not the kind of place the department sends its best street cops.

According to Talley, Frank had shown up at CE&P a couple of times with court orders that authorized her to keep guns that she had seized. Back in those days, after the adjudication of a criminal case, some judges would release a confiscated gun back to the arresting officer as a sort of reward for a job well done. Given Frank's penchant for penning other people's names to official documents, it's questionable whether or not the court orders were real, but no one has ever put a lot of effort into finding out. A judge's authentic signature on a court order removing guns from police custody and slipping them into the hands of a psychotic triple murderer might prove embarrassing.

One of the guns Talley turned over to Frank was a Beretta 9 mm; another was a two-inch Smith & Wesson .38 revolver.

Two weeks before the robbery and murders that would make her the poster child for a police department gone wrong, Antoinette Frank called the 7th District and reported that the 9 mm pistol she'd recently collected from the property room had been stolen. When an officer arrived at Frank's house on Michigan Street to take the theft report, Frank and LaCaze were both there.

Frank told the officer that she'd been at Delgado Community College in mid-city attending class, and had returned to her car—her 1977 Ford Torino—to find that someone had broken into it. Her books and her newly acquired Beretta pistol were missing.

Later, LaCaze remembered it a bit differently. Although he confirmed that the 9 mm pistol Frank had reported stolen was the same one she got from Dave Talley in the property room, he told detectives the report she filed was bogus because the gun had not really been stolen. LaCaze claimed not to know why Frank reported that the gun had been snatched in a car burglary, but when detectives pressed him on it, he mumbled, "She say she might give it to her brother."

**Ernest** J. Smith III was fifty years old and having trouble with his daughter's ex-boyfriend. The kid was a troublemaker whom Smith had seen lurking around the neighborhood ever since his daughter had broken up with him. Maybe it was just a passing thing, but maybe not. Maybe the guy was obsessed. Maybe he wasn't going to get over it. Maybe he was dangerous. Mr. Smith decided to call the police.

The Smiths lived in the 7th District, on Merrywood Court in New Orleans East.

In the early evening of March 3, Smith drove to the district station. He marched through the glass front door and told the desk officer that he wanted to file a complaint about his daughter's ex-boyfriend, whom Smith believed was stalking and harassing her. The deskman said he would call the dispatcher and have a patrol car sent to Smith's house to take the complaint. He told Smith to go back home and wait for the officer.

A short time after Smith got home, a police car pulled into his driveway. Smith met the female officer at the front door. She introduced herself as Officer Antoinette Frank. Tagging along behind her was a young black man carrying a pad of paper, perhaps a legal pad, Smith later recalled, and a stack of police forms. The young man was short, had lots of gold teeth, and wore blue corduroy pants and a striped, multicolored shirt. Officer Frank carried nothing in her hands.

She nodded toward the servile young man. "He's my trainee."

Smith looked at him again. He didn't look anything like Smith's idea of a police recruit or trainee. He showed no identification of any kind, there was no badge clipped to his belt as Smith had seen plainclothes officers and detectives wear, and he wasn't carrying a gun, at least not that Smith could see.

Smith hesitated for a second, then stepped aside and let the officer and her trainee into his home.

Smith and his wife sat with their two guests around the dining room table while they explained the problem they were having with their daughter's ex-boyfriend.

Frank seemed sympathetic, but after listening to Mr. Smith's concerns for about twenty minutes and asking only a few questions, she looked at her watch, then popped to her feet. "There's really nothing I can do for you right now."

Smith was surprised. He'd hoped the police department

would be able to help him. Maybe they could send someone to have a talk with the young man, maybe throw a scare into him. "What if I see him hanging around here again?" he asked.

Frank fished through her combination badge case and wallet and pulled out a business card. She handed it to Smith. "Call the number on there. That's straight to the district. You'll get a quicker response if you do that, and if he comes around when I'm on duty, they'll notify me, and I'll come straight over."

Frank and her "trainee" piled through the door and hopped back into her squad car, leaving Smith standing in the doorway, a police business card between his fingers.

The next day, Saturday, when Smith got home, he walked into his den and found his wife staring at the television. "She was nervous and upset," he later recalled. His wife told him that she'd just seen the police officer and that little man who'd been at their house only yesterday on the news. They'd been arrested for killing three people at a restaurant. Smith sat down with his wife and watched until the TV news showed the footage again of detectives escorting Officer Frank and the man she'd introduced to them as her "trainee," whose name they found out was Rogers LaCaze, to Central Lockup.

Smith sifted through a pile of bills and other scraps of paper on the kitchen counter until he found what he was looking for—Officer Frank's business card. He scooped up the telephone and called the number on the card. When he got through to the station, Smith told the officer who answered the phone that he'd seen Frank and LaCaze together just hours before they'd apparently killed all those people. The officer told Smith to hang up and dial the police emergency number. Using that number, what he said would be recorded on tape.

Smith hung up, then picked up the phone again and dialed 911.

* * *

**Although** her shift didn't end until 11 P.M., Frank was home by nine o'clock. On Michigan Street, Frank's next-door neighbor, Diane Masson, was struggling trying to move a heavy desk in her house. Masson and her husband had lived next to Frank for about a year and a half. "My husband and I were excited knowing we had a police officer next door," she said. "And she always had a lot of cops over there, which made us feel even safer." Masson also knew that Adam Jr. frequently stayed with Frank, and she saw him as a friendly guy who was always smiling.

At around 9 P.M., Masson walked next door to ask Frank if her brother could come over and lend her a hand moving the desk. "I knocked on her door, and she turned all the lights out before she answered," Masson said. "She said her brother wasn't home. I thought it was kind of strange. Now I know it was four hours later that the shootings all took place."

What's even stranger is that Diane Masson went next door to look for Adam Jr. at all. It had been more than two months since a pair of NOPD sergeants had searched Frank's Michigan street home for her fugitive brother and warned Frank that she had to notify the police department immediately if he showed up again. If Mrs. Masson hadn't seen Adam Jr. in more than two months, it seems unlikely she would pop over at nine o'clock on a Friday night expecting that he could help her move a heavy piece of furniture.

Still, there would be even more strange goings-on at the Frank house, including a gruesome discovery.

# EIGHTEEN

**Right** around the time that her next-door neighbor was looking for her brother, Antoinette Frank picked up her cell phone and called the Kim Anh restaurant. "Chau," she said. "This is Antoinette. I wanted to know if I could work tonight."

It was nine o'clock. "You talking about right now?"

"Yeah."

"Why so early?" Chau said. "Did you get off work already?"

"I just got off," Frank said. "You need somebody to work tonight?"

"Ronnie is working tonight."

"But he's not coming in until eleven though, right?"

"Yes, but Robert Miller just called and said Ronnie told him to work from nine until eleven. Then Ronnie will be here."

"Okay," Frank said, then hung up.

A few minutes later, Officer Robert Miller showed up for his two-hour shift. He stood near the bar. Chau, who was working the cash register and making drinks that night, was still a bit confused by Frank's phone call. Antoinette and Ronnie worked the same shift, which didn't end until 11 P.M. Frank had worked at the restaurant Wednesday and Thursday night but wasn't scheduled to work the detail at all this weekend. So why had she called, and why was she already off work?

Chau mentioned the call to Miller, then said, "Why she get out early? What's wrong with her?"

Miller shrugged. "I don't know."

Around 10 P.M., Quoc Vu came in through the back door. He was later than usual because he and his younger brother, Cuong, had been in the vacant field next to the restaurant playing football until long past dark. Cuong had beaten him to the restaurant and was already hard at work. Quoc started helping his mom in the kitchen.

Just a few minutes past eleven o'clock, Ronnie Williams pulled into the parking lot in his Ford Ranger pickup truck. He walked into the restaurant wearing his uniform. He shook hands with Miller, and the two officers chatted for a couple of minutes before Miller left. Williams parked himself behind the bar as he surveyed the dining room.

After about an hour in the kitchen, Quoc piled some food onto a plate and slipped through the dining room and into the convenience store side to eat. Officer Ronnie Williams strolled over to visit with him while he ate, and the two of them started talking and joking around. A bond of friendship existed between them despite the differences in age, background, and culture.

Close to midnight, Chau was surprised to see Antoinette Frank walk through the front door. Business had been slow, and only two tables had customers. Chau was thinking about closing early.

Already changed out of her uniform, Frank had on black jeans, a green blouse, and a black leather jacket. She was carrying her police radio in her hand and seemed to be in a hurry.

Chau smiled at her. "Hey, Antoinette. What are you doing here?"

"Can I get a couple of orange juices to go?"

Chau nodded. "Sure, but where are you going?"

"I'm going to see a show at the Plaza."

After she looked at her watch, Chau said, "Wow. You go to see the show so late?"

"It's a late movie. A midnight movie at Cinema Eight. In fact, we're a little bit late right now."

Frank trailed behind Chau as she headed toward the kitchen. "Who you go with?" Chau asked.

Frank pointed through the windows along the front wall of the restaurant. "With my nephew. He's in the car."

Frank's car sat in the parking lot, and Chau saw the indistinct shape of someone sitting in the front passenger seat.

"Where's your mom?" Frank asked.

"She's in the kitchen."

The two women stepped from the dining room into the kitchen. The three other Vu kids, Ha, Cuong, and Quoc, were there helping Mrs. Vu clean up. Frank rushed up to Mrs. Vu and threw her arms around her. She had been out sick for a couple of days. "How you doing, Mom?"

"I feel much better," Mrs. Vu said.

Chau opened the refrigerator and found that the plastic orange juice bottle was almost empty. She poured what was left into a plastic foam cup, then turned to Frank. "We only have enough orange juice for one drink, but you can get another one from the grocery side."

Frank said goodbye to Mrs. Vu and the kids, then followed Chau out into the dining room. Frank crossed into the convenience store side of the building and pulled a bottle of Hawaiian Punch from the cooler. "Chau, I got to go," she said as she walked back into the dining room. "We're going to be late for the show."

"Okay," Chau said. "Have a good time."

Mrs. Vu hadn't fully recovered from whatever kind of bug had kept her down for the past two days. Just after midnight, her youngest son, Cuong, told her she needed to go home. "It's late. You need to rest," he said. Mrs. Vu's oldest daughter, Ha, agreed. "Go home," she told her mother. The restaurant was empty, and they were going to close early. "We'll take car of everything."

Reluctantly, Mrs. Vu decided to take her children's advice. As she walked out the door, Cuong hugged her and kissed her on both cheeks. It was the last time they would see each other.

At 12:51 A.M., Frank called from her cell phone again. When Chau answered the restaurant telephone, the off-duty policewoman said, "Chau, I'm on my way to the restaurant."

"Why didn't you go to the show?"

"It wasn't as good as I thought."

"What you do now?"

"I want to get something to eat. Can you ask your mom to fix two hamburgers for me?"

"My mom not here," Chau said. "She wasn't feeling that good, but hold on and I ask my sister."

Chau yelled to her sister in the kitchen and asked if she could cook two burgers for Antoinette. Ha said that she was out of French bread, the kind of bread she knew Antoinette liked with her hamburgers.

When Chau got back on the line, she told Frank, "My sister say we are out of the kind of bread you like. Can she fix something else for you?"

"How about steak and fries?"

Chau checked with her sister. Ha said a steak and fries would be no problem.

Ten minutes later, as the Vus were doing their final cleanup for the night, Frank walked through the front door.

This time she wasn't alone. "Chau," she said, "this is my nephew, Rogers."

The man Frank called her nephew was a teenager, about five feet, two inches tall, with a slight build; he wore blue corduroy pants and a striped, multicolored shirt. He carried a cellular telephone in his hand and had a pager clipped to his belt. Because of his neat appearance, Chau at first thought LaCaze must some kind of businessman, but when he smiled, she saw a mouthful of gold teeth and became suspicious. She'd heard that only gangsters had gold teeth.

Someone handed Frank a foam to-go box.

"It's only one box?" Frank said. "We got two people."

Ha Vu hadn't known Frank was with someone and had cooked only one meal. As Chau turned toward the kitchen, Frank reached out a hand and stopped her. "It's late, Chau. Don't worry about it. This will be fine."

While Frank and LaCaze sat at a table and opened their to-go box, Chau locked the front door. She crossed the dining room and dropped the key on the bar next to Ronnie Williams.

The big policeman eyed the little guy who was sharing a meal with Frank. A month before, Williams had spotted LaCaze behind the wheel of a blue four-door Cadillac, driving like a maniac. As soon as Williams stopped LaCaze, he must have realized what he was dealing with. The clothes, the jewelry, the gold teeth, the little man's attitude—all would have screamed out to Ronnie Williams that LaCaze was a dope-dealing thug. Now here was the same guy munching on free food and rubbing elbows with an off-duty police officer. *What the hell is up with that?* Ronnie Williams probably wondered.

Chau stayed behind the bar, cleaning up and putting everything away. Ha and Cuong were in the kitchen, scrubbing dishes and washing down the floor. Quoc was in the dining room, sweeping the floor. Several times he noticed LaCaze staring at him. It made Quoc uncomfortable.

Chau noticed that Frank seemed restless. She kept getting up from the table and pacing around the dining room.

After a few minutes of nibbling at the steak and fries, LaCaze hopped up and went into the bathroom. He was in there for a long time. When LaCaze finally came out, Frank sprang to her feet and snapped the to-go box closed. "Chau, I got to go," she said, the words almost tripping over each other. Frank barreled toward the exit, towing LaCaze behind her. She shoved at the front door but it wouldn't budge. Chau had locked it.

Chau asked Williams to unlock the door for Frank and her nephew. "I don't see the key," Ronnie Williams said. He searched the bar and the floor behind it, but still couldn't find the key.

Each of the Vus had a key to the door, so Chau called Cuong out from the kitchen. The seventeen-year-old hurried into the dining room with his key. He unlocked the door and let Frank and LaCaze out, then locked it back behind them.

Frank and LaCaze didn't leave right away. They stood in front of the restaurant door for a few minutes, talking. Seeing them standing outside made Chau realize that she had forgotten to tell Frank good night. She took a step toward the door, but remembered that her key was missing, so she cut around the bar to the grocery store side—it took a different key and she still had that one—and opened the door. Chau stuck her head outside. "Good night, Antoinette."

Twenty feet away, in front of the main door, Frank nodded. Then she said, "Chau, do you want me to work tomorrow night?"

"Let me ask Ronnie because I don't know." Chau stuck her head back inside and glanced at the policeman. "She wants to know if we need her tomorrow night."

Williams shook his head. "Tell her don't worry about it. I'll take care of it."

Chau looked back at Frank. "Ronnie say he work tomorrow, but if I need you, I'll call you. Okay?"

Frank shot a stare through the glass door at Ronnie Williams, but her voice remained calm and friendly. "Okay, then, I'll see you later."

"Good night," Chau said again.

LaCaze and Frank turned and walked toward her car.

As Frank's jalopy hobbled out of the parking lot, Chau closed and locked the grocery-side door.

When Chau got back to the bar, she could tell that Ronnie Williams was mad.

"Why do you keep giving her free food?" he demanded. "You should make her pay. The most you're supposed to give her off is fifty percent."

"Okay," she said. "Next time."

"Don't let people get over on you. That's why I'm here, so people don't get over on you."

"Okay, Ronnie. I start charging Antoinette. I charge her fifty percent."

"Chau, I'm telling you," the policeman warned, "you just can't trust people." It seemed to Chau as if there was something else about Frank that was bothering Ronnie, something more than her getting free food.

Ronnie pulled the cordless telephone from its cradle on the bar. "What's your phone number?"

"At home?"

Williams nodded.

"Why?"

"Because I want to call your mom and tell her that you are never supposed to give away free food."

Chau gave Ronnie her mom's number.

Williams punched the keypad with his thick fingers.

When Mrs. Vu answered, Ronnie said, "Mom"—everybody called Mrs. Vu "Mom"—"Chau is always giving away free food. I want you to tell her to stop it."

Chau could hear her mom answering—in Vietnamese.

Williams held the phone out to her, and Chau called to her brother Quoc, who had gone to help Ha and Cuong in the kitchen, to come get the phone and act as translator between Ronnie and their mother.

Quoc held the phone to his ear; then, when his mother finished, he looked at Williams. "She say that she will make Chau charge Antoinette fifty percent. She say she tell Chau no more free food."

Williams grinned. He took the phone from Quoc and put it back against his cheek. "Thanks, Mom," he said, then hung up.

Chau didn't mind. Ronnie was there to take care of them, and if he wanted to chew her out for her giving away free food, that was all right. He meant well, and he was always there for them when they needed his help. Late at night, it was his strong presence, standing tall in his uniform on the outskirts of the dining room, that always made Chau and her family feel safe.

Williams worked the security detail almost every weekend. It seemed he was almost part of the Vu family. Frank, too, was close to the Vus. Chau's mom was so fond of Frank that she even helped her out with money, above what she earned at the detail, but tonight Frank had been acting strange. Coming by twice like she had, and bringing that young guy, the guy she said was her nephew. For some reason, seeing the two of them together had given Chau the creeps.

"Why do you keep letting her work?" Ronnie Williams asked. Williams and Quoc were propped up against the bar while Chau finished straightening up.

"She's a nice person," Chau said.

Williams shook his head. "No she's not. Did you hear about her brother?"

Chau hadn't heard anything. She hadn't seen Adam around in a while, not since that night a few months ago when Frank had stormed in and pulled him out of the restaurant, but she remembered the way he would sit at the bar all night scarfing down free food and drinks and sometimes making passes at her, like that one time she'd told Ronnie and Stanley about.

"A couple of months ago," Williams told Chau and Quoc, "we found out that Frank's brother was wanted in Opelousas for trying to kill two guys."

"Did Antoinette know about it?" Quoc asked.

Williams nodded. "He was living with her. She had to know, but when some of the rank went out to her house to look for him, she said he wasn't there. They didn't trust her, so they searched the place anyway."

The idea that Antoinette's brother was a wanted criminal made Chau nervous. "Did they find him?" she asked.

"No. He was gone, but I bet you anything that she's the one who warned him to get out of town."

"How did she know they were going to come and look for him?" Chau asked.

Williams shrugged. "Policemen can't keep secrets. Somebody probably mentioned it to her before those guys went out to her house."

"Do you think he'll come back here?" Chau said.

"No. I'm sure he's long gone, but I don't think you should let Antoinette work here anymore. If you can't trust her, you don't need her coming around."

It was close to one-thirty in the morning when Chau dumped a pile of cash onto a small table in the kitchen. As she started to count, Chau remembered that she hadn't paid Ronnie. She always paid the officers who worked the security detail in cash at the end of the night. If anybody was in need of money, it was Ronnie Williams. Ten days before, his wife, Mary, had given birth to their second son. The twenty-five-year-old father of two was working all the extra-duty security jobs he could.

Chau left the money piled on the table and walked into the dining room. Ronnie stood behind the bar sipping a

Coke, still talking to Quoc. There was a box of envelopes on a shelf under the bar. As she reached for an envelope to put Ronnie's money in, Chau saw headlights flash in the parking lot. She stared through the glass front door to see who was pulling up, glad the restaurant was closed and the doors locked. The car idled in the parking lot for a few minutes, then backed into a parking space. When the driver killed the headlights, Chau recognized the car. It was a very old red and white Ford Torino. It was Antoinette Frank's car.

A knot of fear suddenly formed in Chau's belly. Why was Antoinette coming back again? This was the third time in two hours. Something wasn't right.

The money. The image of all that cash lying on the table flashed through Chau's mind. It almost seemed preposterous, but maybe Antoinette was there to rob the restaurant. Chau turned and bolted toward the kitchen. "Don't let her in," she shouted over her shoulder at Quoc and Ronald Williams. "I don't want her to see all the money."

In the kitchen, Ha was packing up some food to take home. After they closed the restaurant, the Vus usually ate together at home and watched television. Cuong was still busy cleaning the kitchen. He and his sister ignored Chau as she dashed into the tiny kitchen and scooped up the cash. The front door rattled as someone tugged on it.

"Chau, Chau, hurry up," Quoc called out from the dining room. "Antoinette wants me to open the door."

"Don't open it," Chau shrieked from the back. Ha and Cuong were starting to take notice as Chau stuffed the bundle of cash into the microwave and slammed the oven door shut.

"What's going on?" Ha asked.

"Don't worry," Chau told her. She held her hand up, signaling to her sister and brother to stay put. "I take care of it."

In the dining room, Quoc saw Antoinette Frank fumbling with the lock. "Chau, hurry up," he called out. "Antoinette almost get in the door."

As Chau rushed up behind Quoc, the deadbolt on the door clicked. Somehow Frank had unlocked it. She threw open the door and barged into the dining room.

# NINETEEN

**From** where he stood behind the bar, Ronnie Williams stared at Frank as she came through the front door. He must have thought her behavior was strange, but he would have had no reason to be alarmed. After all, not only was Frank a fellow police officer, she was on his platoon. They worked together every day. Still, she was acting weird. "Hey, Antoinette, where'd you get a key to the door?" he asked.

Frank ignored his question and blew past him as she wrapped her arms around Chau and Quoc Vu and herded them back toward the kitchen. Almost frantic, Frank said, "Chau, I need to talk to you. Just come with me, Chau. I need to talk to you."

Ronnie Williams was a big man, just over six feet tall and 225 pounds. He wasn't used to being ignored.

With his back to the front door, he took a step toward the kitchen.

Rogers LaCaze slipped through the glass front door carrying a 9 mm pistol in his hand.

Officer Ronald A. Williams II, twenty-five years old, married, and the father of two young boys, one of them a brand-new baby, never took another step. LaCaze reached across the bar and shot him in the neck.

"That's when I heard boom, boom, boom!" Chau said later.

LaCaze's first bullet entered just behind and below Ronnie Williams's right ear. It tore an almost horizontal path through his neck, shattering his spine and severing his spinal cord; then it ripped an exit wound below his left ear. As Officer Williams tumbled forward, LaCaze fired again. His second shot hit Williams high in the back of the neck, at the junction of the neck and the skull. It cut a channel through Ronnie's brain, traveling upward at a thirty-five-degree angle, and exited above and in front of his left ear. LaCaze fired a third time. The bullet struck Williams in the lower back just to the right of the spine. It cut through the right side of his chest, tearing through his right kidney, his diaphragm, his liver, and his right lung. It exited just below his right collarbone.

Officer Williams hit the floor behind the bar, facedown in a pool of blood.

LaCaze circled the bar and bent over the fallen policeman. He snatched the pistol from Williams's holster. Then the cold-blooded little killer reached into the dead officer's back pocket and stole his wallet.

After the explosion of shots inside the dining room, Frank let go of Chau and her brother and ran toward the front of the restaurant. LaCaze was walking toward her. He handed her the 9 mm pistol he'd just used to shoot the policeman. He had Officer Williams's gun in his other hand.

In the few seconds that they were out of Frank's sight, Chau dragged Quoc into the kitchen and shoved him through the door that led into the walk-in cooler. The cooler could be accessed through a door at each end, one from the kitchen and one from the convenience store. On the side of the cooler adjacent to the store was a set of glass doors, the kind found in almost every convenience store. Just inside the doors were shelves full of soft drinks, beer, and cold snacks. Next to the door on the kitchen side, the door through which Chau and Quoc had entered, was a window. From inside the cooler, the window provided a partial view of the kitchen.

As she pushed her brother into the cooler ahead of her, Chau called for her other brother Cuong and sister Ha to follow her, but they didn't. They stood rooted to the kitchen floor, their eyes wide with terror.

As the cooler door shut, Quoc dashed to the far end and flipped off the light switch, plunging the cooler into darkness. Chau also scrambled down the length of the rectangular-shaped cooler. She wanted to get as far away from the kitchen as possible. The two of them hunkered down in the dark, amid the food crates, the cardboard boxes, and the cases of beer and soda. "We had to go all the way to the back so the bullets couldn't reach us," Chau later recalled. "We were afraid we were going to get shot."

As Chau and her brother huddled in the cold darkness, she thought of the scared faces of Cuong and Ha as the door had closed behind her. She hoped they had hidden somewhere.

Sealed off from the rest of the restaurant, a feeling of isolation, which brought with it its own brand of fear, washed over Chau. She and Quoc peeked through the glass doors and the window that looked into the kitchen, trying to see what was going on.

Chau caught a glimpse of Frank in the kitchen. The policewoman was rooting through an area where the Vus sometimes stashed their money. Through the cooler doors, Quoc saw the man Frank had introduced as her nephew, the short man with all the gold teeth, banging around inside the convenience store. They were searching for something.

A moment later, Chau heard shouting in the kitchen. Voices raised in anger, others in terror.

Inside the cramped kitchen, Ha and Cuong Vu were on their knees on the dirty floor. Frank stood over them, the still-warm 9 mm pistol clutched in her hand. "Where's the money?" she screamed at the terrified brother and sister. Cuong, just seventeen years old, had been playing football with his brother only a few hours before. The Vus were strong Catholics. Cuong planned to enter the priesthood, and Ha was going to become a nun.

Frank leaned forward and clubbed Cuong in the face with the pistol, splitting open his left eyebrow. She shouted at him to tell her where their money was hidden.

A few seconds later, Frank ran to the microwave.

Inside the cooler, Quoc crept over to the window near the kitchen. He looked out with his sister. They saw Frank and LaCaze pawing through the microwave. Chau whispered to her brother that she'd hidden their mom's money in the microwave. "Antoinette couldn't have known where the money was on her own," Quoc said later. "She must have made my brother and sister tell her." The angle from the window wasn't wide enough for Quoc to see Cuong and Ha.

Gunshots exploded inside the kitchen. Quoc and Chau hit the floor, afraid bullets would rip through the walls and kill them both, but not before Quoc caught a glimpse of Frank in profile. She stood rigid in the kitchen, her right arm extended downward, pointing at something below her on the floor. Her right hand clutched a pistol.

Ha and Cuong were still on their knees. Frank held the gun a little more than eighteen inches away from Ha Vu when she fired. Her first shot hit the helpless young woman in the top of the head. The bullet tore through the vital structures of Ha's brain and exited through her mouth. According to Dr. Richard Tracy, who performed the autopsy on Ha, the wound resulted in "instantaneous death." A second bullet struck Ha in the back of the head. It ripped across her skull but didn't fracture it, then exited behind her left ear. Two shots in less than a second, both on target, a double-tap, which is just how police officers are trained to shoot.

Twenty-four-year-old Ha Vu pitched forward until her forehead struck the floor. She died so fast she remained on her knees even in death.

Frank shot Cuong in the chest. The bullet pierced his liver and ripped an exit hole in his back. She later told detectives that when Cuong hit the floor "he kept mumbling something." So she shot him again. This time, the bullet struck the seventeen-year-old in the right shoulder blade. It punched through his lung before exiting the right side of his chest. Still, the young man who wanted to be a priest wouldn't be quiet. Finally, falling back on her police training, Frank double-tapped Cuong in the back of the head. The two 9 mm bullets ripped parallel tracks in his brain and tore through the left side of his forehead. According to Dr. Tracy, who also performed the autopsy on Cuong, the two bullets were fired in very quick succession and were "instantaneously fatal."

**In** the eerie silence following the sound of the last gunshot, Chau and Quoc spotted Frank and LaCaze rushing around inside the restaurant. They were still searching for something.

Quoc peeked through the window on the kitchen side, trying to spot Ha and Cuong. He lost sight of Frank. It made him nervous, not knowing where Frank was. "Where is she?" he whispered to his sister.

Chau crouched down and looked through the glass cooler doors into the dining room. "She's next to the bar." Then Chau saw what Frank was doing. "She's messing with the telephone."

"Can you see Ronnie?"

"No."

The minutes dragged by like hours. Finally, Chau saw

Frank and LaCaze run out the front door. She heard Antoinette's ancient Ford rumble to life in the parking lot. As car headlights flashed across the front of the restaurant, Quoc sprang to his feet and took a step toward the door on the kitchen side. "We've got to call the police."

Chau grabbed his arm. "Antoinette is police."

"Ronnie said Antoinette was not good police."

"Wait," she whispered. "They might not be gone." Chau saw panic spreading across her brother's face.

Quoc tried to pull his arm away, but Chau's grip was firm. He was desperate to check on Cuong and Ha. "That was her car," he said. "You saw it leaving."

"It might be a trick. You go out there, and they going to kill you."

They waited in silence, shaking with cold and fear in the darkness of the cooler. Nothing moved inside the restaurant.

**Frank** screeched out of the parking lot behind the wheel of her red and white 1977 Ford Torino Elite. The car looked a lot like the one Paul Michael Glaser drove when he played Starsky in the 1970s cop show *Starsky & Hutch,* except that Frank's hunk of junk didn't have the racing stripe. Frank's jalopy had been manufactured at about the same time that Rogers LaCaze was born.

On the dashboard, wedged under the windshield, was a tattered cardboard sign. It was about a foot long and six inches wide. Printed on either end of the sun-yellowed placard was a star and crescent—the symbol on the badge of the New Orleans Police Department. Printed in the center of the sign, between the badges, were the words "NEW ORLEANS POLICE OFFICER ON DUTY."

As Frank raced down Bullard Avenue toward the interstate, the valves rattled under the hood as the engine howled, making her car sound kind of like a giant vacuum cleaner set on overdrive.

"One of the bitches got away," she said.

LaCaze sat in the passenger seat, a plastic bag in his lap. In it was the money they'd taken from the restaurant. He still had Ronnie Williams's pistol in his hand. "What are you going to do?" he asked.

Frank turned on the service road that ran beside the interstate. "She saw us. She knows me."

"Who?"

Frank glanced at LaCaze. "Chau."

"Which one's she?"

"The one who runs the place."

LaCaze gripped the bag tighter. "What are you going to do?"

"I'm going to the Seventh District station."

"What!"

"I'm going to tell them I walked in on a robbery. I seen two guys with ski masks running out the back door."

"They're going to think you had something to do with it."

"They ain't never going to believe I had anything to do with this, shooting Ronnie, shooting them Vietnamese."

"What about me?"

"I'm dropping you off."

Frank turned on the little street called Cindy Place. She pulled up outside of LaCaze's apartment building. LaCaze lived there with Renee Braddy, the woman he called his "baby momma," the mother of one of the eighteen-year-old's three kids.

He climbed out of the car, still carrying the plastic bag and the pistol. Frank punched the gas pedal and roared off down the street. She was headed to the 7th District police station to report a crime.

# TWENTY

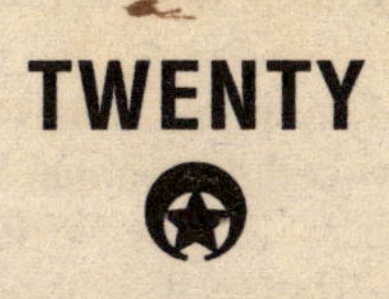

**Chau** signaled her brother to stay put. She told him that she would get to the phone and call for help.

The last gunshots had come from the kitchen, and it was in the kitchen where Chau had last seen Cuong and Ha. Afraid of what she might find in there, Chau scuttled across the cooler floor toward the door on the convenience store side. Still crouching, she eased the door open and peeked out. Although an acrid smell burned her nose and throat, she didn't see or hear anyone inside the restaurant.

Crawling on all fours across the hard floor of the convenience store, Chau held her breath for most of the way, afraid that at any second she would hear one more gunshot, and it would be the last sound she would ever hear. She passed the store counter and rounded the corner into the dining room. The bar loomed ahead, just five feet in front of her. When she was beside it, Chau rose first to her knees, then got her feet under her and crouched, afraid to poke her head over the top of the bar.

Finally, she worked up the nerve to stand just enough to

reach the telephone on the bar. The base station was there but not the handset. She thought back to what she'd seen: Antoinette standing at the bar, doing something with the phone. Frank had taken it with her so that they couldn't use it.

Chau remembered her purse. It was on a shelf behind the bar. In it was her new cellular phone. She crept around the edge of the bar and saw Ronnie Williams lying facedown on the floor. "I saw Ronnie was lying with all the blood around him. That's when all my confidence was gone because the person that protects us was lying right there," Chau later said.

She reached behind the bar, snatched her cell phone out of her purse, and flew back to the relative safety of the cooler and the comfort of being with her brother.

Something was wrong with her phone. Chau was afraid Antoinette had done something to it as well. She thumbed the numbers 9-1-1 on the keypad but nothing happened. There was no ringing at the other end. Fighting her rising panic, Chau punched in her home number. Still nothing happened. The call would not go through.

While Chau tried to call for help, Quoc padded to the kitchen side of the cooler. He eased the door open and peered into the kitchen. His brother and sister were dead. A thick pool of blood reached across the floor from one to the other. Quoc pulled the door shut as tears streamed down his face.

The battery indicator on Chau's cell phone showed that it was almost dead. She dialed a friend's number and waited. The wait seemed like an eternity, but this time her patience was rewarded with the sweet sound of electronic ringing on the other end. The call had gone through.

Her friend answered the phone.

"It felt just like a miracle," she said later. "I was so happy."

Just then, Quoc yelled to her from the other end of the

cooler. "Chau, they're dead. Ha and Cuong are both dead. Everything is covered in blood."

Chau ran to the door that led to the kitchen and threw it open. She saw Ha squatting on her knees, her forehead pressed to the floor. Chau backed into the cooler and away from the carnage, almost tripping over a box of sodas. She looked at the telephone in her hand. Her friend was still there, waiting. "Please call the police," Chau said. "My sister, my brother, and Ronnie, they all got shot. My brother and my sister . . . I think they're dead. The police officer was killed." She told her friend it was Antoinette, a police officer, who had done the shooting, but before she got the full story out, Chau's phone died. She threw her cell phone underneath a soda rack. She didn't want Frank to find it. "In case they came back, they wouldn't know I had already called the police," Chau explained later.

Quoc had heard Chau's end of the brief conversation and wasn't convinced her friend was going to call the police. He wanted to find a phone and make sure help was on the way. He told his sister that he was going to run to a friend's house and use the phone. It was only a couple of blocks away on Pressburg Street.

At first Chau said no. She was sure her friend would call the police.

"But your phone died before you finished talking," Quoc said.

Chau took a deep breath to try to calm down. What her brother said made sense. But someone had to stay with their sister and brother and with Ronnie. If she let Quoc leave, at least he would be safe. And he was right. They needed to make sure that someone called the police. She pointed to the door on the kitchen side. "Okay, but you be careful because they might still be around here."

Quoc hugged his sister and slipped into the kitchen. He tiptoed past Ha and Cuong and tried not to look at their blood-soaked bodies.

The back door, made of thick plywood, stood open. They usually left it open to help vent the heat from the kitchen, but the screen door was hooked from the inside. They always kept it locked at night. Quoc lifted the hook, cracked the screen door open, and slipped into the cool night air. He sprinted to his friend's house.

Meanwhile, all Chau could do was wait. That, and latch the screen door. If Frank and LaCaze came back, she didn't want them sneaking up behind her. "I was so scared she was going to come back," Chau said later. "I was praying and praying, asking God to please help me because I couldn't think anymore."

Chau was terrified that Frank might come back and try to kill her.

She was right.

**Quoc** banged on the door of his friend's house. It was very late, and the lights were out. He pounded the bottom of his fist against the door again and again. Finally, lights started popping on inside. A muffled voice called out through the door. "Who is it?"

Quoc shouted that he needed help right away. His brother and sister had been shot.

Within seconds, Quoc was in his friend's kitchen. He dialed 911 as his friend's family huddled around him.

At 1:50 A.M., New Orleans police communications specialist Sandra Jackson answered Quoc's frantic call. "Nine-one-one operator, what is your emergency?"

"My sister and my brother have been shot!" Quoc gave Ms. Jackson the name and address of the restaurant. Inside the communications center, Sandra Jackson pivoted in her chair and shouted to the police dispatcher that there had been a shooting at the Kim Anh restaurant. The dispatcher started calling 7th District units and advising them of the 34-S (a shooting). The dispatcher assigned three cars to the call and dispatched an EMS unit to the scene.

With the police and EMS on the way, Sandra Jackson turned her attention back to the caller and asked for more information.

"My sister got shot in the head," Quoc said. "Ronnie Williams also got shot. He's a policeman."

Jackson asked for clarification. Ronnie Williams was a police officer? Yes, Quoc told her, and he repeated that the officer had been shot.

"A female officer, her name is Antoinette," he said, "she came in with her nephew, and they robbed the store, and they kill everybody. Me and my sister, we hid in the cooler. She didn't see us. I think my brother and other sister are dead."

The command desk, which coordinates the police department's communication system, upgraded the call from a 34-S to a 108. Officially a 108 means, "officer needs assistance, life in danger," but for requesting assistance with a regular fight, no matter how bad it gets, New Orleans cops use the code 10-55. They save the call of a 108 for when they're being shot at or have already been shot. Since the call came from the dispatcher and not a police officer on the street asking for backup, and because it had originally come out as a shooting, the cops who heard the call knew it meant a police officer was down. Every police car within fifteen miles started rolling toward the Kim Anh.

Quoc hung up the telephone and called his parents. He told his mom that Ha and Cuong had been shot. He thought they were dead. Ronnie Williams was also probably dead.

Quoc could see the restaurant from his friend's house. Everyone in the house stared out the window, waiting for the police to arrive.

* * *

**Frank's** old Torino died as she pulled into the parking lot of the 7th District station. She rolled one tire over the curb and bailed out of the driver's seat. Seconds later, she burst into the empty lobby and dashed up to the front desk. Officer Eric Davis looked up at her. He had drawn desk duty that night.

"I need to borrow a unit," Frank gasped.

"Huh?" Davis said. It was almost two o'clock in the morning. Off-duty officers didn't usually run into the station at that hour demanding to borrow a police car.

"I need a car," Frank said.

Davis glanced at the clock on the wall. "You got a detail or something?"

Frank shook her head. "My car's broke, and I heard on the radio there was a shooting at the Kim Anh restaurant. It might be a 108, and I need to get over there."

Davis shrugged. "I don't have any keys." He half-turned in his chair and jerked a thumb over his shoulder. "You can look in the back, see if they got any keys hanging on the board."

Without even bothering to reply, Frank dashed past the stunned desk officer and ran down the central hallway toward the rear of the station. From a wall-mounted keyboard next to the back door, Frank snatched a set of keys to a marked police car, unit number 709, then bolted through the door.

She found the marked police car beside the station. She jumped behind the wheel, cranked the car up, then sped out of the parking lot. With emergency lights flashing and siren wailing, Frank raced back toward the restaurant. There were two witnesses left.

As she drove the borrowed 7th District police car to the Kim Anh, Frank realized that she'd forgotten her police radio under the seat of her Torino. NOPD cars didn't have radios mounted inside them. Every officer was issued a badge, a gun, and a handheld police radio. Of the three, the most important was the radio, because without it, you had no way to hear what was going on and no way to communicate with anyone. Without a radio, you were on your own.

Frank no longer had the 9 mm. LaCaze had taken both guns. Getting caught with the weapon used to murder a police officer wasn't part of Frank's plan. She had her off-duty gun, a two-inch Smith & Wesson .38 revolver, tucked into the front of her pants. On Bullard Avenue, just a block or so from the restaurant, Frank killed her emergency lights and siren. Bullard Avenue is actually a boulevard with a wide grass median, so Frank had to pass the restaurant and make a U-turn.

She drove through the parking lot but decided not to stop. The parking lot was too well lit. Next door was a State Farm insurance office. Most of its parking lot was in the dark. She backed the police car up against the front of the insurance office and climbed out.

Sirens wailed in the distance.

As Chau shivered inside the dark cooler, Antoinette Frank slipped through the front door of the Kim Anh restaurant. She had come back to finish what she'd started.

# TWENTY-ONE

**After** Antoinette Frank's arrest, Detectives Eddie Rantz and Marco Demma still had plenty of work to do. They didn't even have time to drive Frank to headquarters. The two homicide detectives had to stay at the Kim Anh restaurant to supervise the work at the crime scene, which had to be processed with meticulous care.

Because of the stunning events of the last couple of hours, Rantz knew the case was going to be the epicenter of a media frenzy. He asked Sgt. Robert Boyd, a night watch supervisor at the 7th District, to transport Frank to the homicide office and to baby-sit her until he got there.

With one of the murderers in custody less than three hours after the shootings, Rantz turned his attention to the second suspect—Rogers LaCaze.

Before Officer Frank left—handcuffed in the backseat of a patrol car—she gave Rantz a couple of addresses where he might be able to find LaCaze. The most likely places were the apartment he shared with Renee Braddy or his mother's house. Although LaCaze and his mother didn't share a common last name, Rantz had little trouble in locating her address on Independence Street. He sent teams of homicide detectives to both locations to find and arrest LaCaze.

Rantz also woke up a state district judge. He called the judge at home and told him that a police officer had been murdered. Rantz said that a couple of homicide detectives were on the way to the judge's house. "They've got two search warrants I'd like you to look at."

"Who prepared the affidavits?" the judge asked.

"Detective Marco Demma."

"I'll be ready when they get here," the judge said. Demma's affidavits usually needed very little review. The detective had a genius for homicide investigation.

**Since** kicking out her two sons, Alice Chaney, Rogers and Michael LaCaze's mother, had lived alone at 639 Independence Street in New Orleans. She was a religious woman who spent a lot of time in church. She believed in the principle of early to bed, early to rise. In the wee hours of the morning of March 4, 1995, the sound of someone pounding on her front door jolted Ms. Chaney out of a sound sleep. She lay in bed for a moment, caught in that netherworld between slumber and wakefulness, unsure if she had really heard what she thought she had heard. She hoped it had been just a dream. Loud knocks in the dead of night almost always meant bad news.

The pounding came again.

Ms. Chaney threw back the covers and stood up. She pulled on a dressing gown and hurried to the front door. When she opened it, she found herself looking at two detectives in suits. She didn't have to see the gold star-and-crescent badges clipped to their belts or the uniformed policeman standing behind them on the lawn to know the men were detectives. As a black woman in New Orleans, and the mother of two young sons, both of whom had run afoul of the law, she instinctively knew it. A hollow feeling opened up in the pit of Alice Chaney's stomach.

Neither detective introduced himself. "Are you Alice Chaney?" the light-skinned black one said. He was tall and wore a blue suit.

"Yes, I am."

"Is your son home?"

"I have two sons."

"Is Rogers here, Rogers LaCaze?" the tall detective asked.

Ms. Chaney shook her head. "They don't live here. I put them both out last year."

"Do you know where we can find him?"

"What's this about?" she asked.

They glanced at each other. Then the tall one said, "A police officer named Antoinette Frank implicated your son in a shooting. We need to speak to him to clear it up."

The mention of Frank's name made LaCaze's mother even more afraid. She'd met Frank the day after Thanksgiving the previous year and had always been suspicious of her, had always sensed there was something wrong with her. And now, somehow, Frank had involved her son in some of her craziness. She had warned Rogers to be careful of her.

The detective asked her again if she knew where they could find her son.

"I can beep him for you," she offered. "I'm sure he'll call me back."

The two homicide men stepped inside.

Ms. Chaney picked up the telephone and punched in her son's pager number. After the pager service's connection beeped, she entered her home number.

The three of them stood silently until the phone rang. It was Rogers LaCaze. "Mom, what's wrong?" he asked as soon as his mother answered the telephone.

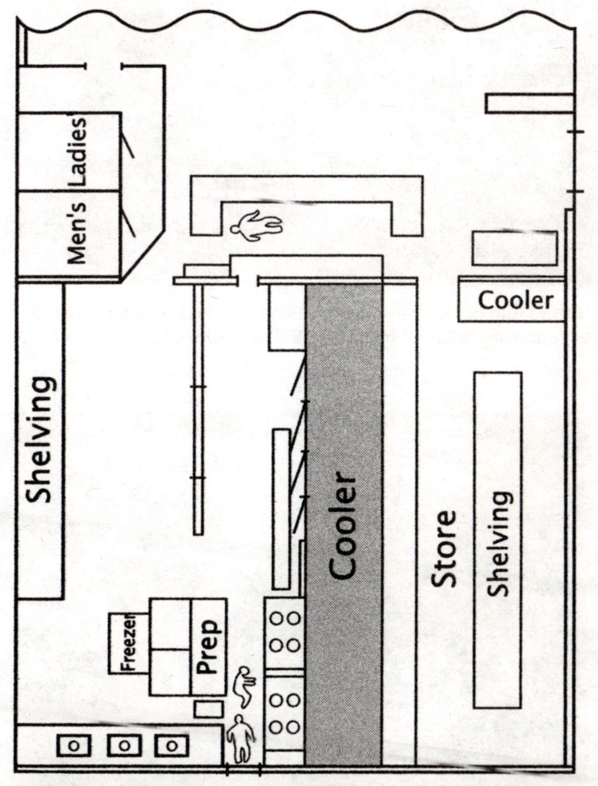


A sketch of the crime scene. The body of Officer Ronald Williams lies in the front of the restaurant while Cuong and Ha Vu lie in the kitchen. *(Courtesy of Jeff Hay)*

The Kim Anh restaurant was the setting for a shocking triple murder in the early-morning hours of March 4, 1995. *(Photo courtesy of Chuck Hustmyre)*

**Mrs. Vu kneels on the spot where her two children were murdered.**
*(Photo courtesy of* Times-Picayune*)*

Mrs. Vu is comforted by her son, Quoc.

*(Photo courtesy of* Times-Picayune*)*

Pictures of Cuong (left) and Ha (right) make up a small shrine in the Vu home. *(Photo courtesy of* Times-Picayune*)*

Antoinette Frank (center, in striped shirt) leaves the Kim Anh restaurant after a visit with the jury. *(Photo courtesy of* Times-Picayune*)*

Rogers LaCaze is led away from the crime scene during the jury visit. *(Photo courtesy of* Times-Picayune*)*

The 7th District Police Station. Both Ronald Williams and Antoinette Frank worked here. *(Photo courtesy of Chuck Hustmyre)*

Eddie Rantz spent 27 years in the NOPD. A cop killing a cop was something he never thought he would see. *(Photo courtesy of Rantz Law Firm)*

Antoinette Frank's home on Michigan Street. After her conviction for murder, a body believed to be her father's was found buried under the house.
*(Photo courtesy of Chuck Hustmyre)*

The final resting place of New Orleans Police Officer Ronald Williams, II. Note the NOPD badge in the upper left corner. *(Photo courtesy of Chuck Hustmyre)*

"They have two homicides here and they say it is urgent that they speak to you because they need to confirm your story with Ms. Frank's story because she has implicated you in a shooting."

"Ma," LaCaze said, "I'll turn myself in, but I don't trust them people. You come with them."

Ms. Chaney turned to the detective in the blue suit. "He says he wants to turn himself in but wants me to come with you. Can I go?"

The detective nodded. "That's no problem."

Ms. Chaney told the detective that Rogers was at his brother's apartment across the river. The uniformed officer, who'd been outside and who had stepped into the house had once lived across the river. He got on the line and asked LaCaze for the address and directions. LaCaze told the officer that he would wait for them at his brother's apartment.

The last time LaCaze had spoken with Antoinette, she said she would take care of everything. She had told him that no one would believe she was involved in the robbery. As far as the police would know, it had been a couple of black guys wearing ski masks. Everything was going to be okay.

Ms. Chaney climbed into the backseat of the detectives' car. Several police cars—marked and unmarked—followed them across the twin spans of the Mississippi River Bridge to the west bank.

Michael LaCaze's Farmington Place apartment was located in the small suburb city of Gretna, in neighboring Jefferson Parish. On the way there, the New Orleans detectives contacted the Jefferson Parish Sheriff's Office and asked for a couple of deputies to stand by in the area to assist. Although they technically had no jurisdiction or police powers in Jefferson Parish, this investigation was about the brutal murder of a New Orleans policeman, and none of the cops headed across the river gave a shit about what parish they had to go in to find the shooter.

The JP deputies who were waiting around the corner from Michael LaCaze's apartment for the NOPD caravan to arrive knew the score. This was a New Orleans case, and New Orleans cops would handle it.

According to a couple of veteran NOPD sergeants, up until the time of the killings at the Kim Anh, no one who had ever murdered a New Orleans police officer had lived to see the booking desk.

**At** 636 Farmington Place, detectives and uniformed cops spread out around the building, covering both the front and back of apartment 100.

As soon as one of the NOPD homicide detectives knocked on the door, Rogers LaCaze opened it. He stood in the doorway wearing a T-shirt and a pair of silk boxer shorts.

Ms. Chaney waited behind the detectives. The tall black one, the one in the blue suit, looked at Rogers and said, "Are you Rogers LaCaze?"

"Yes," LaCaze answered.

The detectives stepped inside and handcuffed him.

"Why are you handcuffing me?" LaCaze whined, as the stainless steel restraints ratcheted tighter behind his back.

"For your safety and for ours," one of the detectives said.

At the Kim Anh restaurant, on the other side of New Orleans, Sgt. Eddie Rantz got the radio call he'd been waiting for—the second suspect was in custody.

**Moments** after the ambulance carrying Ronald Williams rolled up the ramp at the back of Charity Hospital, police officers, both on duty and off duty, started trickling into the hospital's emergency department.

Detective Sgt. Joe Waguespack, Sr., working the night

watch at the 3rd District, was one of the first to arrive. The news was sketchy at best, so Waguespack talked to one of the medics who'd brought Williams in. The medic told the sergeant that if Williams hadn't been a police officer, they would have left him on the scene. There was just nothing they could do for him.

As word spread among the officers at the hospital that Ronnie Williams was definitely gone—and the incredible rumor began to circulate that another police officer had killed him—many of the cops, especially the younger ones, began to get very emotional. A lot of that emotion was anger.

Some of Waguespack's detectives arrived. "We kept the policemen from going crazy," he says.

Sgt. John Rice from Homicide and Detective Herman Cade from the Robbery Division caught the unpleasant assignment of having to go to Charity Hospital and collect evidence from Ronnie Williams's body.

The two detectives stood in examination room number 4, a curtained-off little alcove tucked into a corner of Charity's emergency room. They stared at the lifeless form of a fellow policeman lying on a gurney.

Someone had already pulled off Williams's tie, his black leather belt, the one he wore under his gun belt, a pair of black shoes and a pair of blue socks and had tossed them on the floor. Rice picked them up.

A doctor was there and peeled off Williams's light blue uniform shirt and dark blue pants; he handed them to Cade, who wadded them up and stuffed them into an evidence bag. Next, the doctor pulled off Ronnie's blood-soaked underwear—a plain white T-shirt and a pair of Jockey boxer shorts. A pinky-sized hole, jagged around the edges, stared out of the back of the T-shirt where a bullet had ripped through the cotton fabric.

The doctor lifted Williams's head and unlatched the gold chain from around the officer's neck and handed it over to the waiting detectives. Then he lifted the officer's left hand and tugged at the plain gold wedding band on the third finger. It stuck on the middle knuckle for a second, then slipped off. He handed the necklace and ring to Cade, who stuffed them into the bag.

From a stainless steel tray beside the gurney, Rice picked up the contents of Williams's pockets: a half-empty pack of Marlboro cigarettes and a five-dollar bill.

Ronnie Williams's body lay stripped of everything—his clothes, his dignity, his life. If it hadn't been for the gaping wounds and the smeared blood, he would have almost looked as if he were asleep.

Someone pulled a sheet over him. Rice and Cade walked away. Neither one had anything to say.

**Detectives** Mosley and Lawless asked LaCaze where his clothes were.

"In the closet," he said. "Why?"

They wondered why a man who knew that two detectives were coming over to talk to him at four o'clock in the morning would answer the door nearly naked. They were also looking for evidence.

They searched the closet and pulled out the clothes LaCaze said he'd been wearing the night before.

"Do I need to get dressed?" LaCaze asked.

Lawless nodded, but when LaCaze half-turned and reached his manacled hands up toward the clothes Lawless had pulled from the closet, the detective said, "Not these. We'll find you something else to wear. These are evidence."

"Evidence of what?" LaCaze asked.

"You're under investigation for murder."

"Murder? If this has anything to do with Antoinette Frank, I'll tell you right now, I ain't had nothing to do with it."

"Who said it has anything to do with Antoinette Frank?" Mosley said.

"That's what somebody told my momma."

"What do you know about Antoinette Frank?"

"I know she's crazy."

Lawless and Mosley put LaCaze in the backseat of Lawless's unmarked police car. The drive back across the river was loud. Earlier, Lawless, who'd just transferred over to Homicide from the Crime Lab, had been in such a rush to get to the Kim Anh crime scene that he'd bounced over a curb and knocked the muffler off of his car.

LaCaze didn't have a whole lot to say, but he stressed to the detectives that whatever had happened had been Antoinette's fault. He didn't have anything to do with it.

"He was more afraid than anything else," Lawless says.

The detectives parked in the basement; then they escorted LaCaze up to the third floor, to the homicide office, where they baby-sat him until Rantz and Demma returned.

**The** doorbell rang at 5 A.M. The sound jerked Mary Williams out of a fitful slumber.

She'd only been asleep for a few hours. With a ten-day-old baby, sleep was hard to come by. She'd nodded off sometime around two in the morning. When the doorbell woke her up, she realized that Ronnie still hadn't called her back. When he worked the restaurant detail, he usually got home around one-thirty so when he hadn't shown up, Mary paged him. When she didn't get an answer, she started to get a little mad. Ronnie knew she was up late with the baby and that she couldn't get to sleep until she knew he was on his way home and safe. "I paged him about five times in a row just to piss him off," Mary says. He still didn't call back. Mary decided he was just being a jerk, maybe mad at her for firing off so many pages. "It never crossed my mind that something may have happened to him," she says. "He always carried himself with an air of invincibility, and it reassured me tremendously. I honestly didn't think anything could happen to him." Exhausted, she fell asleep while waiting for her husband to come home.

Mary crawled out of bed and tiptoed to the door. Who could that be at this hour? She looked through the peephole and saw her mother standing outside. They were supposed to go shopping later that morning. Through the fog of drowsiness, Mary thought, *Damn, why is she here so early? I'm not even remotely ready.*

When she opened the door, Mary found out that her mom wasn't alone. There were lots of people outside. Her father. Captain Landry, Ronnie's district commander. The police chaplain. Ronnie's parents and his brother. All standing at her door with sad faces. Then she knew. With the certainty of police wives everywhere. If your husband is hurt, they call you. If he's dead, they come to your house.

# TWENTY-TWO

**The** New Orleans Police Department is housed in a five-story 1960s, cement-and-glass monument to the ugly, nondescript building style known as modern architecture. In 1995, with the police department crumbling and crime—particularly murder—skyrocketing, the city fathers didn't spend a lot of time worrying about the upkeep of city property.

And the police department itself had more important things to worry about than the appearance of its dirty and litter-strewn headquarters building. Dozens of officers had been thrown in jail. The entire Vice Squad had been disbanded the year before after some of its members were prosecuted for corruption. Most of the fleet of patrol cars was falling apart. Officer equipment and support had fallen below even substandard levels. Because of those reasons and others, it seemed inconceivable that officer morale could sink any lower, or at least it seemed so until Antoinette Frank decided to make headlines.

NOPD headquarters sits at the corner of Tulane Avenue

and South Broad Street. It rises above the Criminal District Court building on one side, and municipal court and the House of Detention on the other. In front of the headquarters building is a concrete plaza roughly fifty feet long and about seventy feet wide. In front of the building is a decorative pool with a fountain. In 1995, the fountain didn't work, and the knee-deep pool was bone dry and choked with weeds. In fact, there were weeds and unwanted clumps of grass sprouting up throughout the plaza.

Inside police headquarters, things weren't much better. A dinginess permeated the entire building. Burned-out light bulbs were rarely replaced. Mail slots built into the walls, part of the old-fashioned system that allowed letters to be dropped into the basement mailroom from any floor, were clogged with trash and cigarette butts. At least one of the two front elevators, the ones thc public used, was usually on the fritz. The back stairway was confettied with scraps of paper, discarded coffee cups, and candy wrappers.

The disease of decay and neglect infected those within the building's walls as well. Many of the headquarters staff, police and civilian alike, seemed trapped within its confines. The symptoms of the infection manifested themselves in the sickly pallor that blanched the faces of the employees. The condition created a decayed attitude and a work ethic that reflected the larger malady that contaminated the building, the department, the entire city. By the mid-1990s, it seemed that New Orleans was living up to its nickname, "The City That Care Forgot."

Police headquarters was a depressing place during the day, but at night it was even worse. In the darkness, it took on the appearance of an abandoned building. Inside the drab walls of the third-floor homicide office, Rogers LaCaze and Antoinette Frank sat in separate interview rooms. LaCaze's mother, Alice Chaney, fidgeted in a chair in the waiting area.

There was no one there for Frank. Her mother lived a

hundred miles away, in the small town of Opelousas; and her father, who had lived with Frank for a while, was still missing a year and a half after she reported his disappearance.

**It** was after 6 A.M. by the time Eddie Rantz and Marco Demma got back to headquarters. Chau and Quoc Vu were already there, sitting in the homicide office, sipping sodas. While still at the restaurant, Rantz had ordered a couple of detectives to transport the two surviving victims to headquarters so that he could get complete statements from them. He had also asked the command desk to call Officer Tuac Tran at home and wake him up. Tran was the department's only Vietnamese-speaking police officer. He met the homicide detectives on the third floor.

Rantz didn't know a thing about the Vietnamese language, but he knew enough to know that not everything translates perfectly from one language to another. Anything the Vus said might be important, and if Chau and Quoc started slipping back and forth from English to Vietnamese, as they'd done at their family's restaurant, Rantz wanted someone there who could understand everything they said.

Rantz also had someone from the records room come in and open up early so Demma could get a mugshot of LaCaze from one of his previous arrests. Detective Demma also picked out five other photos of young black males who shared some common facial characteristics with LaCaze and put together a photo lineup.

After having the photos printed, Demma and his regular partner, Detective Norman McCord, along with Detective Richard LeBlanc and Officer Tran, escorted Quoc Vu into an interview room. Quoc was clearly upset. He was shaking, and his face was streaked with the tears he'd shed for his brother and sister and for his friend Ronnie Williams. In the grayness of the interview room, the temperature must have felt like it was forty degrees.

Detective Richie LeBlanc set a cassette tape recorder on the table and slipped a fresh tape into it. He tested it to make sure it was working, then rewound the tape. LeBlanc pressed the record and play buttons simultaneously. The tape started to roll.

"Would you state your name, date of birth, and address for the record?" LeBlanc said.

"My name is Quoc Vu. I was born on March 9, 1976. I live at . . ."

Quoc told the detectives what had happened the night before. About playing football outside with his brother until ten o'clock, then going into the restaurant to help out. About Frank, whom he referred to throughout the interview as "Miss Antoinette," coming in and out of the restaurant. About the guy she brought in with her around one o'clock in the morning, her nephew, the guy with all the gold teeth. About how the guy kept staring at him while he swept the floor. About the guy making Quoc nervous.

"Did you see the person or persons who did the shooting?" LeBlanc asked.

Quoc nodded. "It was . . . uh . . . a black male . . . and Miss Antoinette was there with him."

"Can you explain how she got inside the restaurant?"

"I think she used a key and opened it," Quoc said.

"Are any keys from the restaurant missing?"

"Yes. My sister's set." Quoc thought back to the night before, to seeing Frank fumbling with the lock. "My sister had a key missing when she left, when Miss Antoinette left."

The detectives knew that Quoc and his sister had hidden inside the restaurant's walk-in cooler.

"Did she [Frank] know you were in the cooler?" LeBlanc asked.

"No."

"While you were in the cooler, did you see Officer Antoinette come back into the kitchen?"

"Yes."

"And what did she do at that time?"

"She was digging in the area that we usually hide our money in," Quoc said. "She was digging in our stuff."

The three detectives looked at each other. "Would she know on her own," LeBlanc asked, "or had anyone ever told her that you hid money back there?"

"No. We never told her. We never told anyone."

"What happened after that?" the detectives asked.

"We heard more gunshots."

"After the shooting, after you came out of the cooler, what did you do?"

"I saw my brother . . .,"Quoc said, then paused as he choked back tears, "and my sister laying there, and I told my sister Chau, 'I think they're dead,' and I started running to a friend's house."

Demma laid a manila folder on the table in front of Quoc. He placed a hand on the boy's shoulder. "Quoc," the detective said, "I have some pictures here I want you to look at. I want you to tell me if you see anyone you recognize. Can you do that?"

Quoc nodded. "Yes. I can do it. I do it for my brother and my sister."

"Good," Demma said. Then he opened the folder and slid out six photographs. He spread them on the table in front of Quoc, arranging them into two rows of three photos each. "Take your time. I want you to look at them carefully and tell me if you see the man who was in the restaurant tonight with Antoinette."

"I see him," Quoc said.

"Where?" Demma asked.

Quoc stabbed his finger down on the photo of Rogers LaCaze. "Him. He's the one."

"Are you sure?" Demma asked him.

Quoc nodded. "I will never forget him."

Later, testifying in court about the photo identification,

Detective Marco Demma said, "There was no hesitation whatsoever."

Demma turned LaCaze's picture facedown on the table. He reached into his shirt pocket and pulled out a pen. "I want you to sign your name on the back of the picture and date it." He handed the pen to Quoc, who did as the detective asked. Demma flipped the other five mugshots over so they, too, were facedown on the table. "Now," he said, "I want you to write your initials and the date on the back of each photo."

"But I don't know these other people," Quoc said. He turned over the picture of LaCaze. "I only know that one."

"And that's why you signed that one. Your initials on the other photos are just to verify that I showed you more than one person's picture."

Quoc nodded and started initialing and dating the backs of the other five pictures. When he was finished, Demma and McCord scratched their initials on the backs of all six photos.

Demma walked out of the interview room and told Rantz what Quoc had said. "What kind of witness is he going to make?" Rantz asked.

Nodding, Demma said, "I think he's going to be pretty solid."

While Antoinette Frank and Rogers LaCaze waited in separate interrogation rooms, detectives, who'd spread throughout New Orleans East, were busy rooting through *their* stuff.

**The** search warrants Eddie Rantz and Marco Demma had prepared for the judge's signature were for 6801 Cindy Place, apartment 211, the home of Rogers LaCaze and his girlfriend, Renee Braddy; and 7524 Michigan Street, home of Antoinette Frank, and once home to her fugitive brother and her still-missing father.

At LaCaze's Cindy Place apartment, homicide detectives cracked open the door and jolted Renee Braddy and her baby from their sleep. Bleary-eyed, Braddy demanded to know what was going on. The detectives handed her a copy of the court order. "We have a search warrant for your apartment."

"A search warrant! What for?"

The homicide cops started searching the apartment.

One of the detectives found, lying on the dresser in the bedroom, a New Orleans Police Department summons in the name of Roger (no "S") LaCaze. It had been issued on January 30, 1995 at 2:24 A.M. The summons charged that LaCaze had failed to maintain control of the blue four-door Caddy he was driving. The issuing officer had signed it and written his badge number—Ronald Williams, badge number 1474.

Detectives also found a box of UMC .380-caliber ammunition, the same brand of inexpensive bullets LaCaze and Frank had tried to buy the day before at Wal-Mart. That caliber of ammunition is also identified on the box as 9 mm Luger. Someone not terribly familiar with guns could easily look at the box and think that it could be fired from a 9 mm handgun.

When the homicide cops questioned Braddy about her boyfriend's whereabouts the night before, she told them that he'd been home with her until about 1 A.M., when his brother had driven over and picked him up. Braddy said that she next heard from Rogers sometime between one-thirty and two o'clock (during the exact time of the robbery and murders) when he'd called from Michael's west bank apartment to tell her that he was spending the night there. She didn't explain why LaCaze had left their apartment at one o'clock in the morning and gone all the way across the river to his brother's place just to spend the night.

The next stop for the team of homicide detectives was Frank's rented house on Michigan Street. The house was small, no more than seven or eight hundred square feet, and sat in the middle of a quiet, working-class neighborhood. The house was a wood-framed rectangle, set about two feet above the ground on bare cement blocks. It had a low-pitched gable roof and clapboard siding that was painted pale blue. A set of plain concrete steps led to the front door. Overgrown hedges lined the front wall. In the yard, close to the street, stood a pair of stocky crepe myrtles.

Sometime after sunrise, the detectives pulled up in a couple of cars and parked in the street. The short rock-and-dirt driveway that ran along the left side of the house was empty. There was no garage or carport. The house had an empty feel.

Still, a couple of detectives went to the back door—just in case. The house had no skirting at all. From the front, you could look under the elevated wooden foundation and see into the backyard. Two detectives approached the white wooden door. There was no safe spot to stand as they knocked. The door was offset to the right of the center of the house. The front wall of the small house had five windows, four to the left of the door and one to the right. There was no front porch to stand on, just the narrow concrete steps. A window air-conditioning unit stuck out from the bottom half of the second window to the left of the door.

Rantz had briefed the detectives on what he'd been able to find out about Frank's background, including what he knew about the situation with her brother. Frank and LaCaze were locked up at headquarters, but no one knew for sure if they were the only two involved in the robbery and murders. And given Adam Frank, Jr.'s sordid past, fugitive status, and obvious propensity for violence, the detectives didn't take going into 7524 Michigan Street lightly. They had their guns out and were ready to use them.

After they forced the door open, the detectives found the house empty.

Detective Carlton Lawless, new to homicide and one of

the detectives who'd found and arrested LaCaze, was at Frank's house to help with the search warrant. "The place was very neat," he says. Everything was in its place. After they secured the house—made sure no one was hiding—the detectives started searching.

Lawless decided to go out back. He noticed a pile of fresh dirt in the backyard. Lawless bent down beside the house and peered beneath the flooring. "Under the house was even neater than inside the house," he says. There wasn't the usual collection of junked lawnmowers, busted bicycles, and sundry trash that usually collects over the years under raised homes. In fact, Lawless says, it looked as if it hadn't been that long since someone had raked the ground under the house.

Inside, detectives were busy un-tidying Frank's home. The execution of a search warrant can be a very messy process. Typically, drawers get dumped out, beds get flipped over, clothes get pulled off of hangers and the pockets turned inside out, shoes are searched and tossed out of the closet, and every container is emptied.

Detectives found, lying on top of the dresser in the master bedroom, Frank's gun belt with an empty holster for a .38-caliber revolver. In the top drawer, they found her .38—a Smith & Wesson model 15, with a four-inch barrel. It was loaded with six rounds of ammunition. In Frank's bedroom, they found a plastic package containing a brand-new Safariland double 9 mm magazine holder and a new leather duty holster for a 9 mm pistol, but they couldn't find the 9 mm. They also found a General Electric police radio charger, but no radio.

Rummaging through Frank's stuff, detectives seized her bulletproof vest and two badges: a New Orleans Police Department Explorer badge, number 183, and Frank's silver New Orleans Police Department patrolman's badge, number 628.

After the detectives finished their search, they put the

door back together as securely as they could. Walking across the small yard on the way to his car, one of the homicide detectives noticed that several people who lived nearby had come out of their homes to watch.

Diane Masson, the next-door neighbor who'd come over the night before to ask if Frank's brother could help her move a desk, stood between her yard and Frank's. "What's going on?" she called out.

The detective glanced at his watch. "It'll be on the news soon enough."

# TWENTY-THREE

"**For** the record, state your name and your date of birth," Detective Louis Beard said. The detective glanced at the cogs on the cassette tape to make sure they were turning. They were. He looked at his watch. It was 6:35 A.M.

"My name is Chau Vu."

"And your date of birth?"

"July 15, '72."

"Are you currently employed?"

"I'm the daughter of the owner."

"The owner of what?"

"Of the Kim Anh restaurant."

"Can you read and write the English language?"

"Yes."

"Have you competed high school?"

"Yes, I did. In Vietnam and I go to SUNO [Southern University of New Orleans] for accounting degree."

In one of the cramped interview rooms on the third floor of police headquarters, Detective Beard, Chau Vu, and Officer Tuac Tran, the Vietnamese interpreter, huddled around a small metal-framed table. When Rantz had asked Beard to handle the interview, he'd cautioned the detective, "She's the only person left alive who saw everything, so that little girl is probably going to be the key to this entire case."

In the small interview room, Beard adjusted his notepad. In addition to a tape, a good interviewer takes notes. Tape recorders can malfunction and tapes can break. "Did you know the three people that were killed tonight?"

Chau took a deep breath. "Yes, I do."

The detective, used to dealing with death, spoke in the past tense. The victims were dead. Chau Vu, most likely suffering shock and denial, still spoke of her brother and sister, and of her friend Ronnie Williams, in the present tense.

"How did you know these three people?"

"Ronnie Williams was uh . . . the policeman. He worked detail almost every day . . . every night. He come and check on us. And the other two victims were my brother and my sister."

"Okay. Would you, would you tell me . . . what happened tonight in your own words." Beard pushed the tape recorder a little closer. "Speak loud now so we can hear you."

Chau told the two policemen what had happened at the restaurant earlier that morning. The story took longer to tell than the events themselves took to actually happen. At 7:02, when Chau finished her story, Detective Beard shut off his tape recorder.

**Just** outside the interview and interrogation rooms, the third-floor detective bureau was starting to fill up. Some of the department's top brass were milling around inside the already cramped office space, trying to find out what was going on and if what they'd heard was really true—that a police officer had been involved in the murder of a fellow officer.

Rantz and Demma needed to start their interviews with the suspects, but they would have someone else with them while they talked to Frank. Sitting in on the questioning would be Lt. Richard Marino. Marino was from the department's Public Integrity Division, or PID, the newly formed successor to the disbanded Internal Affairs Division.

Just as in most police dramas on television, shows like *NYPD Blue,* the relationship between working detectives and police department internal investigators is strained at best. Street cops both fear and loathe internal affairs types. They fear them because of the career-wrecking power they wield. They loathe them because the job of the internal affairs cops stands in direct contravention to the bonds of brotherhood that bind police officers to each other.

The reason police officers stand together so strongly and defend each other so passionately is that they define their world as "us against them." It's the good guys versus the bad guys, and the police, no matter what, always see themselves as the good guys. They also frequently see themselves as surrounded by the bad guys. Cops, particularly big-city cops, spend a huge chunk of their time dealing with people who don't like them, who view them as an occupying army. Throw in a dash of racial tension, and you have the makings for a simmering pot of rancor gumbo, one that's nearly always on the verge of boiling over. Like Newton's third law of motion—for every action there is an equal and opposite reaction—the hatred some segments of the public have for the police is matched by the love the cops have for each other.

Internal affairs investigators—the police who police the police—stand separate and apart from other cops. Their job is to investigate their brother law enforcement officers, and in a profession where your very life depends on the trust you have in your partner, most cops don't trust internal affairs people. A lot of cops think that the I.A. types are either out to get them or are acting as stooges for criminals.

One of the fastest and most effective ways for a defendant to shift the focus of a criminal case off of him is to shift it onto the police officers who investigated the crime and who arrested him. All someone has to do is accuse the cops of violating procedure, of planting evidence, or of lying, and it's the police officers who become the defendants. It worked for O.J.

Most police procedural manuals read like the tax code and are about equally as difficult to make sense of and to follow. In the often fast-moving, dynamic situations encountered in law enforcement, like an arrest in which the suspect is resisting or fleeing, it's almost impossible for a police officer to do every single thing right. They're human; they make mistakes.

In New Orleans, most allegations of misconduct aren't even resolved. In the majority of cases, if there's not enough evidence, or perhaps even *no* evidence other than the word of the arrestee or the arrestee's family that the officer did anything wrong, the complaint is simply listed as "non-sustained." The officer is not cleared of any wrongdoing, and the allegation stays on the officer's record forever.

If an officer racks up enough allegations, he or she doesn't get promoted; and if the officer goes to court, it's the officer and the officer's personnel file that go on trial.

A certain number of non-sustained complaints can also be enough to land a New Orleans police officer in PPEP School, short for Professional Performance Enhancement Program, a sort of after-school detention center for police officers, which, according to one veteran officer who's been twice, is "really just a stepping stone to getting fired."

Most of the officers forced into PPEP School are from violent crime and narcotics task forces, the tactical unit, and the Traffic Division, assignments in which officers have the most negative contact with the public. But the theory espoused at PPEP School is that the assignment is not the problem; rather it's the officer who is the problem. According to that line of reasoning, an officer working in the records room—one who hasn't seen a criminal in ten years—has just as much chance of collecting complaints as a task force cop who makes twenty felony arrests per week.

In New Orleans, criminals have been able to use the old I.A. and new PID to proactively get rid of effective cops. Police commanders booted Officer Danny Scanlan out of the 6th District after several "residents" of the St. Thomas housing project complained that he was harassing them. What Scanlan and his team were actually doing was making a lot of solid felony arrests and cutting into the dope dealers' profits.

"At that time, the St. Thomas was where all the dope and guns were, so we were hitting them pretty hard," Scanlan says. He was so effective at his job that a local rap group recorded a song in which they kept complaining about "Blue Eyes," the name local thugs had given to Scanlan.

A few years after the police department transferred Scanlan out of the 6th District, the FBI recorded a couple of local drug kingpins from one of the housing projects talking about a pair of cops that were putting too much heat on their operation. One of the drug dealers said, "We'll just get a bunch of people to file complaints on them and get them kicked out of the project just like we did Blue Eyes."

When the FBI told the police department they'd been duped, Scanlan (now a sergeant) felt a touch of exoneration. In addition to dozens of "non-sustained" complaints, Scanlan has also managed to rack up commendations for bravery for the five shootouts he's been in so far during his career.

Yet, even after taking into account the suspicion and skepticism they hurl at internal affairs investigators, most good cops will admit, although many perhaps grudgingly, that there's a need for I.A., or in New Orleans, for PID. In a criminal case in which a police officer is accused of committing a major crime—like Antoinette Frank—an internal affairs agency lends an air of objectivity to the investigation.

# TWENTY-FOUR

It was just past 7 A.M. when Rantz, Demma, and Marino stepped into Frank's interrogation room. The detectives found the rookie patrol officer—now a triple-homicide suspect—lounging in a chair. She was waiting for them. Her face was an expressionless mask, her eyes vacant. Antoinette Frank looked as if she didn't have a care in the world.

Inside the tiny room were a few chairs and a small table. A mirror was built along one wall so people outside the room could see what was going on. It wasn't much of a trick. Everyone has seen enough movies and TV cop shows to know that a built-in mirror in an interrogation room isn't there so suspects can comb their hair. Everybody knows it's a two-way mirror (some sources refer to it as a one-way mirror). The real purpose of the mirror is to allow additional detectives or witnesses to watch the interview without being seen and without affecting the process. A two-way mirror is a lot like a tape recorder set right in front of the suspect. It's so obvious that it's usually forgotten within minutes.

Rantz took a seat across the table from Frank and looked at her, as a scientist might look at a specimen. Her indifference just reinforced his earlier impression that she was a nut job. Approaching his twenty-fifth anniversary with the police department, Rantz had dealt with a lot of nuts. He knew well that nuts came in both varieties, male and female.

Nearly two decades before, Eddie Rantz had just made sergeant and was serving a mandatory six-month rotation in patrol before going back to the detective bureau as a supervisor. One day Rantz and his partner, Gene Beckmeyer, got a call about a woman screaming for help. When they arrived at the little shotgun house, the two patrolmen stepped up onto the front porch. Beside the door was an open window, a gossamer-thin curtain dangling just inside. As Rantz and his partner paused on the porch, listening for any sounds of commotion inside the house, Rantz peered into the window and saw the partially obscured image of a woman walking toward him.

There was no screaming inside the house, no sounds at all other than the soft pad of the woman's bare feet on the hardwood floor. Rantz waited.

As the woman reached the other side of the window, she raised her hand. There was a pistol in it.

The muzzle was two feet from Eddie Rantz's face when the woman pulled the trigger. The bullet punched a hole through the thin curtain, and the expanding gasses pushing outward from the barrel blew the curtain aside just long enough for Rantz to get a look at the woman. The look in her eyes told him she was totally crazy.

"To this day, I don't know how she missed me," Rantz says nearly thirty years later. As he recalls just how lucky he was, the retired detective-turned-lawyer touches his index finger to his forehead, his chest, and to each shoulder as he makes the sign of the cross.

But somehow she did miss him.

As the bullet whizzed past him, Rantz rolled to the side and pulled his revolver. Through the open window he heard the sound of feet pounding on the floor as the woman ran toward the back of the house. Beckmeyer leaped from the porch and dashed down the alley beside the house to cut off the back door. At the end of the alley stood a chain-link fence. Beckmeyer started to crawl over it. Rantz heard a second gunshot, this one from deeper inside the house. Then a loud curse. It was his partner. "I'm hit," Beckmeyer said. "The bitch shot me."

Beckmeyer loped back to the front of the house. The bullet had ripped through his thick forearm. Both officers pulled back to their squad car. As he crouched behind the car, Rantz reached in through the driver's side door and grabbed the radio mike. He kicked in a 108, then said, "My partner's been shot."

Rantz pushed Gene Beckmeyer into the backseat of the first squad car that arrived on the scene and told the driver to take his partner to Charity Hospital.

Then Rantz turned his attention back to the lunatic inside the house. He was pissed. The woman had almost killed him and had shot his partner.

Within minutes, officers had the house surrounded. Rantz spotted a reserve policeman with a shotgun crouched beside a nearby patrol car. Eddie wanted to rush the house but knew he needed some extra firepower, something more than the six-shot .38 he was carrying. He signaled to the reserve officer. "I need you to go in with me and bring that shotgun."

The reserve cop shook his head. "You can have the shotgun, but I ain't going in there." The part-time officer slid the shotgun across the pavement to Rantz. There were five shells in the tube: four buckshot and one rifled slug.

Rantz knew the woman was still inside the house and that she could almost certainly hear him through the open window. He gave instructions—loud enough so that she could hear—to some of the other officers. He said he was going to empty his shotgun at the house, then they could rush the front door with their revolvers.

After a couple of other cops mumbled that they would go with him, Rantz popped up from behind his patrol car. He laid the shotgun across the hood and blasted four loads of buckshot through the open window. Then he rushed the porch. With the shotgun still cradled in his arms, Rantz, an ex–football player, booted open the front door.

Inside the den, the woman was waiting. Still with the same crazed look in her eyes, still holding the pistol. The muzzle once more pointed at Rantz. The shotgun in Rantz's hands held just one round—a deer slug. The slug was a one-ounce hunk of lead, an inch-and-a-half long and nearly three-quarters of an inch in diameter. When Rantz saw the black hole of the woman's pistol staring straight at him, he rolled backward and fired the big shotgun from the hip. From less than ten feet, the slug hit the woman in the belly and heaved her backward against the wall. She slid to the floor and left a red smear on the wall.

As they searched the house, looking for guns or people, Rantz and another officer came to a closed closet door. Rantz held his revolver in his hand and jerked open the door. A twelve-year-old girl jumped out. She was the woman's daughter. "As keyed up as we were, I don't know how we didn't shoot that little girl," Rantz says.

The girl said that her mom often got drunk, and when she did, she imagined that people were trying to break into the house to rape her. That day, as the alcohol-induced demons began to chase her, the woman had started screaming for help. Someone heard her and called the police. An autopsy later determined the woman had been pregnant.

# TWENTY-FIVE

**In** the interrogation room, Eddie Rantz punched the play and record buttons on the tape recorder. Lieutenant Marino read Frank both her constitutional rights as outlined in the U.S. Supreme Court decision of *Miranda v. Arizona* and those listed under the state's Police Officer's Bill of Rights, which has more to do with firing, discipline, and unfair treatment by internal affairs investigators than criminal investigations.

After the preliminaries were over, Marino asked Frank to tell them what had happened early that morning at the Kim Anh restaurant.

"Well, I went to the restaurant along with my nephew, I think my nephew. I think he's my nephew because a member—"

"What's his name?"

"Roger LaCaze." Even Frank forgot the "S" at the end of LaCaze's name.

"Okay," Marino said.

"We went to the restaurant to get something to eat. Initially, I went there to get something to drink and to order some food to go. I was going to go to a show, so I got a glass of orange juice, and I told Chau, whose family owns the restaurant, that I would be back to order some food and I'd call and let her know what I would like to have after I come from the show."

Frank knew the schedule at the Kim Anh restaurant. She knew they closed at one o'clock in the morning on weekends. Her story, even in the early stages, wasn't showing a lot of forethought. If the Kim Anh closed at one, how could she expect to go there to eat after seeing a midnight movie, which wouldn't have let out until sometime after 1:30 A.M.?

"So we were going to go to the show," Frank continued, "and then we decided, well, we'll just go get something to eat instead of going to the show 'cause it was getting kind of late and I was getting kind of tired and so was he. So I called Chau, and I told her to order a couple of hamburgers and fries, and she said she didn't have hamburgers; she had something else . . . so I told her that's fine. I'll pick that up and we'll eat that over there. We wanted to get something in our stomachs for the night. So we went back over there and went inside. Ronnie was there."

*Ronnie was there.*

After a rambling explanation of how she picked up drinks at the restaurant and about her aborted attempt to go to see a movie with someone she believed was her nephew, Frank finally mentioned the name of the murdered fellow police officer, an officer from her platoon, with whom she worked every day.

"I spoke to everybody. I normally do that, so we got the food and we asked for it to go. He [LaCaze] said no. He wanted to eat there. We needed something to drink, so I went back in to get something to drink. I spoke to Ronnie. I told him hello. I spoke to him, and I went to the back to talk to Chau, told her I wanted something to drink and thanked her for the food and everything, and I turned around and I heard the gunshots, about six or seven . . . and I could see Ronnie falling, so I just told everybody in the store to get out. I went around trying to gather everybody else together. A couple of them ran in the back, so I ran after them telling them to calm down, calm down. I told them just to stick with me. I was going to get them out."

"Who was firing the shots?" Marino asked.

"Roger."

Marino leaned closer. "I'm sorry?"

"Roger."

"Roger LaCaze," the PID man said, "the man you brought in there, went in there with, to the restaurant?"

Frank took a deep breath. "Yes."

The detectives recognized what they were hearing. It was a typical, almost textbook, attempt at deception. A person trying to lie, especially one trying to conceal his or her own culpability in a crime, typically provides great detail about the unimportant events leading up to the crime but will then give only vague information about the crime itself.

The reason for that is that most people can't lie well under pressure. Lying is a creative process. And unlike telling the truth, which relies simply on memory, most often only short-term memory, lying is a complicated process that involves not only memory but also creativity and logic.

Creating lies is also a process that becomes more difficult as the pressure increases. Sitting in a homicide office interrogation room, facing three counts of first-degree murder and three angry, experienced detectives is a high-pressure situation, one that can defeat even the most competent liar. Because most suspects feel the need to talk, the pressure to say something, to explain how they couldn't possibly have done what the police think they did, they spend most of their time on the trivial details that really happened, things they can actually remember; and they gloss over the parts that they're forced to make up.

Frank faced two conflicting forces: the need to explain what she could and the need to withhold incriminating details. Because of those opposing pressures, the detectives found out that Frank liked orange juice, that she was too tired to go to a midnight movie, that she wanted to order hamburgers and fries but settled for steak and fries, that she normally talks to everyone at the restaurant when she goes there, that she's polite and that she made sure to thank Chau for the free food and drinks; but what the detectives didn't hear, at least until Lieutenant Marino asked her directly, was who was doing all the shooting.

What was also absent from Frank's dry recitation of the facts was any sign of shock or outrage at the brutal murder of three innocent people, which happened virtually right in front of her eyes. Ronnie Williams was a fellow police officer, on the same shift with Frank. The two of them worked together daily. The Vus treated her like family. They fed her, bought her gifts, gave her money when she needed it. Frank was with all three victims when they died. She spoke to them literally seconds before the bullets ripped through them and silenced them forever.

She said she had nothing to do with it, yet she didn't seem dazed or stunned at all. Most people who witness something so terrible are almost immediately engulfed in a fog of denial. They say things like "I can't believe it," or "I was just talking to him (or her)," or "They can't really be dead." But none of that rolled off of Antoinette Frank's tongue. She prattled on about orange juice and movies and hamburgers and saying hello to everyone and thanking people and then something about hearing gunshots . . . until someone finally pinned her down and asked, "Who was firing the shots?"

"Roger," she said. *No big deal.*

"Okay," Marino said. "What happened next?"

"I put them [Ha and Cuong] in a corner in the kitchen. I told them to calm down, calm down . . . everything was going to be all right. I told them I was going to get them out. He [LaCaze] came around to the back [the kitchen], and I ran to the front to check on Ronnie, and I heard some more gunshots go off, and I ran back in [the kitchen] and said, 'What you doing, what you doing?' "

Although she admitted going back into the kitchen after hearing a second volley of shots, Frank didn't say anything about Ha and Cuong, who, if Frank's story were true, would have been lying in plain sight—dead on the floor.

"He kept saying, *'Where's the money?'* So he was pushing me saying, *'Where's the money?'* I said, 'What money?' I thought Chau had got away. I was glad for that, but he kept pushing and pushing me to tell [him] where's the money. He told me if I say anything he'd kill me."

"Did you locate any money in the place?"

"No. I wasn't trying."

"Did Roger ever locate any money in the place?"

"I don't think so 'cause he was mad when we left."

Frank told the detectives that she drove LaCaze back to his apartment on Cindy Place. She claimed that he again threatened to kill her if she talked. Then she told them, "I went to the Seventh District station and was screaming that Ronnie's been shot, Ronnie's been shot . . . call it in, call it in. He's been shot, he's been shot."

Rantz noted in his final report that the desk officer, Eric Davis, said that Frank didn't say anything about Officer Williams being shot.

"The gun you saw Roger shooting, can you describe it for me, please?" Demma asked.

"The handles were black. I don't know what caliber. I wasn't paying any attention. I know it was loud."

"I would take you as being an experienced policewoman, after two years, that you would know a little bit about guns. Was it an automatic?"

"Oh, it was a semiautomatic weapon."

"Was it similar to our Beretta in size?"

Frank shook her head. "It was bigger than the Beretta. I had one. That's the one I had that was stolen."

"How many shots did you initially hear?"

"Six or seven," Frank said, "and they were rapid."

"And then when you went out front, did you then see Ronald down, shot?"

Frank shook her head. "I didn't. When I heard the shots, I didn't initially run right to the front. I gathered, I told everybody to get out. I started gathering everybody up."

"How were you going to get out?"

"The back door."

"Then you went to the front area and passed Roger? Roger was going to the back?"

"Okay, okay." Frank pushed her hands out in front of her in a "slow down" motion. "I ran to the front and said, 'Roger, what are you doing, what are you doing?' And he goes, *'Where's the fucking money, where's the fucking money?'* And I go, 'What money, what money?' So he comes running back, he comes to the back. I'm looking at Ronnie, and I'm . . . my head is messed up."

At this point in Frank's story, she and LaCaze were separated. LaCaze had run into the kitchen where Ha and Cuong were trying to make themselves small, while Frank was in the dining room, near the bar, looking at Ronnie Williams. She had not yet mentioned anything about the .38 revolver tucked into her pants.

"And then at some point," Demma said, "Roger goes into the back area, in the kitchen?"

"Yes."

"And you heard shots again?"

"Yes." Frank said that she couldn't remember how many shots. Her head was too messed up. "I know it was more than one," she said. "More than two."

Marino then switched to the topic of the getaway. Frank

said LaCaze forced her to drive him to the apartment on Cindy Place. She told the detectives that as she drove away from the restaurant, LaCaze had his gun "sitting on his lap."

Frank explained that after she left LaCaze on Cindy Place, "The first thing that hit me, I said go to the Seventh District and tell everything that happened. So when I get there, I got too scared to say anything." Moments before, Frank told the detectives that she'd screamed to the Seventh District desk officer that Ronnie Williams had been shot.

"Did you ever put your hands on any gun and fire it tonight?" Marino asked.

"No."

"You haven't fired any guns tonight?" the PID man repeated.

Maybe it occurred to Frank how ridiculous it sounded, that an armed police officer didn't even touch her weapon after seeing a fellow officer gunned down. "No," she said. "I have my two-inch that I thought about shooting him with, but I tried to take the gun from him at one point in the kitchen when he told me he was going to shoot me, and I know he would because I saw Ronald."

Her rambling answer didn't impress Rantz, who had dropped the hammer on more than a dozen people who'd tried to kill him or his fellow cops.

Rantz started asking questions about what LaCaze had been wearing at the restaurant. He knew LaCaze had been wearing nothing but shorts when he was arrested. Blood spatter from any of the victims on LaCaze's clothes, if they could find the clothes he'd been wearing, would send LaCaze to the death house.

Frank was evasive, at one point saying, "I can't remember what he was wearing."

"Who's he live with on Cindy Place?" Rantz asked.

"His girlfriend or somebody. He has a bunch of girlfriends."

Rantz's stare was cold enough to freeze the air between them. "Who's he live with on Cindy Place?"

Frank shifted in her seat. "His girlfriend."

The difference in the interrogation style between Marino and Rantz was already starting to show. Rantz wasn't going to put up with a lot of bullshit.

"What is your relationship with Rogers?"

"Well, I handled a couple of incidents with him, and we started talking, and he used to come over where I work a detail and talk. He mentioned a couple of relatives of his that seem the same as mine, and we determined that somehow—"

Rantz cut her off. "I'm just trying to figure out why it is that you and Rogers would be going out to the movies on a Friday night, leaving his girlfriend at home."

"She has to go to work early in the morning, about five o'clock in the morning."

"Where does she work?"

"Shoney's."

"When you saw the police officer lying on the floor," Rantz said, "did you notice if his gun was in his holster?"

"I didn't even look. I was looking at the overview of it. I don't—"

"And you don't recall if you saw two guns being carried by Rogers?"

Rantz grilled her about the gun LaCaze had, about where she thought he might have put it and Ronnie Williams's gun after the shootings, about where LaCaze usually parked his car, about her car, about how many times she and LaCaze went to the restaurant.

"When you all came back the third time," Rantz said, "who was driving your car?" A simple question, but apparently one without a simple answer.

"I think I was. Let's see, he drove, he drove, I drove the first time; he drove when we came back."

"The third time, when the shooting happened, he was driving?"

"Yeah. I was on the passenger side. I think I was."

One of the problems a criminal has with lying to the police during an interrogation is that he or she can't be certain what the police already know. A lot of questions tossed out during an interrogation are really just test questions. The cops already know the answer; they just want to see how truthful the suspect is going to be. They're called control questions.

The driver of a car usually has a certain amount of power over the passengers. Frank was trying to show that she was in no way in control of what happened.

"You think you were on the passenger side?"

"Yes. I really think I was."

"Is it common for him to drive your car?" Rantz said.

"When I'm . . . by driving all day . . . I was kind of stressed out with driving today, so I rather him drive. I wanted to relax."

"When you all got back the third time, were the doors locked or unlocked, to the business?"

"It was unlocked," Frank said. "I found that unusual 'cause when I walked up, I knocked on the window door. I looked up at the counter, and he [Ronnie Williams] beckoned me to come in, so I pushed the door and the door was open, so when I walked in, the first thing come out of my mouth was 'Why wasn't the door locked?' and he said, 'Oh, we're getting ready to leave in a little while,' and I said, 'You still should have the door locked.' "

"At that time, where was Ronnie?" Rantz asked.

"Ronnie was behind the counter, right at the edge of the counter. He had keys in his hand. They must be getting ready to leave." Frank told the detectives that she was looking for a drink to take home with her free food. "I went in the back to tell her [Chau] good night and tell her I was taking a drink out of the cooler, and that's when all hell broke loose."

Frank told Rantz that she was talking to Chau in the kitchen, facing her, with her back to the dining room when the gunshots rang out. "I didn't see anything behind me," she said.

Just a few minutes before, Frank said that after Officer Williams was shot, she had seen him falling.

"I pushed her [Chau]. I said, 'Come on, let's go.' The first instincts that came to my mind was to push her and go out the back door, and I started yelling for everybody to go. I said, 'Let's go, let's go.' "

"Now you were trying to push everybody," Rantz said, "you were saying come on, let's go, let's go out the back door?"

"They all scattered every which way, and I'm trying to gather everybody together."

"What made you change your mind," Rantz said, "about getting them out the safety of the back door?" With the back door, and presumably safety, only a few feet away, the detective wanted to know why Frank turned around and ran back into the dining room.

"Because they didn't listen to me. I kept telling them let's go, let's go. I was running for the back door, and they all scattered. I said, 'I am going to make sure everybody gets out safe.' Then I ran to the door, and the next thing I know that's when Roger come running through. And when he come running through, I said, 'What are you doing?' My head is all screwed up. He said, *'Shut up. Where's the money?'* I said, 'What money?' So I'm running to the front—"

"Now stop," Rantz said. "I heard all that before."

Frank slumped in her chair.

"Where was Chau?"

"I don't know," Frank said. "She vanished."

"When was the next time you saw Chau?"

"When we came back on the scene. When I came back," Frank quickly corrected herself.

"When you went up front, then heard more gunshots, you had no idea where Chau was then?"

"I thought they [Chau and Quoc] got away somehow. I was happy to know they got away."

"When you heard the second volley of shots," Rantz said, "when the two Vietnamese victims were shot in the kitchen, where were you when you heard those shots?"

"I was running back to the kitchen."

The answer was too vague for Rantz. He pressed her. "You were in the kitchen?"

"When I heard the first shot, I ran back to the kitchen, and I told Roger, 'What are you doing, what are you doing?' "

Still, Frank refused to give a clear answer. Rantz asked again. "Were you in the kitchen? Did you see the shooting?"

"It was over when I actually made it back to the kitchen. I heard the shots and I ran back. All I heard was, my mind . . . I don't know how many I heard, but I know I heard more than two, one or two, so I immediately ran back up in there. I was trying to gather everybody together. I just wanted everybody to get out."

Her answer did not make clear whom she was still trying to get out. Frank had already explained that she thought Chau and Quoc had gotten out. She already knew that Ronnie Williams was dead, or at least seriously hurt, behind the bar; and after that second volley of shots, when she ran into the kitchen, she must have seen Ha and Cuong dead on the floor. So from Frank's perspective, the only people still alive in the restaurant were she and LaCaze.

# TWENTY-SIX

"**When** you initially were in the kitchen talking with Chau or getting your drink or whatever it was, you heard a shot or shots, correct?" Sgt. Eddie Rantz asked a tired and confused Antoinette Frank.

"Yes."

"Were you armed?"

Frank's eyes bulged. "Me?" Three detectives and one murder suspect were jammed into a tiny interview room. Frank wanted to make certain Rantz was talking to her.

"Yes, were you carrying a weapon?"

"My two-inch revolver."

"What did you think when you heard those shots going off in the restaurant?" Rantz asked.

"I had no idea it was Roger shooting. I thought somebody had bust through the door shooting, so I figured let's get everybody out of the door."

"As a police officer, armed, did you think to pull your weapon to defend yourself against some unknown aggressor?"

"When I pulled my weapon, he had his gun sticking in my face. He said he would shoot me."

To the detectives, Frank's answer didn't make sense. She heard shots coming from the dining room, where she knew LaCaze and Ronnie Williams were. She didn't know who was doing the shooting, yet she dashed into the dining room without drawing her own gun. Earlier, when she mentioned running into the dining room after hearing the first shots and seeing LaCaze, Frank didn't say anything about him jamming a gun in her face. It was only after the detectives asked why she hadn't used the two-inch .38 they'd found on her that she added that little detail.

"So did you pull your weapon?"

"I had it here," Frank gestured toward her waist. "I unzipped [my jacket], and he saw me going for it. He said, *'I'll kill you. I know where you live, and I'll kill you. All I want is the money.'* And he had the gun drawn on me the whole time."

"But he didn't take your gun away from you?" Rantz asked, skeptically. Frank's statement was drifting more and more into the realm of fantasy.

Frank shook her head. "He didn't take it away from me."

Rantz wanted to be clear he was hearing her right. "Rogers knew that you had a gun?"

"After I showed him."

"Then he left you and shot the two additional victims?"

"No." Frank wagged her head. Her story was getting less clear by the minute. "Let's get this straight. After I heard the gunshots the first time, the first six or seven gunshots, my immediate rush was to get everybody out. They wouldn't listen to me. Everybody was going too slow, so when he ran into the kitchen area screaming, *'Where's the money, where's the money?'* he has his gun on me the whole time."

Frank's inconsistency about what happened right after the first shots were fired was maddening. In one version, after hearing the gunfire in the dining room, Frank ran up front to see what had happened. In the dining room, she managed to see Ronnie Williams fall and encountered La-Caze, who held a gun on her and demanded to know where the money was. In the other version, she was in the back trying to rescue everyone when LaCaze burst into the kitchen and held a gun on her.

Frank continued, "I am frantic, saying, 'Well, I don't know, I don't know [where the money is],' so I just immediately ran to check on Ronnie. When I saw Ronnie laying on the floor, my head, I freaked out. My head was messed up. I ran; that's when I heard the other shots going up in the kitchen, so I ran back saying, 'What are you doing, what are you doing?' He turned the gun on me. I unzipped my jacket, and he said, *'I'll kill you. I know where you live. I know how to get to you.'* So after that . . . he had the gun drawn on me the whole time. I wasn't able to draw down on him as easy as it seems."

Frank told the detectives that she saw Ronnie Williams standing behind the bar seconds before the first shots. She said she ran to him, bent down and shook his back a little. "I could just see the pool of blood, and that's when I jumped up and I was going to run back to the kitchen when I heard more gunshots." She said she ran into the kitchen and confronted LaCaze. "That's when he wheeled around to me with the gun. I just unzipped my jacket, and he said, *'Don't try it! I'll shoot you.'*"

It was another evolution of her story. In this one, she heard gunshots, crossed paths with her wild-eyed, two-gun-toting "nephew," ran to the side of a dead fellow officer, heard more gunshots, sprinted back into the kitchen to ask LaCaze to explain why he'd just murdered one of her partners, found him pointing a gun at her, and *only then* did she think about drawing the revolver tucked into her waistband. And again, no mention of seeing the bodies of Ha and Cuong heaped on the floor.

Rantz was tired of it. "Where is your police department radio at this time?"

"In my car. Locked in my glove box."

Rantz ran a hand through his iron-gray hair. "It is in your red and white Ford Elite?"

Frank nodded helpfully. "I usually keep it there. I usually take my gun, my radio with me even when I go out, in case incidents happen when I'm out, I'll have it, but I locked my glove compartment when I put it in there. When I go to the show, I leave it because I don't want anybody going in my car, breaking into my car and taking it. At least they would have to break my glove box to get to it."

"So it is in your glove box right now?

"Right."

There seemed to be no end to how stupid Frank's story could become. "Why is it when you went out and got in the car, to . . . Once you dropped him [LaCaze] off on Cindy, you didn't use your police radio to call in the incident?"

"I was frantic. I just headed for the district."

"But why would you head to the district rather than just put it over the radio and get assistance at a quicker pace?"

"I was just . . . I was just frantic."

"At any time before you and Rogers went into the place, did he tell you he was going to rob the place?"

A subtle shift from interview to interrogation.

Frank looked down at the table. "No."

"Did he go there with plans to rob the place?"

"If he would have told me he was going to rob the place, I'd have never gone there."

It couldn't have escaped the detectives' notice that Frank didn't say she would have tried to stop LaCaze from robbing the Kim Anh or arrested him, only that she wouldn't have gone there.

"When you saw he shot Ronald and then realized he shot the two Vietnamese people in the back, can you explain to me why he would have left you alive if he had just killed everybody else in the place?"

"I don't know. You'd have to ask him that."

"You can't answer that?"

She shook her head. "I can't answer that."

"Why didn't you inform us," Rantz said, "when we first arrived on the scene that Rogers, that you knew who the perpetrator was?"

" 'Cause he told me he'd kill me." It must have occurred to Frank right then that if she had immediately told her fellow officers what had happened and they had arrested LaCaze for three counts of first-degree murder and armed robbery, he wouldn't have posed much of a threat to her because she added, "And he'd find somebody that would kill me if I did."

Longtime homicide detective Marco Demma chimed in. "When you all left after the shooting, who drove?"

"He did, no, no, no, I drove. He had, he initially jumped in the driver's side, and then he said, 'No, you drive.' "

Demma said, "So you drove?"

"And he told me to go on Cindy Place."

Rantz wanted a clarification. "And it's just you and Roger? There's nobody else in the car?"

"No," Frank said. She was alone with LaCaze. She was armed. She drove to Cindy Place. LaCaze jumped out of the car. She repeated to the detectives LaCaze's threat that if she told anyone what had happened, either he would kill her, or he would get someone else to kill her.

"I'm going to ask you a question," Rantz said. "Once . . . You said that you were scared of him—"

Frank opened her mouth to speak, but Rantz didn't want to hear any more of her bullshit.

"Let me finish the question," he snapped. "You said you were scared of him. He got out of the car; once that threat was gone, why didn't you notify someone of what just happened?"

"I was going to the Seventh District station. I was going to notify," Frank stammered. "I was one-and-a-half minutes away."

Yet, in contrast to the minute-and-a-half Frank claimed it took her to get to the station, it only takes about one-tenth of a second for a radio signal to travel to the station and to the command desk and to every other police car in the district.

"But you didn't, you didn't notify anybody at the Seventh District that you knew who the perpetrator was who shot Ronald."

"Oh," Frank said, with a flash of insight. "That's your question."

Rantz kept his cool. "Right."

"Because I was so much . . . He said he would kill me if I told anybody he was the perpetrator."

The detective took her back in time a few hours, to the moment she entered the 7th District station. "But you are now safe; you're in a police station among friends and police. You felt that threat was greater than your obligation as a police officer to identify the perpetrator and stop him before somebody else got hurt?"

"No, I never looked at it like that," Frank claimed.

Marino jumped in. "How did you look at it?"

"How long have you been a police officer?" Rantz demanded.

"Two years," Frank said, looking back and forth from Marino to Rantz. "Not quite two years, a year and a half on the street."

Demma wanted to take her off the hot seat for a minute, ease the pressure. If she asked for a lawyer, the interview was over. "The restaurant," he said, "do you know the name of it?"

Frank took a hard swallow. "Kim Anh."

The detectives alternated, taking Frank through her work on the restaurant detail, finding out she had worked

Wednesday and Thursday nights. Was she supposed to work Friday? No, she told them. Ronnie always worked the weekends. Weekends were busier.

"Did you help Roger set this whole thing up and kill all those people?" Marino asked.

"No," Frank said. "I realize how this may look to you all, but I didn't."

"If we go to Roger's house, we are not going to find any gun that's yours or the stolen gun that you told us about at Roger's?"

"No. Not unless Roger broke into my car when I was at school a couple of weeks ago, but I doubt that seriously."

Frank was leaving herself a way out, and all of the detectives picked up on it.

"You doubt he did?" Marino asked.

"I doubt he did because they stole my schoolbooks, and I don't think he wanted my schoolbooks." Evidently, LaCaze was not a big reader.

"How long have you known Roger?"

"About a year, maybe not even a year, maybe seven or eight months."

She had actually known LaCaze only since the end of November, just over three months.

"Were you dating Roger or intimate with Roger?"

"Never." Frank was still trying to maintain the fiction that LaCaze was her nephew. "It was after a couple of incidents he got into, I started talking to him. I even tried to help him find a job."

Rantz wanted to know how much Frank would admit to knowing about the diminutive criminal. "Tell me what kind of incidents he got into."

"He was involved in a shooting when he got robbed, and he got shot, and that's when I really started talking to him." Frank held her thumb and forefinger a half inch apart. "He was that close from death, and he's a young man, so I figured well maybe I could turn him around, find him a job.

He took a liking to me; I took a liking to him. He's a nice clean-cut-looking character, but we started talking, and we found out through mentioning relatives, this, that, and the other; and he thought that one of my uncles was his uncle or some sort like that, so he said, 'Well, maybe you must be my aunt.' Maybe so."

"You said that you were going to turn him around, turn him around from what? What was wrong with him that you had to turn him around?" Rantz asked.

Frank's eyes rolled from one detective to another. "I mean, I didn't know his total background, but he had six gold teeth in his mouth. I mean, a good average citizen is not going to have all of that. I wanted him to get all those gold teeth removed. He's eighteen years old. I told him to be on the right track and just, you know, get a job."

Frank admitted to the detectives that she'd run LaCaze in the NOPD's computer system and knew he'd been arrested several times. "I know it was for traffic, and recently he was arrested for aggravated battery, but I think he was supposed to be a witness or he was an accessory, something like that."

The interrogators didn't bother to tell her that there was a huge difference between a witness to a crime and an accessory to a crime. Witnesses don't get arrested.

"Does he use drugs?" Marino asked.

"Not to my knowledge." Frank's answer was vague, one that left a lot of wiggle room. "He never appeared to."

"Do you use drugs?"

"No, I don't." Her answer was much more sure than the previous one. The NOPD routinely administers random drug tests to its officers.

"Why would he have not killed you and left you lying there, too?"

"I don't know. I really don't know," Frank said. "I thought he was going to kill me. I really did."

Rantz asked what Frank would have done if she could have gotten her gun out.

"I would have shot him . . . but I couldn't," she said.

Again, Rantz asked her what happened after LaCaze got out of her car at the Cindy Place apartment.

Frank claimed LaCaze stood beside the car with his gun drawn and made sure she drove away.

"So he stood in the street pointing a gun at you?" Rantz asked, unable to hide the sarcasm in his voice.

"Exactly."

"Then you drove away from there?"

"And went straight to the Seventh District."

"Straight to the Seventh District and frantically reported that Ronald was shot?" Rantz wanted to pin Frank down on exactly what she told Officer Eric Davis at the 7th District station.

"Right," Frank said.

Rantz retraced her movements. "You took a policc car, drove back over there, and changed your mind about reporting any of this and could calmly and quietly sit there and deny any knowledge of any of this. Explain how you could do that for me."

Frank folded her arms across her chest. She must have felt the noose tightening. "I didn't calmly do anything."

"Well, you seemed mighty calm when I got there, but tell me how you could sit there calmly or upset, having seen a good friend of yours just murdered, two other people you know murdered and would choose not to tell fellow officers who committed this brutal murder?"

"I was very upset. I was in tears, scared, shaken, very emotionally disturbed."

Rantz hadn't seen any tears. As far as Frank being emotionally disturbed, that he believed. "How is it that you couldn't tell anyone?"

"And I was also in fear of my safety after seeing that he did brutally kill four people in cold blood, what he would possibly do to me if he really wanted to."

Rantz let Frank's miscount of the number of bodies

slide. "But wouldn't the avenue to take have been to get him off the street so he couldn't hurt you?"

"That's what I'm trying to do now."

Rantz and the other detectives had heard enough. They ended the interview at 8:03 A.M. Between them, Rantz, Demma, and Marino had seventy-two years of combined police experience. That's seventy-two years the three of them had been listening to people lying. They'd heard good liars and bad liars, and all three were in agreement—Frank was a lousy liar. Nothing about her story made sense, and very little of it was even consistent, but as bad as Frank's story was, it stood as a shining example of sheer brilliance compared to what Rantz and Demma would soon hear from Rogers LaCaze.

# TWENTY-SEVEN

**When** he stepped out of the interview room after taking Frank's statement, Eddie Rantz almost blew a gasket. Packed around the viewing window, peering through it at Antoinette Frank, as if they were looking at some freak in a carnival sideshow, stood at least a dozen people who did not belong in the Detective Bureau. Included in that group were a couple of deputy chiefs and some of the department's public affairs people.

Rantz was worried about solving a triple homicide, about getting justice for the victims and their families; these guys were worried about how they were going to spin the story so the department didn't take such a vicious hit.

The police department's fucked-up hiring practices weren't Rantz's problem. His problem was figuring out who committed this murder and putting them in jail. His job was to wreak vengeance for the victims.

"You know what a homicide detective is?" veteran murder cop Joe Waguespack, Sr., says. "We are the voice of the dead. We speak for them. We demand justice for them."

Rantz had a history of irreverence toward department brass. Once, an incoming chief decided to have a meeting with all the division heads, so he set up a roundtable discussion. The chief had been hired from outside the department and didn't know anyone on his staff, so naturally he wanted to meet everybody and learn a little bit about them. Eddie Rantz was the assistant commander of the Armed Robbery Division.

Once everyone filed into the conference room, found a seat, and got themselves situated, the new chief stood up. He gave a canned spiel about himself, told everybody what a great cop he'd been at his former department, and how glad he was to be in New Orleans . . . blah, blah, blah.

When he finally finished talking about himself, the chief asked the officers at the table to stand up one at a time, to introduce themselves, and to give a little background on themselves and their career. As the procession went around the table, Rantz drummed his fingers on the wooden top. He'd seen this show before. The new guy was from out of town. He would be in New Orleans for a couple of years; then he'd leave and move back to wherever he came from. The new chief had already been briefed on everyone's background. This was just a touchy-feely bunch of bullshit. Rantz had armed robbers to catch.

Finally, it was Rantz's turn. He stood up, smoothed his imported silk tie, and looked the new chief right in the eyes. "Hello. My name is Eddie Rantz, and I'm an alcoholic."

The polite corporate smile the chief had had plastered on his face since the introductions began dropped away. His brow creased. The bureaucrats around the table cringed. The detectives busted out laughing.

Rantz raised a hand to his forehead. He shook his head like he was trying to clear it. "I'm sorry. I must be at the wrong meeting."

As Rantz took his seat, the new chief turned to one of the aides flanking him. "Who the fuck is this guy?"

The detectives laughed harder. Eddie wasn't trying to be an asshole. That was just his style.

When Rantz saw the crowd that had gathered in the homicide office during Antoinette Frank's interview, he stomped up to the deputy chiefs, the PR people, the other brass hats. He pointed to the door—the one that led out of the Detective Bureau. "You all have to get out of here."

One of the deputy chiefs gave him a hard look. "Eddie—"

Rantz shook his head. "Chief, you all gotta go. This is a homicide investigation, not a press conference." He jabbed his finger at the floor. "In here, I'm in charge. I'll let you know what happens."

The squad room grew quiet. The group standing by the viewing window looked at the deputy chief who'd spoken up. Maybe he would overrule the detective, tell him the department command staff had every right to be wherever they wanted, whenever they wanted. Maybe he'd just tell Rantz to shut the—

The deputy chief nodded. "All right, Eddie. Come see me when you get done. I need to keep on top of this situation." He turned and nodded at the others. "These guys got a job to do. Let's let them do it."

The brass hats filed out of the room.

Narcotics detective Wayne Farve lounged at a desk across the room. He'd seen what had just happened. He wished someone would kick him and his wife out so they could go home. It had been a long and terrible day for the Farves. But Wayne understood the process. Eddie would need a taped statement from both of them. Besides that, Wayne's wife had practically adopted Chau Vu. The girl from the restaurant wasn't comfortable if Yvonne got more than a dozen steps away from her.

A little before nine o'clock in the morning, Eddie Rantz, Marco Demma, and homicide detective Patrick Young—a thirteen-year police veteran—stepped into the interview room with Rogers LaCaze. LaCaze, who would later make a big deal about Detective Young's presence in the room, sat hunched against the table.His big eyes darted from one detective to another as they came through the door.

The detectives sat down around the table. They introduced themselves; then Demma set a tape recorder in the center of the laminated plastic tabletop. He punched the buttons that started the wheels of the tape spinning.

"For the record," Demma said, "would you state your full name, please?"

"Rogers Joseph LaCaze."

"Your date of birth?"

"Eight-thirteen of seventy-six," the nervous teenager said.

"How far did you get in school? What's the extent of your education?"

"Tenth grade."

The eighteen-year-old high school dropout, who had a lower-than-room-temperature IQ, found himself staring across the table at three pissed off veteran detectives. Patrick Young, the most inexperienced of the three, had been a cop since LaCaze was in kindergarten. Although he lacked much in the way of formal education, LaCaze possessed a sizeable amount of street smarts. He'd been a criminal for several years. He had to realize how high the stakes were and that in this contest it was his life that was on the line.

"He was scared," Rantz recalls.

LaCaze had every reason to be scared. Under Louisiana law, Title 14, Section 30 defines first-degree murder as the intentional killing of a human being under any *one* of the six special conditions laid out in the statute. What Rantz suspected LaCaze of doing at the Kim Anh restaurant met not just one but three of the special conditions:

- The killing of someone during the commission of certain enumerated felonies, including armed robbery

- The killing of a police officer
- The killing of more than one person

The punishment would be up to the jury but included only two options—life without parole or death by lethal injection.

Demma read LaCaze his Miranda rights and asked him if he wanted to answer questions without an attorney present.

"Yes, sir." LaCaze mumbled.

"Okay, Roger, would you at this point explain to me what happened tonight at the restaurant in the 4000 block of Bullard?"

LaCaze took a deep breath. He talked fast, his words tripping over each other, his voice high-pitched and squeaky. "Antoinette and the child [Chau] had words. She [Frank] said, 'I'm gonna to get that motherfucker.' And when we came back, she say, 'Look, when you hear the signal, come in. Stand by the door and lock it. Don't do nothing else. And don't shoot my gun 'cause it's registered in my name.' I heard the gunshot. I went in. I stood by the door, locked the door and put the key in my pocket. I heard more gunshots. I stood by the door. She came back and said, 'Damn, one of the bitches got away.' We left out the restaurant, got in the car, and she dropped me home. I called her. I got a ride with my brother and went to the pool hall. Antoinette said she was going to the station 'cause they ain't no way nobody would ever believe she had anything to do with it."

*End of story. Can I go home now?*

That may have been what LaCaze was thinking, but the detectives had just a few more questions.

"Did she [Frank] pick you up tonight?" Rantz asked.

"Yes, sir."

"What time was that?"

"Around eleven-twenty." LaCaze told Rantz that Frank

had picked him up from his apartment on Cindy Place. Although it was his apartment, LaCaze said he didn't know the address or the apartment number.

"How long have you known Antoinette?"

"About a month. A month and a week." He was only two months off.

"How did it come that Antoinette came to pick you up tonight?"

"She took me to get a job at the Plaza Towers."

"When did she take you?"

"Around six o'clock this evening." That was right in the middle of Frank's shift. LaCaze said that she dropped him back on Cindy; then later, after the end of her shift, she picked him up again, and they went to the Kim Anh to eat dinner.

"Did you eat there or take the food to go?"

"We stayed there for around three to four minutes. I didn't like the food, so we left."

"Did you all take the food with you?"

"Yes."

Demma asked if LaCaze saw a police officer at the restaurant. LaCaze answered that there was a uniformed policeman sitting behind the bar.

"Did you know that officer?"

"No, sir." LaCaze told Rantz and the other detectives that when he and Frank got to back to his apartment, Frank was in a rage. LaCaze insisted that Frank was fuming over Chau and Ronnie Williams shutting her out of the detail. LaCaze claimed that Frank had said, "Why he gotta take care of it every weekend when the money flowin' and I gotta get it Monday through Wednesday when no money ain't comin' in."

Rantz glanced at his two detectives. He kept his face straight. LaCaze was winging it, but winging it badly. The homicide cops had already searched his apartment on Cindy Place and talked to his girlfriend. Renee Braddy had said that she and LaCaze had been home with their daughter until about 1 A.M., when LaCaze suddenly sprung out of bed and announced that he was going all the way across town and across the river to his brother's apartment.

LaCaze's story also demonstrated a complete lack of understanding of how details worked. Police officers working a detail were paid a flat hourly rate. In 1995, it was somewhere around $20 per hour. It didn't matter how much business the place had on a particular day.

"She went in the trunk, and she got her gun," LaCaze said. "And she give me her gun. She told me to hold it and don't shoot it unless I have to because it's registered in her name. So she went in—"

"Okay. Let me stop you there," Demma said. "You said that. It was then at the apartment she decided to go back?"

"Yeah."

"All right. That's when she gave you her duty weapon?"

"Uh-huh."

"All right. What kind of weapon was that?"

"A thirty-eight."

"Did she have a gun?"

"Yes."

"What kind of gun did she have?"

"A nine."

"You're saying a nine-millimeter?"

"Yes."

"So y'all went back to the restaurant?"

LaCaze nodded. "Uh-huh."

"What did she tell you to do?" Rantz asked.

"She told me to lay down in the car because the lady [Chau] wasn't going to open the door. As soon as she went in, I still was laying down, and two minutes after, I heard the gunshots. I got out the car, got on the passenger side, and went inside, locked the door, put the key in my pocket and stood by the door."

"Where was the key?"

"In the door."

"What prompted you to go into the restaurant?"

"She told me that . . . when she . . . When I hear gunshots, come in."

Rantz wanted it on tape step by step. "So you heard the gunshot and you went in?"

"Uh-huh."

"And you brought in her revolver with you when you went in and you locked the door?"

"Yes."

"And you put the key in your pocket?"

"Uh-huh."

"Okay, and what happened next?"

LaCaze glanced up at the ceiling, his eyes cutting to his right. Scientists say that the right side of the brain is the creative side. Interview and interrogation experts say that glancing up and to the right is a sign that a person is not relying on memory but is creating something. "I heard more gunshots, like five . . . five to seven minutes later. After that, she came back to the front. It was all over. She was like, 'One of the bitches got away. They don't have no money here. Come on, let's go.' "

"Did you ever go in the back, in the kitchen?" Rantz asked. He knew that both Chau and Quoc said they had seen LaCaze ransacking the kitchen.

"No, sir," LaCaze said.

"You didn't go look for any money?"

"No, sir."

"Okay," Demma said. "Was it just you and Antoinette Frank at that business tonight?"

"She said they had two other people in the back."

Rantz gave LaCaze a sharp look, thinking he must be talking about Ha and Cuong. "What two other people?"

"With masks on."

The detectives glanced at each other. Masks?

"Did she say who these two people were?" Demma asked.

"No."

"Did she say where these people came from?"

LaCaze shook his head. "No. She said they came out the back door."

# TWENTY-EIGHT

**As** the interview progressed, LaCaze seemed to get more confused. He seemed to be trying to shift some of the blame for what happened onto Frank's phantom gunmen, despite having just told the detectives that he and Frank had entered the restaurant with guns so that Frank could get revenge on Ronnie Williams and Chau Vu for cutting her out of the security detail. LaCaze couldn't seem to get his intellect around the idea that he needed to stick with one story or the other. Either he and Frank had stumbled upon some masked gunmen in the midst of an armed robbery, or Frank had gone off the deep end and dragged him into a bloody vendetta against Officer Williams and the Vus.

LaCaze's attempt to merge the two stories was creating the highly improbable scenario that he and Frank had stumbled upon an armed robbery in progress when they burst into the restaurant armed with a couple of pistols so that Frank could get even with Williams and the Vus.

For Rantz and the other two detectives, the story was getting very confusing. "About how many shots did you hear, total?"

"About seven or eight."

"The weapon you had," Rantz asked, "did you fire it at all?"

"No, sir."

"You mentioned that Antoinette had an argument with Chau. Do you know what the argument was about?"

"About details."

"Did she [Frank] say more specifically what it was about?"

"She was saying that Ronnie always be fuckin' over her. That's what she kept saying his name was. He be messing over her, and they do anything he say."

When Rantz asked LaCaze where he went while he was carrying a gun around inside the restaurant, LaCaze admitted he walked over to the bar and peeked inside the cash register. "Did you see the policemen lying on the floor?" Rantz said.

"I glanced over there . . . but he was leaning to the side."

"Could you see any blood?"

"No. I didn't see no blood."

With three gunshot wounds, one of which was to the base of his brain, Officer Ronnie Williams was found facedown on the floor behind the bar, lying in a sea of blood.

"Could you see if the police officer had his gun on?"

"Yeah," LaCaze said. "He had a gun on. I seen the gun."

"Do you know what happened to that gun?"

"No."

"What happened to the key?" Rantz said.

"Probably still in the car."

"When you all left, who was driving?"

"She was driving because she dropped me off at Cindy Place. She say, 'I'm about to go to the Seventh District 'cause I just seen two armed guys with masks on was coming through the back door.' "

"When she left the restaurant, did she still have that gun with her?"

"Yeah. She had her nine."

"Did she have any other guns?"

"No."

"What did you do with her revolver that you said she gave you?"

"Brought it back to her house," LaCaze said.

"When did you bring it back to her house?"

"My brother came and got me to go shoot pool. I told him, man, I gotta go bring something to Antoinette's house." LaCaze claimed that his brother drove him to Frank's house on Michigan Street, that he used a key she kept hidden under a mat by the back door to get inside, and that he put Frank's revolver in the top drawer of her dresser.

"You put the key back under the rug?" Rantz asked.

"Uh-huh."

"Is that key still there?"

"No. I don't know. It should be." One question, three answers.

Detectives who executed the search warrant at Frank's house didn't turn up a key hidden under the doormat, although they did find Frank's Smith & Wesson service revolver in the top drawer of her dresser. Where Frank kept her gun was a detail that LaCaze, a frequent visitor to her house, could easily have known.

The idea that immediately after being dragged into an armed robbery and murder plot, and after witnessing Frank gun down three people, LaCaze decided to drop Frank's duty weapon off at her house, then go shoot a little pool with his brother struck Rantz as beyond ludicrous. It was just the sort of half-baked hodgepodge of excuses and lies he'd heard thousands of times before.

"Did you tell your brother what happened?" Rantz asked.

"No."

"Did you tell your brother you were putting a gun in Antoinette's [house]?"

"No."

"The nine-millimeter that Antoinette had tonight, do you know where she got it?"

LaCaze nodded. "She got it from downstairs in the recovery room."

*The recovery room?* Rantz scratched his head over that one. Then he understood. "When you say downstairs in the recovery room, you're talking about the New Orleans Police Department *property room*?"

"Yes, sir."

"How do you know that she got it from there?"

"She told me."

"All right. Do you know when she got the gun?"

"No, but she say she been having it; and like around a week ago, she reported it stolen."

"She reported it stolen?"

"Uh-huh."

"How do you know that?"

"Because I was there when the man came . . . the officer came and took the report."

"Where did he come to take that report?"

"At her house."

"And she reported that gun she got from the property room stolen?"

"Uh-huh."

Frank had told Rantz and Demma about her duty weapon—her Beretta 9 mm—being stolen, but LaCaze's version of the story came as something of a shock. It hinted at the extent of her planning to rob the Kim Anh.

"Did she say why she was doing that?"

"No. She say she might give it to her brother."

"Is this the first time you know of her getting a gun from the property room?"

"No," LaCaze said. "She already got a little bitty thirty-eight from there, too."

"Do you know who she's getting them from?"

LaCaze shook his head. "His name is 'D' if I'm not mistaken."

"Have you ever seen this person before?" Demma asked.

"Yes, sir."

"Where?"

"Dillard's." LaCaze was talking about the department store where Frank worked another security detail.

"Is he a policeman or a correctional officer?"

"A policeman."

"What's he look like?" Rantz asked.

"Kind of fat, real chubby."

Detective Young had a question. "Roger, you knew when you and Antoinette were going back to the restaurant, you knew at that time that you were going back to shoot somebody. Is that correct?"

"I didn't know she was gonna shoot 'em. I knew she was upset."

The detective shook his head. "When she gave you that gun and told you don't shoot unless you have to, you knew at that time that she was planning to shoot someone, am I correct?"

LaCaze shifted around in his chair. "I guess so. I didn't know what was going through her mind."

"Did she give you a gun?" Rantz asked.

"Uh-huh."

"Did she tell you don't shoot unless you have to?"

"Yes."

"So you knew she had a gun with her, right?"

"Yes."

"And you knew on the way there that she was going to pay someone back," Young said. "Am I correct?"

Under the stares of the three detectives, LaCaze wilted in his chair. "Uh-huh. Uh-huh."

"So you knew she was going to shoot someone?"
"Uh-huh."
"Yes or no?" Rantz snapped.
"Yes," LaCaze blurted.
"In fact," Demma said, "just to clarify, you heard a shot and you knew that was the signal to come in. Is that correct?"
"Uh-huh."
"And that's what you did; you came in and locked the door behind you."
"Uh-huh."
"Weren't you worried that you were going to this restaurant knowing that they have a uniformed police officer on duty there?"
"I guess so."
"After she dropped you off at Cindy Place, what did she tell you she was going to do?" Detective Young asked.
"She was going to the Seventh District and let them know that they had two armed guys with masks on in the back, coming through the back door when she was going inside. They would never suspect her."
"Why?"
"I don't know."
"Is it because she was a police officer?" Rantz asked, already using the past tense.
"Yeah, I guess so," LaCaze conceded.
Rantz had heard enough but knew he had to give his suspect the last word. "Is there anything you wish to add or delete from this statement?"
"That um . . . I didn't shoot at nobody."
"Okay," Rantz said. "Is that it?"
LaCaze nodded. "I guess so."
Demma leaned forward and switched off the tape.
Based on what LaCaze had told them, Rantz knew they had to have another go at Frank. Would she cooperate, or would she ask for a lawyer?

# TWENTY-NINE

**Outside** the interview room, things were semi-normal. Rantz's tirade was still having the desired effect. The brass hats were probably huddled up in a conference room somewhere waiting for word about what was going on. *Let them wait,* Eddie Rantz thought. *It's almost nine-thirty in the morning, and I still don't have a confession.*

In their statements, Frank and LaCaze had implicated each other. Neither had admitted to shooting anyone.

Frank had tried the phantom masked gunmen story when Rantz had first talked to her out on the scene, but by the time they got downtown, she had given up on it.

LaCaze didn't know which way was up. There were no gunmen, then there were gunmen, then there were no gunmen—he couldn't decide. According to LaCaze, Frank was upset about not getting enough hours at the restaurant, so she decided to kill everybody. After hearing gunshots, he carried a loaded revolver into the restaurant and locked the door. Then he saw a dead policeman, he peeked into the cash drawer, he dropped Frank's NOPD-issued revolver off at her house, he shot pool with his brother. Later, LaCaze was surprised to hear that the police wanted to talk to him. Just another wild and crazy night with his new friend Antoinette Frank.

Rantz didn't have much hope LaCaze would provide any more details. Looking back on the case, Rantz says, "He was an absolute moron."

Frank had to be the one to crack.

At about a quarter to ten, Eddie Rantz, Marco Demma, and Richard Marino walked into Antoinette Frank's interview room. The detectives found her sitting in almost the exact same position they'd left her in. She was relaxed. She looked like she didn't have a care in the world.

Demma started the tape recorder. Marino advised Frank again of her rights, both constitutional and the Police Bill Of Rights. The lieutenant advised Frank that the nature of the investigation was still suspicion of armed robbery and murder. Incredibly, Frank didn't ask to speak to an attorney; she waived her right to remain silent, and agreed to answer more questions about what had happened at the Kim Anh restaurant.

Rantz gave Frank a brief rundown on what LaCaze had said, stressing LaCaze's claim that she had been the one who'd entered the restaurant and shot everybody.

Finally, Frank started to show a little concern. She said she wanted to set the record straight.

"Start off with whenever you and Roger LaCaze got together, and tell me what happened tonight," Marino said.

"Okay," Frank said, "after I got off work, we discussed that he needed money real bad. I had been looking for a job for him, but I couldn't find him a job."

"He said, *'Doesn't that restaurant on Bullard make a lot of money?'*"

"And I said, 'Well I don't know; I guess they do okay. They have a lot of business. I work a detail there sometime.'"

" *'Do you think I could rob that place tonight?'* he said."

"I said, 'I don't know. I wouldn't suggest you do nothing like that. Besides, there is a policeman working a detail there.' "

"And he said, *'So, I'll take care of that.'*"

"I said, 'Well, what do you mean?' He showed me the gun, and I said, 'No, no, we can't do that, we can't do that. You are going to have to wait until we find you a job,' and I would have had him a job lined up for Monday . . . valet parking. Well, he couldn't wait for Monday. He needed money, but I finally talked him into not thinking about it. I said, 'Look, we are going to go over there; we're going to get something to eat. I just came home from work. I'm hungry.' "

*No, no, we can't do that . . .*

According to Frank's own words, as soon as LaCaze suggested robbing the Kim Anh and showed her the gun he intended to use to do it, she put herself not in the position of a police officer sworn to uphold the law, but in the position of a fellow conspirator. Then, according to what she told detectives, instead of taking LaCaze to jail for carrying a gun and plotting an armed robbery and the murder of a police officer, she insisted on taking him to the Kim Anh to eat.

It took a lot to shock Rantz, but the sheer stupidity of Frank's statement was doing it. He wanted to make sure he understood exactly what Frank meant. "What did he imply by showing you the gun?"

She shrugged. "You could interpret it any way, but I would think he meant shooting up the police officer and whoever else."

"Shooting Ronald Williams?" Rantz pressed.

"The police officer, right," Frank said.

By not using Ronnie Williams's name, Frank was distancing herself from him.

"Ronald Williams, you knew was there?"

"Right."

"Okay, go ahead," Marino said.

"So I told him we can't do that. I work a detail there a lot, too, and I don't want anybody to come up in there and do me anything, and I sincerely meant that. I said, 'You need to put the gun away and stop waving it around like that. We are going to go over there, and we are going to eat.' "

Rantz let Frank ramble on.

"So when we were in the car, I went there the first time to get some orange juice because we were going to try to catch a movie first. I told Roger to put the gun on the floor panel of the car, and I told him, 'I'm going to take it from you because I don't want you waving that thing around.' "

Frank claimed they went to the movie but got there after it started. They went back to the restaurant to eat, nibbled on some food, then decided to leave. "I could tell he was on edge because he kept looking around. I said, 'You did leave that gun in the car?' He said, *'Yeah.'* I said, 'I'm going to make sure.' So I went and looked in the car. The gun was in the car, so I felt safe that he wouldn't do anything crazy."

They packed up the food. Frank said she told Ronnie and everyone goodbye; then she and LaCaze walked to her car. According to Frank, as they were about to pull away in her Torino, LaCaze said he needed something to drink. Frank said she tried to persuade LaCaze to wait until they got to her house, but he insisted that he wanted a drink right away. They walked back inside to ask Chau for some juice. Frank said she knocked on the door, expecting it to be locked, but Ronnie Williams signaled her to come in. She pushed the door open.

Frank said she gently chided Williams for leaving the door unlocked, then walked into the back to bum a couple of drinks from Chau. "All of a sudden, I hear the shot ring off," she told Rantz. "So I grabbed Chau. I looked back; I see Ronnie Williams fall to the ground." Frank told the detectives that she realized that LaCaze had said he wanted to leave just so he could go out to the car and get the gun; then he came up with the drink ruse as a means to get back inside the restaurant.

Frank again launched into her story about wanting to save everyone. "My first instinct was to run and get everybody to safety."

Rantz held up his hand. "Let me stop you a second. Let's not try to exaggerate the story."

"I'm trying to tell you stuff," Frank protested.

"Wait. Let's not go with another lie. We don't need a replay of saving everybody like the hero if you actually knew what was going on in there, okay."

"I was trying to get everybody out."

"But at this point, you knew what was happening."

"I knew he was about to rob the place when I heard gunshots go off, so I wanted all of them out, and I was going to go out with them."

"So you knew he was robbing the place and had already shot Officer Williams?"

Frank swallowed hard. "I heard the gunshots. I saw Williams fall to the ground."

"You must have seen Rogers."

She shook her head back and forth. "I didn't see Roger nowhere, nowhere. I swear to God, I didn't see him nowhere in sight."

Frank said that as she was trying to force the frightened Vu family through the back door, LaCaze appeared behind her. "He goes, *'Shoot the motherfuckers, shoot the motherfuckers.'* I was all hysterical and screaming and stuff, and he has this runaway gun. He has one gun in one hand and the other gun in the other hand. He puts one of the guns to me and goes, *'Shoot the motherfuckers.'* I told him no I'm not doing it, and he put the gun in my hand and he had the other gun and he said, *'Shoot 'em, shoot 'em.'*"

Rantz said, "Which gun did he give you?"

"The one he had. The big black one. I don't know. It was

big, and he had Ronnie Williams's gun in his other hand. He put the gun to my head, and he said, *'Shoot 'em, shoot 'em, shoot 'em.'* And it went off."

*And it went off.*

"You shot them?" Marino asked.

"Yes."

There was the confession Rantz needed. But there was no joy in it, just a hollow feeling in the pit of his stomach.

"How many times did you fire the weapon?" Rantz asked.

Frank's shoulders sagged. "I have no idea."

"About how many?"

"I have no idea," she repeated.

"You shot the two Vietnamese victims in the kitchen with Officer Williams's gun?"

"No, with one of the other guns. He put the gun in my hand, and next thing I know, it went off."

Frank told the detectives that LaCaze took the gun from her immediately after she killed Ha and Cuong Vu; then he forced her to search the restaurant for money. "He was right behind with the guns. I couldn't pull my gun out. I didn't have the right opportunity."

The detectives asked Frank about the money.

"When he jumped out of the car," she said, "he had a little plastic bag in his hand, and he was just throwing stuff in the bag. He had both of the guns facing the car." Frank claimed that LaCaze threatened to kill her entire family if she told anyone the truth. "He said, *'You tell the police that some guys came in with masks and they robbed the place and you were in there.'* So I flew off and went straight to the Seventh District station."

Rantz said, "So he had both guns when you dropped him off on Cindy Place?"

"Yes."

"Where do you think the guns are now?"

"I don't know what he does with his guns."

"So he came back with Ronnie Williams's gun and his gun and put one in your hand?"

"He said, *'I'm not going down by myself. If I'm going down, you're going down.'* I said, 'I don't even want these people's money. Let's go, let's go.' " Frank shook her head. "I don't even remember pulling the trigger. It happened so quick."

Marino asked if she was sure that her bullets had hit the two Vietnamese victims.

"Yes," she said. "Then the guy, the boy, he kept mumbling something; then Roger looked over and shot him a couple more times."

Ballistics tests later confirmed that all the shots fired that night in the Kim Anh restaurant were fired from the same 9 mm pistol, the same type Frank reported stolen in the weeks leading up to the robbery.

"How long before you all went there did Roger discuss wanting to rob the place with you?" Lieutenant Marino asked.

"This was about the fourth time he mentioned that, and I kept telling him to leave those people alone. I feel police officers should try to take young people, turn them around, try to do right. I knew what he was doing, and I guess once a bad apple, always a bad apple, and sometimes—"

Rantz cut her off. "During these numerous times that he indicated that he would like to try and rob this particular business, did you—"

"I really didn't take him seriously," Frank said.

"Did you notify any law enforcement agencies, including the NOPD?"

Frank shook her head. "Because he didn't actually say, 'I'm going to go rob it,' but he kept asking me if they make a lot of money."

"In any of the three or four times that he discussed how much money and indicated that he thought it was a good place to rob, did you ever feel that it was incumbent upon you to warn the police officer who worked the detail there for his own safety?" Rantz asked.

"Well, I worked there, and that could have happened to me. If I would have thought it was that dangerous, I wouldn't have worked it myself, because he could have came in there on me one day."

"Did Roger know Ronald before he killed him?" Marino asked.

"No, Ronald never met me with Roger until today, and I actually introduced them together."

"So he had no idea what the police officer looked like that he was going there to rob and kill?"

"Oh, he [LaCaze] knew him [Williams] from getting stopped by him a couple of times. He never put him in jail or anything. There was no bad blood. I mean, he was doing his job."

Demma asked about the gun Roger stashed under the seat, the one Frank said she was so worried about that she left the restaurant briefly to go outside and check on. "Why didn't you, at that point, take control of that gun and diffuse the situation?"

"Because it was in my vehicle. I thought I was safe."

"Okay. You're afraid of Roger?"

"I wasn't afraid of him until he actually opened fire."

"After he did the shooting, you did everything as he instructed you? Is that correct?"

"Pretty much."

"Did you or did you not say that he instructed you to go to the police and tell them that two masked gunmen came in and robbed the place and shot the people?"

"Wait a minute now," Frank said. Apparently, she took offense to Demma's question. Perhaps she didn't want him to think that she did *everything* LaCaze told her to do. "He didn't instruct me to go anywhere. During the time I was riding with him from the business to his home, I told him

I'm going to the police because Chau saw me. I said, 'You're going to get me in trouble.' "

*You're going to get me in trouble.*

After being spotted slaughtering three people during an armed robbery, it occurred to Frank that she might get in trouble. Nearly three years before, Dr. Penelope Dralle, under contract to the NOPD to evaluate police applicants, had described Frank as "naively avoidant, denying, and evasive." It appeared to Rantz that Frank was living in her own little world.

"The point I'm getting to," Demma said, "is that you said you were so fearful [of him], that when you got to the Seventh District station, you didn't tell the police about the two masked gunmen. You took it upon yourself to say something else."

"All I said was that gunshots rang out. I told you everything that happened. The only thing I didn't say is that Roger is the one that did the shooting, and he made me shoot the two in the kitchen."

By Rantz's standards, that was a pretty big omission.

Demma asked, "Are you now saying that he did not instruct you to tell the police that there were two masked gunmen that came in?"

Frank held her hands up, pushing them in a "slow down" motion. "On the way from the restaurant to his house, I would tell him I'm going to the police because they saw my face."

*Because they saw my face.* Not because it was wrong to murder three people.

Frank told the detectives, "I said, 'You're going to have to take your charge.' Then he says, *'You better not say anything. This is between me and you. When you go to the police, you tell them that two people with ski masks on did that and you just happened to be there. I know where you work. I know where you live. I'm going to kill you.'* "

"So you left there fearful of him after having him just

tell you to say that two men with ski masks robbed the place?"

"And I did not say that." Frank wanted to make it clear that she had not complied with LaCaze's last demand. She defied him by not mentioning any of this at the 7th District station or when Rantz questioned her at the crime scene. Perhaps LaCaze had pushed her a bit too far when he forced her to execute Ha and Cuong. She wasn't going to let him handle her that way anymore.

Rantz wanted some clarification. "So between the time of you leaving Cindy Place with him, getting to the Seventh District, and going back to the [restaurant], you left out what he told you to say about two masked men robbing the place?"

"Because it didn't happen, and I wasn't going to say that." She seemed almost proud of herself. She wasn't going to lie for Rogers LaCaze. After all, she was a police officer. Apparently, it slipped Frank's mind that at the scene she told Wayne Farve about the masked gunmen.

"But you didn't say what happened, did you?" Rantz asked.

"I was scared. I was scared that if I did say anything, he was going to get somebody to kill me. He probably still will."

If Frank thought she was going to get any congratulations from the men in the room for stepping forward and telling the truth despite the danger she faced, she was sadly mistaken. Rantz wanted to wring her neck.

"Okay," Marino said, "Antoinette, you tried to diffuse the situation when he was in the car waving the gun around."

"You say waving the gun around. He showed me the gun. He wasn't saying, *'I'm going to go rob the place.'* I didn't say that."

Frank had forgotten part of her own story. One of the difficulties with lying and having to repeat those lies is that you have to remember what you said, which is a lot harder than remembering what you actually experienced. Frank had said, on tape, that LaCaze was waving the gun around and that he'd said he was going to rob the Kim Anh. She also admitted that he'd talked to her on at least a couple of prior occasions about robbing the restaurant.

The detectives knew what she'd said and weren't letting her off the hook. "You said waving the gun around," Marino explained. "I'm repeating your words."

Frank slumped a little more. "I know what happened. I can't get the right words out of my mouth."

"Well, dear," Rantz said. "No one's trying to stop you or alter your words. We're trying to understand them, but you said, *'I told him to put that gun down and leave it there, so I could get it and put it away later.'* "

"I was going to handle it," Frank insisted. "I was going to throw it [the gun] away or turn it in or something. I know he wasn't going to have it. I wasn't going to let him keep it. It could have been stolen. I was probably going to have the serial number checked or something. I know I just didn't want him to have it in his possession. Maybe bring it back here."

A slip? The Beretta 9 mm pistol Frank had reported stolen had come from the NOPD property room, four floors below the homicide office. She had claimed not to know where LaCaze had gotten the 9 mm he used, so if LaCaze's gun ever found its way into evidence, it would not be coming *back* to police headquarters. Her statement almost amounted to a direct admission that the 9 mm they'd used in the restaurant was the one she'd gotten from the property room and had reported stolen.

"Why didn't you all kill the girl, the other two people?" Marino asked. "Why didn't you kill the little girl? Chau, is her name? And the other man who was working there? What's his name?"

Frank shook her head. "I don't know his name." She knew Quoc's name well. More than likely, she just couldn't bring herself to say it.

Marino persisted. "Why didn't you kill those two? How did you miss killing them?"

"He didn't see them, I suppose."

"Did you?"

"I think I saw Chau in the freezer. I wasn't sure; I could have been just hysterical. All I wanted to do at that point when he had me looking for the money, I kept saying, 'Let's go. Let's get out of here.' The back door was locked. I knew no one could get out that back door. It was locked from the inside. I said, 'Look, Chau knows where all the money is.' He said, *'Well, Chau's in here because nobody went out that front door.'* Then I knew they had to still be in there."

According to Frank, eventually LaCaze felt the pressure of the clock, and they left the restaurant, Frank driving him in her beat-up Torino.

Rantz leaned in close to her. "Why did you tell him that Chau was still alive, that she knew where the money was, and that she was in there?"

"It was just instant reaction when he said, *'Where's the money?'* I said, 'Chau knows where all the money is.' I wasn't trying to get her hurt. If I wanted to, I could have."

"Isn't it a fact," Rantz said, "that the only reason you went back over there was because you knew two survivors know who you are, so you had to come back and concoct some story?"

Frank got indignant. "That's crazy. I went back to help."

"Don't you think it's crazy to come back and tell all these lies since two o'clock this morning?"

"Because I wanted to tell the truth from the beginning, but I was scared. I kept asking, 'Did you all get my nephew?' Nobody wanted to tell me did they get him yet, and I was scared. Well, if they didn't get him, then he's going to come and get me."

"So you wanted to tell the truth at two or three o'clock this morning?" Rantz said. "You wanted to tell the truth at seven or eight o'clock this morning, and now you want to tell the truth again at ten o'clock this morning?"

"Well . . ." Frank said. "I mean, all I can do . . ."

Rantz was disgusted, and he was finished. "Do you have anything else you want to add or delete from this statement?"

Frank hesitated, then said, "I'm sorry."

"Is this statement true and correct to the best of your knowledge?"

"Yes, sir."

"Is this the whole truth?" Rantz said. "It's the third one I've heard. Is this the whole truth, or is there more that we should know?"

"Nothing."

"Nothing else, this is the whole truth?"

"Yes."

Detective Demma shut off the tape recorder at 10:19 A.M., but Frank had one more thing to say.

"Sergeant Rantz, can I ask you something?"

"Yeah, sure."

"Do you think I'm going to lose my job?"

Rantz almost fell out of his chair. "Baby," he said, "I think that's the least of your problems."

When Eddie Rantz stepped out of the interview room, a weariness settled over him. He was bone tired. He'd worked more than a thousand homicide cases, but this was one of the worst. The murder of a police officer was always bad, but this one was even more so. He'd never even heard of a police officer being involved in the murder of another police officer—in any city.

His impression of Antoinette Frank after spending several

hours with her was that she was totally crazy. But there was something else. Nearly a decade after the murders at the Kim Anh, and after twenty-seven years as a street cop in one of America's most violent cities, Rantz says, "She is, without a doubt, the most coldhearted person I've ever met in my life."

# THIRTY

**Narcotics** detective Wayne Farve was still waiting in the homicide office. He was waiting for his turn to give a statement. Farve watched Frank's interviews through the viewing window. "It was like a game with her," he says. "She'd lie about something, and then when the detectives pressed her on it, she'd just smile and say, 'Okay, I'll tell you what really happened.' "

During his career, Sergeant Rantz had taught many classes on interviewing and interrogation. His training and experience told him that he'd gotten everything out of Antoinette Frank that he was going to get. "At best," he says, "you're only going to get eighty-five to ninety percent of the truth. Once I get that, I'm done."

He says there are basically three categories of people you encounter during an interview. There are those who hang tough, who won't budge from their story. There are the confessers, those who feel guilty and want to get whatever they've done off of their chests. Then there are the braggers, those who want to tell you all about it. "One of the tricks to interviewing someone is that you've got to figure out which type you're dealing with," he says.

Antoinette Frank almost created a whole new category. "She didn't think she had done anything wrong," Rantz says.

**Shortly** after finishing her second interview, Antoinette Frank did what's known in police circles as "the walk." In New Orleans, Central Lockup is in a sprawling jail complex behind and slightly to the side of police headquarters. In high-profile cases, reporters and photographers wait outside headquarters for detectives to walk the suspects the half block down South White Street to Lockup.

The reporters are looking for quotes, but the detectives rarely say anything. They generally hate the media and are savvy enough to know that anything they say will probably come back later to bite them on the ass. Suspects, though, are a different story. Every once in a while, one of them wants to talk. Typically, it's just to protest their innocence, or to claim that the police beat them up, but Antoinette Frank was a little different—nor did she disappoint.

Eddie Rantz assigned detectives Yvonne Farve and Marco Demma to haul Frank to jail. The detectives left the third-floor homicide office with Frank in tow. They took the back elevator to the first floor, then snaked their way down the twisting corridor to the covered parking garage on the South White Street side of the building. As soon as the door opened, the camera flashes started popping and the news video started rolling. Reporters shouted questions.

Frank wore her black leather jacket zipped up almost to her throat. Her black hair brushed her shoulders. Her hands were cuffed behind her back. Farve and Demma flanked her. On Frank's right, Yvonne Farve gripped the upper sleeve of her jacket, while on her left, Demma had his hand wrapped around her upper arm.

Most criminal suspects come out the garage side of the building with their head hung low, ashamed, maybe not at what they stand accused of, but at least of being dragged past the news media in handcuffs. Not so with Antoinette Frank. As the photographers backpedaled down South White and across Perdido Street to the Sheriff's Central Lockup, Frank walked with her head held high. She stared straight into one of the news cameras, a half smile playing across her lips.

Just before the procession reached the sally port at Lockup, Frank bent forward and tugged at her two escorts, almost as if she was trying to get away. Demma squeezed his grip tighter. Yvonne Farve, perhaps because she really needed to do it in order to maintain control of Frank, or perhaps because she'd spent so much time with Chau Vu, used a different technique. She yanked Frank's wrists up with her left hand and cranked down on Frank's tricep with her right forearm.

Upstairs in the homicide office, Wayne Farve saw "the walk" live on television. Years later, he still chuckles as he remembers the incident. "Frank tried to pull away, so Yvonne slapped an armbar on her sorry ass."

No one in the New Orleans Police Department felt too sorry for Antoinette Frank.

**That** night, Mary Williams got a call at home. When she answered, she heard someone crying on the other end of the line. Then the caller asked for "Mrs. Ronnie." Family, friends, and policemen filled the Williams house. Mary stepped into the garage. She sank into a corner near the garage door and sat behind a pile of boxes. "Who is this?" she asked.

"Mrs. Ronnie, Mrs. Ronnie, I am so sorry," the pitiful, almost childlike voice said.

They had met only once or twice, but Mary recognized the voice. It was Chau Vu. The two women cried together as they spilled their grief into the telephone. Every time Chau called her Mrs. Ronnie, Mary Williams cried even harder. Chau kept asking if Mary was mad at her. Mary kept telling her that no, she wasn't mad at her or her family. She was very sorry for their loss.

"It was terrible," Mary recalls.

**Sunday** night, March 5, 1995. Eddie Rantz and several homicide detectives were sprawled out in chairs at the Miracle Mile, a bar on Tulane Avenue, across the street from the Criminal District Court building and just half a block from police headquarters. Not surprisingly, given its close proximity to the police department and the courthouse, the Miracle Mile was a popular hangout for cops and prosecutors.

Rantz and his detectives had been working nonstop on the Kim Anh case since Saturday. Eddie still had on the same suit he'd worn to work Friday afternoon. Even though both suspects had been in custody since early Saturday morning, there had been—and still was—a lot of investigative work left to be done. The detectives had to build a profile of the two killers. That meant interviewing people who knew them or had seen them together.

In theory, motive isn't an element of a crime; it's not something the prosecution has to prove at trial. It's enough to prove that the defendants committed the crime. The prosecutor doesn't have to explain why they did it. In theory.

In reality, everybody—and that includes jurors—wants to know why. Why someone did something. The crazier the thing done, the more intense the curiosity to find out why it was done. It's human nature. Often, if a prosecutor can't explain why a defendant did something—particularly something seemingly out of character—jurors have a hard time believing the person really did it. Rantz knew that for the jury that would hear the case against Frank and LaCaze, for the police department, for the city itself, he needed to find the answer to the burning question—Why?

To do that, he had to rip apart the history of Antoinette Frank and Rogers LaCaze, and that meant he and his detectives had to work almost around the clock. But not tonight, at least not for the next few hours. Ronnie Williams's funeral was the next day at noon. Earlier in the evening, the close-knit team of detectives who were working the case had paid their respects at the wake. They'd seen Ronnie laid out in his coffin, dressed in a fresh police uniform, one without the holes and without the blood. Tonight it was time to mourn the loss of a brother. Tonight it was time to get drunk.

The murders at the Kim Anh had been the climax to one of the bloodiest weeks in New Orleans's already blood-soaked history. In this city of just under a half million people, twenty-one of them had been murdered and nine more wounded between Saturday, February 25 and Saturday, March 4. The city had seen an orgy of shootings, stabbings, and strangulations. The homicide detectives had been run ragged even before they got the call to respond to the Kim Anh restaurant.

Rantz was slurping a drink when his pager went off. *Aw fuck,* he thought. *Not again, not a-fuckin'-gain.* The motherfuckers out there couldn't still be killing each other. The bloodlust had to abate one day. He'd lost count of how many drinks he'd had. Rantz looked at the number displayed on his pager. He didn't recognize it. Good. That meant it wasn't the command desk.

He stood up from the table he and his detectives had surrounded and walked behind the bar to use the telephone (it was before the days when everyone carried a cell phone). Rantz cradled the handset between his ear and shoulder, held his pager out in front of his face, tried to focus his tired and bloodshot eyes on the tiny display screen, then punched the numbers into the telephone touch pad. On the other end, a woman answered. It was Mary Williams, Ronnie's wife—now widow.

She was crying. "Do you know where Ronnie's ring is?" she asked. "At the funeral home, he didn't have his wedding ring on."

Rantz knew exactly where it was. He'd seen it listed in the property and evidence section of one of the police reports. It was in Central Evidence and Property, he told her. It was standard procedure. Detectives took everything from a homicide victim, including jewelry. Anything could turn out to be a crucial piece of evidence.

"I want to bury him tomorrow with his wedding ring," Mary Williams said.

A lump welled up in Rantz's throat that threatened to choke him. "I'll get it for you" was all he managed to say before he hung up.

Rantz went back to the table and snatched his suit coat off the back of his chair. He told his detectives he'd be right back. "Where you going?" they demanded.

"I gotta take care of something," he said.

In the basement of police headquarters, Rantz pounded on the locked door at CE&P. Finally, a girl—one of the civilian clerks—opened it a crack. "Can I help you?" she asked. Her tone left no doubt in Rantz's slightly pickled brain that helping him was the last thing she wanted to do.

"I need to get a piece of property out."

The girl looked at her watch. It was after midnight. She shook her head. "You're going to have to come back in the morning. We don't check property out this late at night."

"You don't understand. It's not evidence, it's property, and I need to get it right now."

"Like I said, you are going to have to come back in—"

"I'm Sergeant Rantz. I'm in Homicide. I'm the lead detective on this—"

She shook her head again. "I know who you are, but I can't just let you come in—"

"You know the policeman who got killed? It's his wedding ring. His funeral is tomorrow, and his wife wants to bury him with his ring. We don't need the damn ring. I know; it's my case."

She wouldn't budge. "Besides," she said, "that property is locked up in the safe. I couldn't get it even if I wanted to."

The CE&P door opened out. When the civilian clerk tried to close it, Rantz pulled it all the way open. "I'll get it myself."

"You can't come in here! I'm going to call the captain."

"You call whoever you want, honey. I've got to get that ring tonight."

The safe turned out not to be a real safe at all, at least not one with a combination lock. Instead of a big dial and tumblers and all that, it was just a big steel box with a chain wrapped around it. The chain was clipped together with a heavy-duty padlock.

The clerk, who'd followed Rantz through the labyrinth that was the property room, folded her arms across her chest and struck a defiant pose. "I told you."

Rantz wandered around for a minute until he found what he was looking for—a three-foot metal pry bar.

When he got back to the lockbox, the girl started screaming, "You can't do that! You can't do that!"

Ignoring her, Rantz slid the pry bar behind the padlock, between the chain and the door of the safe, and started rotating it. When it got tight, he turned one hand over, palm up. He took a deep breath and pushed down with one hand and pulled up with the other. The bar moved another quarter turn. Rantz turned sideways, shoving his body weight down on the hand that was pushing, and pulled back on the other hand with all his strength. The clerk kept screaming at him.

The lock popped. The chain flew off. The lockbox door sprang open.

"I want you to witness this," he told the girl.

"Witness what?"

Rantz knelt on the floor and pawed through the lockbox until he found the property envelope with Williams's name printed on it. He tore open the seal and fished out the dead officer's gold wedding band. As he stood to leave, the property clerk held a ledger book out to him. "You got to sign this."

"No problem," he said.

The clerk laid the logbook on top of the lockbox and flipped it open. The pages of the book were white with red margins, and about twenty-five blue horizontal lines per page. The record for each item of property spanned two pages. The left page recorded the entry of the property into the safe; the right page recorded its removal.

Rantz patted his shirt pocket but seemed to have misplaced his pen. The smug little clerk handed him one. "You gonna get in trouble for this," she said.

He nodded. "Maybe." Then, with the clerk's pen, he scrawled across both open pages of the logbook, in huge letters, "EDDIE RANTZ WAS HERE!"

He went back to the Miracle Mile to get a drink.

**The** next morning, the telephone woke Rantz up early. It was Chief Pennington. He wanted to know about Rantz's midnight raid on the property room.

"Chief," Rantz said, "normally I'd lie about something like this, but I'm too hungover, and I have too much work to do. So I'll just tell you straight out, I did it. Mary Williams wanted her husband's ring, so I got it for her."

Silence hung on the line. The new chief had been a Washington, D.C., cop for a long time. He'd lost brother officers, he'd investigated their murders, he'd dealt with grieving widows—he'd walked in Eddie's shoes. "Don't worry about it," the chief said. "But, Eddie . . ."

"Yes, sir?"

"Sometime today, go back and sign the logbook properly."

"Yes, sir."

"I'll see you at the funeral," the chief said, then hung up.

# THIRTY-ONE

**On** the way to the funeral home, Rantz passed City Hall on Loyola Avenue and, across from it, the old Howard Johnson's Hotel (now the Holiday Inn). Rantz was a young rookie patrolman when U.S. Navy veteran and Black Panther Party disciple Mark Essex entered the high-rise hotel and started shooting people with a .44 Magnum semiautomatic rifle.

Essex's rampage had started at 11 P.M. on New Year's Eve 1972. Carrying his rifle, he drifted like a phantom through the night shadows surrounding police headquarters and eventually opened fire on Central Lockup, killing an unarmed police cadet and wounding a lieutenant. Just before midnight, Essex gunned down another police officer who was investigating a silent alarm call. Once the bullets and the shell casings were compared, the New Orleans Police Department realized there was a shooter stalking their city and preying on police officers.

A week later, on January 7, 1973, Essex walked into an uptown grocery store and blasted the owner, a man whom he suspected was a police informant, then fled on foot. A few blocks from the store, Essex found a 1968 Chevrolet Chevelle idling in front of a house. He shoved the muzzle of his rifle through the open car window and ordered the driver, Marvin Albert, a black man and Vietnam veteran, to get out of the car. "I don't want to kill you," Essex told him. "I'm just killing honkies today, but I will kill you, too."

Essex was an ardent racist. On one wall of his two-bedroom apartment he had scrawled, "HATE WHITE PEOPLE."

Moments later, Essex crashed the hijacked car, but he still managed to reach the seventeen-story Howard Johnson's Hotel. From the parking garage, he climbed a stairwell and burst onto one of the guest floors. Then he started shooting. He killed twenty-seven-year-old Dr. Robert Steagall; then he shot Steagall's wife in the back of the head as she cradled her dying husband. The Steagalls, visitors from Virginia, had been married for just seven months.

To create confusion, Essex set several rooms on fire by lighting telephone books and tossing them under the drapes. As he dashed through the hotel corridors, blasting away with his rifle and lighting fires, calls started coming in to the hotel switchboard. Two hotel managers went to investigate. Essex shot and killed them both.

As firefighters and police officers arrived at the hotel, Essex started shooting them. Fireman Tim Ursin tried to climb a ladder to reach one of the burning rooms. Essex leaned out from a balcony and shot him. A policeman who had been following Ursin up the ladder fired at Essex with a shotgun and drove him back far enough so that a second police officer could reach the wounded fireman and lower him to safety.

Patrolman Kenny Solis took a .44 slug in the shoulder. His partner, Dave McCann, who'd been a medic in Vietnam, pulled Solis behind the cover of an oak tree and started treating the wound. Solis survived.

Essex shot and killed Patrolman Phil Coleman as the officer stepped from his patrol car. Motorcycle officer Paul Persigo took a round through the face. His dead body toppled onto paramedic Henry Luckow.

Patrolman Eddie Rantz and his partner Johnny O'Brien were just leaving Charity Hospital. Some guy they'd arrested had fallen down and hurt himself and needed a few stitches. When they got to their police car, they heard the radio popping with reports of a shooting at the Howard Johnson's. The two officers already had one unruly prisoner; they didn't need any more. At Lockup, Rantz heard more about the Howard Johnson's. Apparently, several people had been shot. By the time Rantz and O'Brien got back to their car, they heard the hotel was on fire. "Fuck it," Rantz said. "Let's go." They went screaming down Tulane Avenue toward Loyola.

When they turned onto the street in front of the hotel, the two officers rolled up on a scene from a war movie. Police cars, fire trucks, and ambulances littered the street. Dozens of people—emergency personnel and civilians caught in the crossfire—had taken cover behind whatever they could find. Essex was on the roof firing down on everyone with his big gun.

Rantz and O'Brien pulled out their .38 revolvers and started shooting up at the roof, but all they managed to do was knock out a few windows. Police officers traded shots with the gunman for several hours. Eventually, a police commander handed Rantz a .30-caliber carbine and told him to get on the roof of a building to the east of the hotel. From there he could fire down at the sniper.

Meanwhile, Louis Sirgo, the forty-eight-year-old deputy police superintendent, had arrived on the scene and pulled together a group of officers armed with rifles and shotguns. Sirgo led the hastily assembled tactical team up one of the hotel's two stairwells. As the deputy superintendent and his men neared the roof, Essex was waiting for them. When he spotted the policemen coming up the dark, smoke-filled stairwell, Essex took aim at the lead officer and fired. His bullet hit Sirgo in the back and tore out a chunk of his spine. The other officers carried their fallen commander down the stairs, but it was much too late. Louis Sirgo was the third New Orleans police officer Essex killed that day and the fifth in a week.

By the time Rantz worked his way around the kill zone and made it up to the roof of the building to the east of the hotel, night had fallen. As he took up a firing position at the edge of the roof closest to the Howard Johnson's, Rantz saw a U.S. Marine helicopter, a big twin-rotor CH-46, Sea Knight, beating the air overhead as it circled the hotel. The sight of the military helicopter, the rain, the smoke from the fires inside the hotel, and the tear gas only added to the surreal war-torn look that had been cast over downtown New Orleans within the span of one afternoon.

The Marine pilot, Lt. Col. Chuck Pitman, who had flown more than twelve hundred combat missions in Vietnam and had been shot down seven times, carried a load of heavily armed New Orleans policemen in the belly of his aircraft. Pitman made two sweeping passes over the roof of the hotel. On each pass the officers in the chopper fired down at Essex, who was holed up inside a cinderblock rooftop cubicle he was using as a makeshift bunker. Essex fired back at the helicopter each time it roared overhead, but Pitman and the police officers he carried refused to give up. It was do or die.

Bullets from the helicopter had riddled the cubicle and busted open a water main. Pressurized water spewed across the roof and dowsed the officers crouched in the stairwell below Essex's position and on the balconies.

The helicopter swept in again. Bullets, ricochets, and chunks of concrete flew through the air. This time the gunfire pouring from the policemen inside the helicopter was so intense that it forced Essex out from his hole. He dashed across the roof, his rifle clutched in one hand, his other fist raised defiantly in the air. Rantz and the other policemen stationed on rooftops surrounding the Howard Johnson's opened fire. Their bullets joined those raining down from the helicopter and caught Essex in a deadly crossfire. The former Navy man and Black Panther was cut to pieces, his body riddled with more than two hundred bullets.

It was Rantz's first shooting, and although he couldn't tell if he hit Essex or not, one thing he was sure of was that the sniper was dead. "That guy was so shot up," the retired detective says, "he had to be picked up with a scooper."

**On** the morning of Ronnie Williams's funeral, Rantz and Demma drove to the funeral home and found Mary Williams in the viewing room, standing beside her husband's coffin. She had the stunned look of someone who'd been in a deadly crash but had survived—just barely. Her eyes implored Rantz. "Did you get it?" she said.

Eddie reached into the pocket of his suit coat. When he withdrew his hand, he turned it over and opened it. Lying in his palm was Ronnie's gold wedding band.

Mary Williams snatched it up like it was a life preserver. "Thank you so much," she said. Tears ran down her face as she leaned forward and kissed first Rantz, then Demma, on the cheek.

The two detectives faded away into the crowd.

Mary Williams slipped her husband's wedding ring back on his finger.

The evening before, the funeral director had called her at home and asked her to bring clothes for her husband. He told her not to forget underwear, socks, and shoes. She was so dazed she argued about the shoes. "What's it matter about his shoes? No one's going to be able to see his feet."

In her laundry room, she found that she'd accidentally washed a load of Ronnie's white undershirts and boxers with a red shirt. All of his whites had turned pink. She thought how embarrassed her husband was going to be to get buried in pink underwear. Then she realized, it didn't matter. Her husband wasn't going to be embarrassed. He was dead. She broke down in tears.

It was that same night, just before the wake, while Mary was writing her husband's obituary, that she overheard someone say that another police officer had been involved in her husband's murder. The news stunned her. Her mind raced. *Is this for real? Is it just rumors? I don't believe it.*

Mary's eyes met those of the funeral planner. He seemed as stunned as she was. She held up her hand to the person who'd said it. "I don't want to hear any more until I get through with the obituary." Although she didn't want to hear about it, she found that she couldn't stop thinking about it. Throughout the wake, Mary found herself wondering things like *Is it someone I know? Did Ronnie know them? What did Ronnie say? How terrible for him to be betrayed like that.* She also wondered what the Vus must be thinking, to have discovered that it was a police officer who killed their children.

When Ronnie and Mary's oldest son, five-year-old Christopher, found out they were going to put his daddy in a special box, called a coffin, he asked if it was dark in the coffin. "Yes," his mother said.

"Is Daddy going to be scared in the dark?"

"No," Mary told him. "God gives Daddy all the light he wants in heaven."

At home following the wake, Mary found Chris by the front door. He was cracking up with laughter and moving around all crazy-like. "What in the world are you doing, Chris?" she asked.

The boy smiled at her. "Daddy is tickling me."

Monday morning dawned wet and gray. The temperature was in the sixties but felt colder. At the funeral service, Ronnie Williams's body rested in his open casket at the head of the chapel. To Mary Williams, standing beside her husband, the line of people passing by to pay their last respects seemed unending.

Several people stood to speak. New Orleans police chaplain Sam Allen was one of them. "Who could have thought that one of the most heinous and cold-blooded murders in the history of the city could be committed by another police officer? Let us hope others who come to the department as a Trojan horse, ready to disgrace the force with their criminal acts, are stopped at the gates."

When the chaplain demanded "swift justice" for Ronnie Williams's killers, the word "Amen" swept through the throng of police officers. It was a call for vengeance.

The mayor showed up, but he was mobbed by reporters, and to Mary he looked like he was holding court, not grieving. During a break, she found the new police chief in an anteroom. When she introduced herself, the chief's face showed his compassion and his sincerity, but Mary Williams hadn't sought him out to hear compassion. She had sought him out to correct him.

"Why did you say that about Ronnie's detail not being authorized by the department?" Mary asked.

Chief Pennington looked a little stunned. He shook his head. "I didn't say that. Someone must have misinformed you."

Mary held firm. "I saw the TV news broadcast myself. Last night, during an interview, you said that the Kim Anh was not a department-approved detail, but I have copies of the papers Ronnie filled out to work there. They were approved by the department."

"Mrs. Williams, the news sometimes takes things out of context. They try to mold or shape things to come out the way they—"

"But I am right," she said. "My husband was working an approved detail."

"Yes, ma'am."

"I don't want people thinking he was doing something he wasn't supposed to have been doing."

"I'm sorry for the confusion. I didn't mean to imply that he—"

"Can you tell the news people that? That Ronnie was on an approved detail when he died?"

Chief Pennington looked at Mary Williams for a minute. He must have admired her spunk. "Yes, ma'am, I will."

At the end of the funeral service, as the funeral director stepped up to seal the lid on Ronnie Williams's coffin, Mary Williams leaned over and kissed her husband one last time. She laid two photographs on top of his chest—their wedding picture and one of Ronnie and his two sons. Then the six pallbearers carried Ronnie Williams's casket outside and eased it into the back of the waiting hearse. From the chapel, the funeral procession snaked its way through the light drizzle to the mausoleum at Lake Lawn Cemetery, where the twenty-five-year-old body of Ronald A. Williams II was to be entombed.

More than a hundred cars trailed behind the hearse. Mixed in with the cars carrying friends and family were police vehicles from across Louisiana and neighboring Mississippi. When the procession neared the gates of the cemetery, cars passing on an interstate overpass pulled to the side. Men and women, people who didn't even know Ronnie Williams, climbed out of their cars and stood in the rain in silence. Many held their hands over their hearts.

The graveside service was awash in police uniforms. All of the badges had a strip of black tape across them, signifying the loss of a brother. Like most cops, New Orleans policemen don't spend a lot of time crying. For the older guys, a generation older than Ronnie Williams, it just wasn't something they did. They'd been raised on John Wayne movies; they'd seen too much misery at work. There were only three things that could make those hardened men cry:

the sight of their paycheck, last call at the Miracle Mile, and a police funeral.

When the pallbearers unloaded the flag-draped coffin carrying Ronnie Williams from the back of the hearse and took that long, solemn march toward the gaping vault in the mausoleum that would be his final resting place, even the most grizzled and toughest men in that crowd broke down. Many of them cried openly.

They cried in grief, and they cried in shame. "It was real hard when I got up this morning to polish my badge to come to this," a police officer with eighteen years on the job said while attending the funeral. "I wanted to be a cop since I was a kid, but now I'm just hoping to find something else and get out."

One of the patrolmen from the 7th District, who'd eaten lunch with Ronnie Williams the day he died, wore a suit. "I'm too embarrassed to wear my uniform," he said during the funeral.

Another eighteen-year veteran said he, too, was thinking of leaving the department. "If I'm going to take a bullet from my partner, forget it."

As the last strains of taps echoed across the cold stone monuments, the police department honor guard raised their rifles toward the sky and fired the final salute to Ronnie Williams—policeman, husband, father.

As the honor guard removed the flag from Ronnie's casket, an officer approached Mary Williams. He came from where Chief Pennington stood. The officer bent close to her ear. "Would you like the chief to present the flag to you, or would you prefer someone else do it?"

She wiped at her sore, red eyes with a handkerchief. It really didn't matter to her. She knew many of the officers at the funeral but didn't know the chief. Outside of their brief conversation in the funeral home anteroom, she'd hadn't spoken to him before. He had told her that he would correct what he'd said about her husband being killed while working an unauthorized detail—something that was flat-out untrue—but would he? Was the new chief a man of his word, or had he just been trying to get out of a tight spot with a grieving widow? She didn't know—yet. "I'd rather someone else do it," Mary said.

The officer nodded and walked back toward the chief.

Another officer, to this day Mary Williams can't remember who, marched to her and handed her the triangular folded American flag, the white-starred blue field on top. Mary's stoic wall collapsed as she slipped one hand under the folded cloth and placed one hand on top of it. She hunched forward, sobbing, as she laid the flag across her lap.

The worst day of Mary Williams's life finally, mercifully ended. "I was exhausted, our families were exhausted, but it was such a calming experience to see all the love and support," Mary says. "How wonderful people are in times of need."

That night on television, Mary saw a report on the news. Chief Pennington had issued a correction. The newscaster said that according to police department records, Officer Ronald Williams had been working an *authorized* security detail at the time of his death. A faint smile cracked across Mary's lips as she fell asleep. Chief Pennington was a man of his word, a man she could trust.

**Later** that same week the Vu family said its final goodbyes to Ha and Cuong. The brother and sister had lain in cold and stony silence during the extended visitation. Their open caskets stood side by side with only a golden crucifix between them. Banks of gladiolas and carnations surrounded them. Ha was dressed in white, Cuong in a suit. Hundreds of people flocked to the funeral home to pay their last respects and to say goodbye.

La Rai Smith, Cuong's friend and fellow student at Sarah T. Reed High School, came with six members of

Cuong's school soccer team. Smith said she and Cuong had been joking around together about something the previous Friday, the day before Cuong died. Seeing the body of her classmate and his sister brought little comfort or understanding about the senseless act of violence. "I'll never understand why," Smith said.

Hung Tran, a friend of Ha's from Delgado College, cut class to attend the wake. He said Ha was planning to work at the restaurant just long enough to help her parents save some money; then she was going to become a nun. "She was always talking about religion," he said.

Many of the visitors were Vietnamese; many were not. Several of them were police officers. Lt. Joseph L. Riche, Jr., stopped by the funeral home. He didn't know the Vus, he hadn't known Ronnie Williams, he didn't know Antoinette Frank. But he understood their pain, and he felt their loss.

Mary Williams was there for the wake and for the funeral.

Father Dominic Luong delivered the funeral Mass at St. Mary, Queen of Vietnam Catholic Church. At the Mass, Chau and Quoc stood beside the caskets. They had white strips of mourning cloth tied around their heads and held photos of their dead brother and sister in their hands. Thirteen hundred people packed the church. Mrs. Vu stood beside her two fallen children, wailing in Vietnamese, "My daughter, my son, my daughter, my son, I'm here. I'm standing next to you."

Mary Williams says, "Mrs. Vu was the saddest, most devastating sight. Her pain was almost touchable."

At the end of the service, Father Francis Schulte, archbishop of New Orleans, blessed the caskets before a group of New Orleans police officers escorted them to the cemetery.

# THIRTY-TWO

**Two** days after they saw Ronnie Williams rolled into a four-foot-wide by three-foot-tall marble-faced tomb, Eddie Rantz and Marco Demma got a chance to look inside Antoinette Frank's car. The 1977 red and white Ford Torino Elite had been locked up in the basement at police headquarters since Saturday morning. Armed with a search warrant, the detectives took the elevator down to the basement. They carried a camera and a variety of evidence bags.

Standing on the driver's side, the first thing Rantz saw was the nearly worn-out cardboard placard resting on the dashboard. The one that said, NEW ORLEANS POLICE OFFICER ON DUTY. "Motherfucker," he mumbled.

"What's that?" Demma said. He had Frank's keys in his hand and was opening the trunk.

"Nothing."

They went over the car in meticulous detail, searching every square inch of the passenger compartment, the trunk, even the under the hood. They found Frank's NOPD radio stuffed under the driver's seat. As Rantz bagged and labeled the radio, Demma spotted something shiny glinting from the bottom of a cup holder mounted on the front floorboard. He put one hand on the steering wheel to brace himself as he leaned toward the floor. The steering wheel was sheathed with a cheap plastic wrap, a sort of sports car grip.

Demma dipped a couple of fingers into the cup holder and pulled out an unspent 9 mm cartridge. He straightened up and rolled the cartridge around on his fingertips. The head of the shell casing, where the primer was, bore the stamp R-P. A 9 mm Remington-Peters. He showed it to Rantz. At the Kim Anh, Rantz and Demma had recovered eight spent 9 mm shell casings. All of them had been Remington-Peters.

**On** Friday afternoon, March 24, nearly three weeks after her husband's funeral, Mary Williams sat at her kitchen table, going through a stack of mail. Images of Ronnie came almost constantly, unbidden, into her head. Since March 4, she'd been living day-by-day, sometimes just hour-by-hour. The struggle to carry on was sometimes almost overwhelming. She found some comfort in routine. Like opening the mail.

Like most of their household bills, the Chevron Oil Company credit card statement was addressed to Ronnie. She tore open the envelope and idly scanned down the list of purchases. The last entry leaped out at her—$15.29 on March 4, 1995. The day Ronnie died.

Mary looked at the location: 585 Terry Parkway, Gretna, Louisiana. Gretna was across the river. Ronnie had been alive for less than two hours on March 4 and he'd been at the Kim Anh the entire time. Mary picked up the phone and paged Eddie Rantz.

Once Rantz had the Chevron gas bill in hand, he and Marco Demma headed across the bridge to the west bank.

The Chevron station at 585 Terry Parkway in Gretna sat at the corner of Terry Parkway and Farmington Place. Three blocks from Michael LaCaze's apartment. Three blocks from where Rantz's detectives had snatched up Rogers LaCaze the morning of the murders.

"We need a warrant for that apartment," Rantz said.

Demma nodded. "You want me to call JP Homicide?"

"Yeah, but first let's find out what we can from the gas station."

Inside the Chevron station, the night manager thumbed through back copies of his schedule. "John Ross was working on March 4," he said. "He worked from ten o'clock the night before until six that morning."

Rantz glanced at the Chevron bill in his hand. LaCaze had been picked up at around four or four-thirty. Williams had been shot between one-thirty and two. "Was Mr. Ross the only one working between midnight and say about four o'clock in the morning?"

"Yes, sir."

"When is he supposed to work next?"

The manager checked the current schedule. "Won't come on again until Monday night at ten o'clock."

Rantz would have pursued the gas station attendant at home, but he wanted to get another look inside Michael LaCaze's apartment. Neither the gun used to kill Ronnie Williams nor the money had turned up. If LaCaze had been dumb enough to use a credit card three blocks from his brother's apartment that he'd stolen off the body of a policeman he'd just murdered, maybe he was dumb enough to give the credit card to his brother, or dumb enough to stash the money or the gun at his brother's apartment. If Michael had helped his brother in any way at all, he was looking at accessory after the fact to three counts of first-degree murder. He was looking at going to prison.

The morning Ronnie and the Vu children had been murdered had been a maelstrom of activity and emotion, and

Rantz wasn't sure how thoroughly Lawless and the other detectives had searched Michael's apartment.

Rantz rounded up a couple more homicide detectives and told them to meet him in Jefferson Parish; then he and Demma contacted the Jefferson Parish Sheriff's Office Homicide Division. Detective Sgt. Maggie Snow assigned one of her seasoned homicide investigators, Deputy Grey Thurman, to the case. By midnight Friday, the detectives, both JP and NOPD, had finished putting together an affidavit in support of a search warrant for Michael's apartment. Detective Thurman called the duty judge and woke him up. He told the judge that he was helping NOPD Homicide get a warrant for a residence in Gretna. It was about the murder three weeks ago of a New Orleans police officer. "Come on over," the judge said.

Jefferson Parish district judge Patrick McCabe didn't ask a lot of questions. The New Orleans detectives were on a mission. He glanced over the affidavit and found no problem with it. Homicide cops, especially New Orleans homicide cops by virtue of their unsurpassed experience, knew how to write affidavits. The judge pulled out a pen.

"We'd like it to be a no-knock warrant, judge," Sergeant Rantz said.

Judge McCabe looked at him, his pen poised over the sheet of paper in front of him. "Why's that?"

"We're looking for a murder weapon used in a triple homicide. The guy whose apartment it is, the brother of one of the suspects, has got some arrests involving guns, and as of right now, we don't know what his involvement in this case is."

The judge nodded. "Okay." He signed the search warrant and added to it the no-knock provision.

About 2 A.M., a combined team of Jefferson Parish and New Orleans Police homicide detectives stood outside Michael LaCaze's ground-floor apartment door. One of the JPs had a steel battering ram.

Battering rams weigh forty or fifty pounds; they have a square cross section and are usually two to three feet long. Most have steel handles fixed to the sides and a circular steel plate welded to the front. A good ram man can take a door down with one hit. Any more than that, the guy swinging the ram is in for some teasing from his partners.

As soon as the JP detective took down the door, Rantz and Demma led the team into the house. All of the detectives had their guns drawn. No one was sure how involved Michael LaCaze was in what his brother had done.

Michael LaCaze, his girlfriend, and their baby daughter were asleep in the bedroom when the apartment door burst from its hinges. Within seconds, detectives flooded the small apartment. LaCaze, groggy and bleary-eyed, shouted from the bed, "What's going on here?"

Once Rantz knew the apartment was secure, he made the introductions. "I'm Sgt. Edward Rantz, and this is Detective Marco Demma, Mr. LaCaze. We're New Orleans police homicide detectives."

"You here about my brother?"

"Yes, sir."

The detectives started searching. Almost immediately, Rantz and Demma found a letter from the telephone company lying on the dresser in the bedroom. On the back of the sheet of paper were a bunch of handwritten notations. The writing was flowery, as if from the hand of a young girl. It was supposed to be a chronological record of Rogers LaCaze's activities the night of the Kim Anh murders.

*8:45—Rogers LaCaze was present at Shoney's restaurant in the 5700 block of Crowder (New Orleans East).*

*9:00–9:10—Rogers's beeper was missing, and he went to Antoinette Frank's house.*

*9:20—Rogers was at home watching TV and talking on the phone as well as watching daughter.*

*12:45–1:00—Michael LaCaze came to pick up Rogers LaCaze to go to Mr. C's pool hall.*
*1:05–1:55—Need to know. Rogers and Michael played pool at Mr. C's.*
*2:00–2:15—Rogers returned home stating that he was going with his brother to his home.*

"Mr. LaCaze," Rantz said, "would you mind if we asked you a few questions?"

"About what?" LaCaze asked.

"Just about what happened with your brother the night of the murders."

Michael shrugged. He was sitting up, leaning his head and back against the wall behind his bed. "I guess so." His girlfriend took the baby into the living room.

Rantz pointed to Michael's wheelchair beside the bed. "Would you like sit there?"

Michael shook his head. "I'm more comfortable here."

Demma got his briefcase from the car. He set a handheld tape recorder on the nightstand beside Michael. Demma started the tape rolling and asked Michael to tell him what happened in the early morning hours of March 4.

Michael said: "My brother, Rogers LaCaze, paged me about two o'clock, and I called him back. He stated that he needed me to come get him, that something was fucked up, him and Antoinette. So I came to get him, and he was shaken up. When he got in the car, I asked him what had happened. He said that something had went down on Bullard—an incident with him and Antoinette. And they had did something. So he told me how it happened. He said that Antoinette knocked on the door and the police officer came to the door and he shot the police officer, and Antoinette went in and shot the other people. And somebody got away and hid and saw. She dropped him off, and she went to the precinct to play it off. So I picked up my brother and I—we—came straight here. Then afterwards, he went and got some gas, and at three o'clock, I left and went and picked up my girlfriend, and at four o'clock, Homicide came and picked him up."

Rantz and Demma looked at each other. They could hardly have asked for a better statement. The detectives knew the brother would turn on them in court. By the time he worked out a lie with Rogers's defense attorney, he'd have a different story, but they could use the taped statement—made right here, right now—to impeach his testimony and prove that he was lying if he took the stand and tried to create an alibi for his brother.

Demma probed for details. "It was once he got to the car that he told you what happened?"

"Yes, sir."

"Did he tell you why they went to that restaurant?"

"He stated they had a lot of money," Michael said.

"All right. What did he do? Did he do anything while he was here?"

"He called Antoinette's cellular phone several times."

"Did he ever get an answer?" Rantz asked.

"No, sir."

"You mentioned when you got back over here Rogers went and got some gas."

"Yes."

"Do you know where he went?"

"To get the gas?" Michael asked.

Rantz nodded.

"Around the corner," Michael said.

"Why was he going to get you gas?"

"Because I came and picked him up, and he just . . . he felt like, you know, he should get some gas for coming to pick him up."

"So he was helping you out by putting gas back in your car?"

"Yes."

"Did he say how he paid for the gas?"

Michael pushed himself up a little higher along the wall, inching away from the questioning detectives. "No, sir."

Rantz held the telephone company letter up with his hand. He showed the handwritten notes on the back to Michael. "I want to ask you about this sheet of paper that I have here. Do you see what I am talking about?"

"Yes, sir."

"There are some times that are mapped out on this paper, and then they go through nine o'clock, nine-twenty, twelve-forty-five, one-oh-five, and two o'clock. Do you see what I'm talking about?"

"Yes, sir."

"All right, who wrote this?"

"Renee Braddy."

"What purpose did she write this for?"

Michael LaCaze took a deep breath. "So that we could basically have the same times, say the same things so that he [Rogers] could have a set time where he was during the scene of the crime."

"You were trying to alibi him?" Demma asked.

"Yes, sir."

"Renee was trying to help by writing this out for you all to memorize?"

"Yes, sir."

"Okay. When did Renee give you this?"

"About the second day," Michael said.

"All right," Demma said. "When you say the second day, do you mean the second day after Rogers was arrested?"

"Yes, sir."

"Okay. She told you what the purpose of this paper was?"

"Yes. The purpose was to . . . so that our times would be the same if we were questioned."

"So your times and Renee's times would be the same, that you have the same story?"

"Yes."

Demma shut off the tape recorder. If Rogers LaCaze

was relying on his brother to help him beat these murder charges, he was in deep trouble.

Rantz slipped the phone company notice into an evidence bag and signed it. Then he and Demma rode back to police headquarters and logged it into Central Evidence and Property.

# THIRTY-THREE

**On** Monday night, Demma drove back across the river. It was around eleven o'clock when he pulled into the parking lot of the Chevron gas station on Terry Parkway in Gretna. Night attendant John Ross had come on duty at ten o'clock. Demma stepped inside the station and introduced himself. Ross was a twenty-five-year-old black man. He worked nights at the Chevron and days as a shift manager at the Burger King across the street.

Demma showed Ross a photocopy he'd made of Ronald Williams's Chevron bill, then said, "I'm looking for a copy of the receipt for this transaction, something with a signature if I can get it."

Ross took the bill from the detective's hand and studied it. "This was outside. The customer used the card reader."

Demma glanced through the window at the eight pumps. "What's that mean?"

"They stick their card in the slot at the pump, the computer authorizes it, and they pump their gas. They don't have to sign anything."

In 1995, that technology was fairly new.

Demma asked about security tapes for March 4, but the store didn't keep the videotapes that long.

"Is there a way to find out what time this card was used?"

Ross handed the credit card bill back to Demma and pointed to a plastic trash bag at his feet. He lifted it onto the countertop and opened the bag. It was stuffed with used rolls of receipt tape. "These are journal rolls," Ross said. "Every time someone uses the card reader outside, the computer prints out a copy of the transaction. We keep them for a couple of weeks then throw them out. I was just about to put them in the Dumpster."

"Does it record the time?"

"Yes, sir."

Demma reached into the bag and pushed some of the receipt rolls aside. There had to be thousands of transactions recorded on those rolls. He looked at Ross. "You think March 4 is in here?"

Ross nodded. "It's in there somewhere."

"You mind if I look through them?"

"No, not at all," Ross said. "I'll help you." Ross dumped the bag onto the counter, and he and Demma dove in. Demma estimated that some of the tapes were as long as a city block. For two hours, they pored over the contents of the bag. They found the dates leading up to March 4 and dates after March 4, everything but the date Demma needed. "You sure it's in here?" the detective asked.

"Right here!" Ross said. Triumphantly, he held up a section of receipt tape.

"Let me take a look," Demma said.

Ross flattened the tape out on the counter. Demma laid the copy of the credit card bill next to it. The two men scanned down the tape together, looking for Ronnie Williams's credit card number.

"Bingo!" Demma said. They had a match. He jabbed a finger at a ten-digit number on the tape that matched the account number on the billing statement. Ross took a green marker from behind the counter and highlighted the transaction. He explained the jumble of numbers on the receipt to the detective. That Chevron account number had been charged for a card-reader-activated purchase of $15.29 on March 4, 1995, at 2:29 A.M.

Demma slipped the receipt into a brown paper evidence bag. He had John Ross sign and date the bag. According to the timeline Demma and Rantz had recreated, someone had used Ronnie Williams's credit card less than forty-five minutes after Rogers LaCaze shot the policeman down and stole his wallet.

Now all Demma had to do was prove who used the credit card. They hadn't found the card, there was no signature for a handwriting comparison, and there was no surveillance video. There was no direct evidence linking LaCaze to the card, but there was circumstantial evidence. By his own admission, LaCaze was at the Kim Anh during the murders and when Officer Williams's wallet was stolen. About thirty-five minutes later, the stolen credit card was used at a gas station three blocks from LaCaze's brother's apartment. An hour and a half later, detectives found LaCaze at the apartment. Michael LaCaze said his brother had taken his car "around the corner" to buy gas.

Demma still needed a witness.

The detective reached into his briefcase and pulled out a photo lineup that included a picture of Rogers LaCaze. The lineup included five other photographs of young, clean-shaven black males. Demma laid the lineup on the counter in front of Ross. "Can you take a look at these and tell me if you recognize anyone?"

Ross scanned the pictures, then tapped his finger on one. "I know this guy." It was Rogers LaCaze.

Demma slipped his excitement behind a mask of objectivity. "How do you know him?"

"I been knowing him a while, him and his brother." Ross

pointed to the Burger King across the street. "I work over there, too. They come by sometimes to eat. I also see them here sometimes." He tapped the picture again. "His brother is in a wheelchair. I've helped him pump gas sometimes."

"When was the last time you saw him, the guy in the photo not his brother?"

Ross was quiet for a minute. Concentration showed on his face. "He was here that night, that night he got arrested. Matter of fact, I'm sure that was him that used that credit card."

"How do you know that?"

"When somebody uses the card reader and the register starts printing out the receipt, I usually check to see who it is; and when I saw it was him, I went to the intercom and just made a little joke."

"What'd you say?"

"I asked him when he got a credit card because I'd never seen him use one before."

"Did he say anything?"

"No. He just smiled and did his shoulders like this." Ross shrugged, demonstrating what he'd seen LaCaze do that night.

"You said he smiled. Did you notice anything unusual about him, about his mouth, the way he smiles, anything at all?"

Ross pointed to his own mouth. "He's got—I think it's about four—three or four gold teeth that I know of."

"Was there anybody with him?"

"No."

"Any other cars getting gas at the same time?"

"Just him."

Demma turned the photo lineup facedown. "Can you sign and date the back of the photo you've just identified as being that of the man you saw pumping gas the morning of March 4?"

At Demma's instruction, after Ross signed and dated

the back of LaCaze's picture, he initialed and dated the backs of the other five photos. Demma initialed all of six of them. The detective dropped the photo lineup into an evidence envelope.

Now he had a witness.

"**New** Orleans is a city of saints and sinners," says former New Orleans assistant district attorney Glen Woods. "During its history, fires have destroyed the French Quarter at least twice, and both times only two places were saved from God's wrath—Ursuline Convent and Lafitte's Blacksmith Shop. One place for saints and one for sinners."

Like a lot of black kids growing up in New Orleans during the 1950s and '60s, Glen Woods viewed the police department with suspicion. He also had his share of run-ins with them. When he was sixteen, Woods and some friends were cruising around in a car. They were a diverse-looking group of black kids, some light-skinned, some dark, some with long hair, some with short.

Blue lights started popping behind them. *Oh, shit,* Woods thought. *Here we go.* It was a carload of cops from the Felony Action Squad. They pulled Woods and his friends out of the car at shotgun point and spread-eagled them on the hood of the police cruiser. There, in full view of all the traffic going by, the police made the kids empty their pockets. They searched and prodded them. They questioned them. Finally, Glen asked one of the officers what was going on. "We just had a robbery. Nigger who did it looked just like you guys." Woods glanced at his friends. Not one of them even looked the slightest bit alike.

"It was like a line out of a Richard Pryor movie," Woods says.

Another time, Woods was on a bus, coming back from a high school sports event. The bus blew past a police car. A kid on the bus yelled something out the window at the cops.

The cops pulled the bus over. "We got our asses kicked at the corner of Esplanade and Broad," he says.

Glen Woods is a soft-spoken, contemplative man, but he has a mind like a scalpel, a tool he has used to slice people apart on the witness stand. He was born and raised in New Orleans. The city is as much a part of him as his skin, and he wears them both with pride. Although he moved away to attend college, earning a bachelor's degree at the University of Southwestern Louisiana in Lafayette and a law degree from Southern University in Baton Rouge, staying away from New Orleans was never something he seriously considered.

While in law school, Woods returned frequently to the city. One night, he took his books with him to one of his favorite spots in the French Quarter. He was struggling with property law. Soon he found his mind wandering. "As I watched the fog roll in off the river," he says, "I was worried that somebody was going to be murdered that night—it was a vampire night."

New Orleans has a lot of vampire nights.

Although he eventually passed his property-law course, Woods's real interest was crime. "I wanted to be a defense attorney," he says, "but then I learned about bad guys." So he became a prosecutor instead.

From 1985 to 1989, Woods served as a full-time assistant district attorney in New Orleans. His boss was Harry Connick, Sr., father of actor/singer/songwriter Harry Connick, Jr. Connick Sr. had been the New Orleans D.A since the 1960s. He was elected after the previous D.A., Jim Garrison, dragged New Orleans businessman Clay Shaw to trial for conspiracy to assassinate President John F. Kennedy. Known as a farce of a trial, it was nevertheless given serious consideration in the Oliver Stone film *JFK*.

In 1989, as Woods was packing to leave the D.A.'s office for more lucrative work in private practice, Connick asked him to serve as a special prosecutor, working mainly on homicide cases. During his four years as an assistant D.A., Woods had racked up an impressive record of murder convictions. The offer was unprecedented. In nearly twenty-five years in office, Connick had not had a special prosecutor. "I guess I was kind of like the Mounties," Woods says. "I always got my man."

He accepted the offer.

Although he specialized in homicide cases, Woods was occasionally asked to handle other cases the D.A. considered sensitive. Like the arrest and prosecution of the entire NOPD Vice Squad. Vice was hitting the French Quarter, looking for "B-girls." The bar girls would suck up to customers for overpriced drinks, but the bar served them sodas instead and made an enormous profit. The vice cops were using marked money. When they busted the bar, they took all the cash from the register, but only the marked money made it into evidence. The rest fell into the vice cops' pockets.

Although Woods occasionally socialized with two or three of the vice detectives, Connick still gave him the nod to prosecute the case. The Vice Squad case was an emotional one for Woods. One day, he was out socializing with some guys from the squad; a couple of months later, he was indicting them.

The weekend that the news broke about the Kim Anh murders, Woods got a call from Camille Buras, the first assistant district attorney. She asked if he could come into the office. "Frankly, I had no idea why she wanted to see me," Woods says. He had seen the case on the news but didn't put it together with a weekend summons to his boss's office.

Buras told him that Connick wanted to know if he would handle the case. Woods said yes.

Immediately, the prosecutor started talking to witnesses and tracking down evidence. Woods also cast his eye about for a suitable co-counsel. He needed someone sharp, someone the jury would like, someone very experienced in homicide cases, someone who wouldn't cave under the intense scrutiny and pressure that was sure to come with this case. He picked Assistant District Attorney Elizabeth Teel. She was smart, pretty, and determined. Although several years younger than Woods, Teel was already an experienced trial attorney and, more importantly, an experienced homicide prosecutor.

In May, LaCaze's attorney, Willie Turk, filed a motion to sever the two trials. Riding around with Frank in her police car, playing with the lights and siren, was one thing; going to trial with her was quite another. LaCaze, it seemed, suddenly wanted to get as far away from Antoinette Frank as he could.

Ten days after the motion was filed, the presiding judge, Frank Marullo, granted the motion and severed the cases. LaCaze and Frank would stand trial separately.

Woods decided to try LaCaze first. "Frank was the big fish," he says. "LaCaze was a murderer, but in terms of culpability, I felt like she was more responsible than him, mainly because she was a police officer." Woods wanted to take his opening shot at LaCaze. Antoinette Frank could sit in her jail cell and sweat.

As he prepared the case against LaCaze for trial, Glen Woods kept hearing about a pool hall out in New Orleans East called Mr. C's. According to the scribbled note on the back of the telephone company letter the police seized at Michael LaCaze's west bank apartment, Rogers and his brother claimed to have been at Mr. C's at the exact time of the murders.

Then in June, a month before LaCaze's trial was set to begin, Woods got a whiff of a rumor. He heard that a pair of girls, one of them lugging a baby, had gone to Mr. C's and had been talking about Rogers LaCaze.

Woods started nosing around. He went to Mr. C's to see

if he could find out anything. From what he heard, it sounded like the girls had been trying to fabricate an alibi for LaCaze. The day after his fishing expedition at the pool hall, Woods called Eddie Rantz.

Woods had known Eddie for years. The two of them had worked together on several big cases and had become good friends, although it hadn't started out that way. "The first time I met Eddie Rantz, he and I almost got into a fistfight," Woods says.

Woods was at the Miracle Mile, the bar across Tulane Avenue from the courthouse and a frequent watering hole for cops and prosecutors. Sergeant Eddie Rantz and a group of robbery detectives were pounding down drinks at a nearby table. One of Rantz's detectives was a loud-mouth. He was talking shit, peppering a lot of his stories with the word "nigger." Woods didn't know Rantz, but he had seen him around the courthouse and knew who he was. He also knew Rantz was a sergeant and was in charge of most of the men at the table. Woods slid his chair back from his table. He stood up and walked over to the detectives. He stood beside Rantz. "What is this, nigger night?" he said.

The bar fell silent.

Rantz rose to his feet. "Who the fuck are you?"

One guy at the table wasn't a detective. He was a lawyer, a man who later became a state judge in neighboring Jefferson Parish. The lawyer looked at Rantz. He tried to smooth things over. "He's not talking to you."

"The fuck I'm not," Woods said.

The sergeant and the prosecutor stood toe to toe. "It was kind of a dangerous situation," Woods says, "because Eddie can knock a motherfucker out."

Inside the Miracle Mile, the seconds dragged by like minutes. Finally, Rantz nodded. "I'll take care of it."

Woods walked back to his table. Rantz was as good as

his word. For the rest of the night, the loudmouth detective kept his mouth shut.

Woods told Rantz about the pool hall and asked him to send a detective to check it out. Woods needed to find out what was going on. Rantz sent Marco Demma.

# THIRTY-FOUR

**Demma** arrived at Mr. C's Pool Hall at 6510 Morrison Road at about 3 A.M. on June 9. He stepped through the door and got slammed by the wall of music blowing out of the speakers. Fifteen feet inside the entrance, a man sat behind a raised counter. From his perch, he commanded a view of the entire pool hall and could watch all fifteen tables. He looked like a man who was used to trouble, and like a man who knew how to handle it.

"I'm here to see the manager," Demma said.

The man gave the detective the once-over. "That's me." He stuck out his hand. "Name's Patrick Mazant."

Demma cupped a hand to his right ear. He was having trouble hearing what the man said.

Mazant reached under the counter and dropped the music volume a bit. "What can I do for you?"

"Do you know a guy named Rogers LaCaze or his brother Michael?"

"Sure I know 'em."

"How?"

"They come in here sometimes. They're a couple of my regulars."

"Has anyone been in here lately asking about them?"

Mazant nodded. "A couple young ladies came in here the other day. One of them carrying a baby. They were asking about him."

"Do you know their names?"

"No."

"What did they want?"

"They came in, asking around for me. I walked up to them, told them who I was and that I was the manager. One of the girls, she takes me over to the side." Mazant pointed to a spot near the wall, away from the pool tables. "She pulled a picture out of her purse, a picture of Rogers LaCaze and his brother. They look like twins to me. She said she wanted to talk to me about Rogers."

"And you recognized him?"

"Yeah, from seeing him on the news."

"So what did she want to talk about?"

"She asked me if I remembered seeing him in here the night he got arrested."

"Did you see him?"

Mazant shook his head. "No. I don't remember seeing Rogers in here at all. I remember seeing Michael that night. He was with a lady friend."

"What made you notice Michael LaCaze?" the detective asked.

"Because he's in a wheelchair. You can't help but notice him. He has to shoot sitting down, but I tell you this, he can shoot pool pretty good in a wheelchair. Also, someone else paid for his table that night. I remember it was $4.10."

"Who paid for the table?"

"I don't his name, but it wasn't his brother. I'm sure of that."

"When was Michael in here?"

"I think it was from like about ten o'clock until about

eleven. I'm not exactly sure of the time, but I know it was just for an hour 'cause the tables cost four dollars an hour."

"What did you tell the girl who was asking about Rogers?"

"That he wasn't here that night."

"What'd she say?" Demma asked.

"She said for me not to say that. She told me I couldn't be sure that he wasn't here that night."

"Do you think she was trying to get you to say that Rogers was here even though he wasn't, trying to get you to make up an alibi for him?"

"Probably, but I wouldn't do it."

"Did you tell her anything else?"

"I told her, I said, 'I'm going to tell you straight off, he was not here.' She didn't like it, but that's what I told her."

"What's the procedure?" Demma asked. "How do people get a table?"

Mazant tapped a finger on top of the counter he sat behind. "I keep all of the balls up here. If I know you, I don't ask for I.D., but if I don't know you, you got to leave your I.D. to get a rack of balls."

"Did Michael get his own balls that night?"

The pool hall manager shook his head. "Somebody else got them for him, but it definitely was not his brother. I know his brother. They always come in together, but that night Michael was here with some other dude and that lady friend of his."

"How many customers do you usually get a night?"

"It varies, but I'd say anywhere from one hundred to two hundred per night."

"What are your work hours?"

"I come on at about seven o'clock and close pretty much whenever I feel like it."

"How sure are you that the night you saw Michael here without his brother was the night he got arrested?"

"Because the next day was Saturday and I saw it on the

twelve o'clock news that afternoon. I told my girlfriend, 'He's one of my regular customers in the pool hall.' "

Demma was impressed by the manager's confidence. "You always keep such a close eye on the place?"

Mazant nodded. "My job is to maintain and watch all of my pool tables, and make sure that no one puts any alcohol on my pool tables, and to check my door for I.D.s to make sure I don't have no juveniles coming through here."

LaCaze's girlfriend, Renee Braddy, later denied she'd ever been to Mr. C's Pool Hall, but police speculation was strong that one of the two women who went to see Patrick Mazant at Mr. C's was either Braddy or the mother of LaCaze's other two children, Renetta Marigany, or that the two of them had gone together.

**Part** of a prosecutor's job is anticipating defense strategy and staying ahead of it, and that includes shooting down made-up alibis. Demma called Woods and told the prosecutor what he'd found out. Woods was pleased. Preparing to go to trial in what was bound to be the most scrutinized case of his career, Woods was glad he had rock-solid investigators backing him up. Rantz and Demma were two of the best in the business. "I think one of the things that convinced Antoinette Frank to tell the truth was Eddie Rantz and Marco Demma's unassuming manner. She was one of them and could tell them what happened," Woods says.

Still, it was going to be up to Woods to make sure that justice was served, that there were no mistakes in the case, that nothing stood in the way of Frank and LaCaze paying for what they'd done to the Vus and to Ronnie Williams. Recalling what he used to tell detectives who worked for him, Woods says, "When crunch time comes, I don't need you to fuck up, I don't need you to lie, I don't need you to suppress evidence. All I need you to do is tell the truth. I'll handle the rest."

The investigation might belong to the cops, but the prosecution belonged to Woods. Preparing for a homicide trial, Woods once warned a detective, "On the street, I'll listen to you. You tell me to jump in a trash can and cover myself with beer cans, I'll do it; but when we're in the courtroom, you do what I say."

Eddie Rantz and Marco Demma didn't need such warnings. Woods, Rantz, and Demma knew each other well. They'd worked together, and they'd partied together. Sometimes they met at a place on Bourbon Street, a place Rantz liked to frequent, a place called Lafitte's Blacksmith Shop. Lafitte's claims the title of the oldest bar in the United States. The building was once owned by, and is named after, one of New Orleans's most infamous criminals and perhaps its greatest savior, the hero of the Battle of New Orleans—the rogue and pirate Jean Lafitte.

One night after work, Woods strolled into Lafitte's. Rantz wasn't there but Demma was. The homicide detective sat at a table inside the dark bar with a few other cops: fellow detective Archie Kaufman, a captain from a nearby sheriff's office, an ATF agent, and an FBI agent.

The Blacksmith Shop is housed in a squat, single-story brick-and-mortar building on the corner of Bourbon Street and St. Philip Street. Built between 1722 and 1732, the building was constructed in the old French provincial style with a slate roof. It's called a Creole cottage. It was the building's slate roof that kept it from being torched during the two great fires that swept through the French Quarter during the second half of the eighteenth century.

By 1809, the Lafitte brothers, Jean and Pierre—pirates, scoundrels, and all-around scallywags—operated a blacksmith shop in the building, but it was only a front for their real business, which went on behind the shop, out in the courtyard, among the oleanders and date palms. The courtyard was a market for pirated goods and for the auctioning off of what the locals called "black ivory," or slaves.

After Napoleon Bonaparte sold Louisiana to the United States in 1803, the legal slave trade ground to a halt. Although the ownership of slaves remained legal, the new government banned the importation of any more slaves into Louisiana. It was a crippling blow to an economy based on slave labor. Nature abhors a vacuum, so it was quite natural that someone would step in to fill the void in the once-thriving flesh trade. If slaves couldn't be brought into Louisiana legally, then they could be brought in illegally—and sold at a much higher price. For the Lafitte brothers, already pirates and purveyors of stolen goods, it was a golden opportunity. One that they seized with gusto.

In 1813, the first governor of Louisiana, W.C.C. Claiborne, was so fed up with pirates, smugglers, and black marketeers that he ordered copies of a proclamation posted in public places throughout New Orleans, offering a $500 reward for the capture of Jean Lafitte. The day after the proclamations were posted, Lafitte, a tall, slim man with a pale complexion, large, dark eyes, and a narrow face that sported a goatee, was seen standing on a street corner reading one of the notices. He had an amused smile on his face. The very next day, Lafitte posted copies of his own proclamation around town. The pirate captain offered a $1,500 reward—a king's ransom in those days—for the capture of the governor and his delivery to Lafitte's stronghold on Grand Terre Island, at the mouth of Barataria Bay.

To this day, Lafitte's Blacksmith Shop is lit by candlelight. The only electric lights are behind the bar and in the restrooms.

In the murky half light of the bar, Glen Woods dropped into a chair at the table with Demma and the other cops and ordered a drink. A French Quarter local, a gnarled black man by the name of Marty, knew Woods was a prosecutor and was always telling him bizarre tales about government cover-ups and alien conspiracies. Marty wandered into

Lafitte's. He knelt beside Woods and whispered in his ear. "Glen, did you hear about that doctor who got killed in Jefferson Parish?"

Dr. Robert Snapp had been discovered lying on the bedroom floor of his Jefferson Parish home the day before. His ankles and wrists were bound; he'd been severely beaten, then stabbed to death. The case had been all over the news.

"Yeah, Marty, I heard about it," Woods said.

"Well, the guy who did it is in here right now."

Woods thought Marty was just having another one of his alien delusions again, like the extraterrestrial abductors or the *real* gunmen behind the JFK assassination he'd told Woods about. Woods ignored him and took another sip of his drink. He kept talking with his friends. Marty wandered off.

About fifteen minutes later, Marty came back. Again, he crouched beside Woods. "Glen, the guy who killed that doctor is sitting right over there at that table." Marty pointed to a table across the bar, one next to a set of French doors that let out onto Bourbon Street.

Woods glanced to where Marty pointed. There was a guy at the table sitting with a transvestite. Woods had seen the newscasts about the murder. The suspected killer's face had been plastered all over the television. The guy sitting across the bar did look something like the picture Woods had seen. Still, this information was coming from Marty.

"Look!" Marty said, tapping the prosecutor's shoulder. "Look up there."

A television mounted near the ceiling, powered by an extension cord from behind the bar, was replaying the news story of the murder. The suspect's picture flashed across the screen. Woods looked at it, then looked back at the guy sitting with the transvestite. *Jesus Christ,* Woods thought. They did look a lot alike. "All right, Marty, we'll check it out."

After Marty disappeared, Woods leaned over to Marco

Demma. "Listen, I need you to do me a favor. Just go stand over there by the cigarette machine." Along the front wall of the bar, near the possible suspect's table, stood an old-fashioned pull-handle cigarette machine. Demma had heard Marty's rantings. He knew what was going on, but didn't believe the French Quarter wino. Still, the detective stood up, strolled over to the cigarette machine, and made a show of looking for change for a pack of smokes.

Meanwhile, Woods rambled over to the piano bar so he could get a look at the guy from a different angle. It was the guy. Woods caught Demma's eye and nodded. They met back at their table. Woods looked at the other cops. "Houston, we have a problem," he said. Then he asked, "Any of you got your gun on you?"

In New Orleans, police officers are barred from carrying guns into an alcohol beverage outlet—a bar—while off duty. All the law officers at the table shook their heads. None of them had a gun, or so they claimed. To have admitted to carrying a gun would have been confessing to a criminal offense.

"Well," Woods said, "if you don't have them right now, you may want to go get them." He nodded toward the table. "Because we got a '30' man right there." Police code for a murder.

As one, the cops cleared from the table. They stepped outside through the St. Philip Street door. A few seconds later, not nearly enough time for them to have gotten to their cars and grabbed their weapons, they walked back in. Miraculously, they had their guns. The cops started to spread out, one at the front door, one at the back, a couple in the middle of the bar. No one went to the French doors beside the guy's table. The guy noticed the sudden activity and saw his only chance of escape. He jumped up from the table and bolted through the French doors. He moved so fast that his shoes fell off his feet. Demma caught him just outside and put him facedown on the Bourbon Street sidewalk.

His name was Timothy Osborne, a homosexual hustler. In his pocket was the dead doctor's stolen wallet. Osborne had ordered his drinks on the doc's credit card. Under the table at which Osborne had been chatting with the transvestite was a pair of the doctor's much-too-big shoes.

By the time Woods stepped outside, Osborne was spewing his confession to Demma. The hustler admitted that he had beaten and stabbed the doctor to death. Woods shut him up for a minute and made sure someone had read the man his Miranda rights.

"It was just one of those nights," Woods says. "I looked up to see if it was a full moon."

# THIRTY-FIVE

**Rogers** LaCaze's trial began on Monday, July 17, 1995. Early Monday morning, a pool of potential jurors poured into Judge Marullo's courtroom. Fourteen would be selected, twelve actual jurors and two alternates. Jury selection—the mysterious pseudo-science lawyers like to call voir dire—took all day.

Outside the courthouse, the temperature soared to ninety-five degrees. New Orleans rests six feet below sea level. The city is a bowl surrounded by water. There's a one-thousand-square-mile lake to the north, a muddy, mile-wide river to the south, and hundreds of square miles of swamp to the east and west. New Orleans's concave geography traps the air and sucks in the surrounding moisture. On the first day of Rogers LaCaze's trial, the air was thick, wet, and still. Barely a breath of breeze stirred the leaves of the oleanders and azaleas standing on the front lawn of the looming, cement-gray courthouse. It was the kind of day on which sopping wet shirts had to be peeled from sweat-soaked backs.

Inside the courtroom, despite the cool hum of the air-conditioning, the thermometer rose steadily because of the flaring tempers. The first thing Judge Marullo had to deal with was defense attorney Willie Turk's outrageous comments to the press over the weekend. In violation of Marullo's gag order, which barred everyone involved in the case from making any public statements about it, Turk claimed that Officer Ronnie Williams had been under secret federal grand jury indictment for "unspecified charges." To bolster his allegation, Turk fired off subpoenas over the weekend to U.S. Attorney Eddie Jordan, FBI Special Agent in Charge Neil Gallagher, and NOPD Superintendent Richard Pennington.

The U.S. attorney quickly set the record straight. Ronnie Williams had not been under indictment or investigation by his office. Turk's story was bullshit.

Glowering at Turk from behind his bench, Judge Marullo fumed. He accused Turk of deliberately disobeying his order. "I'm sorry, Judge," the lawyer said. "I forgot about the gag order."

Judge Marullo was a thick man with jet-black hair, a jowly face, and a bit of a double chin. He'd earned a law degree in 1968, spoke fluent Italian, was a member of the Louisiana House of Representatives, and had been a New Orleans criminal judge for more than twenty years. He also didn't take any crap from defense lawyers, cops, or prosecutors.

Although Turk recalled his subpoenas, Judge Marullo wasn't satisfied. He wanted his pound of flesh. "This is not southern California," Marullo said, "and I am not Judge Ito." And to prove it, he found Turk in contempt of court and sentenced him to six months in jail and a $500 fine—the maximum penalty allowed under Louisiana law. However, despite the sentence looming over Turk's head, the judge proceeded with the trial.

Turk's smear caught Officer Ronnie Williams's father

off guard. "I suppose he thinks he should do whatever it takes, but doesn't he have to tell the truth?" he told a newspaper reporter on the first day of the trial.

By the end of that day, after much legal wrangling and objection after objection from defense attorney Willie Turk, the judge managed to empanel a jury. Marullo warned them not to discuss the case, not to read the newspaper, not to watch the news. He told them to be back at 10 A.M. and to be ready for a long day. Then he sent them home.

The two prosecutors, on the other hand, didn't get to go home. They worked through the night, going over documents, witness statements, again laying out their strategy for the case. They poked and prodded at it, looking for holes, looking for any weaknesses. They prepared objections to likely defense moves; they planned counters to anticipated defense tactics. Both prosecutors knew that these two trials were going to be the most difficult of their careers.

If they lost LaCaze—if the jury acquitted—the door was wide open to lose Frank. And that was something that could not happen. Glen Woods was not going to let a murderer walk. He'd followed closely the O.J. Simpson case. "As a prosecutor, I was not going to give the jury a reason to find Frank or LaCaze not guilty the way the prosecutors did in the Simpson case," Woods says.

As Glen Woods stepped into court the next day, the fatigue from the long night dropped from him like a cloak. Woods was a dapper man with close-cropped hair. He wore a charcoal-gray suit and burgundy tie. He looked sharp, he felt sharp, he was ready to go.

Rogers LaCaze shuffled into the courtroom wearing dark pants and a print shirt. He sat beside his attorney, Willie Turk.

Once the court was ready, everyone stood as the jury filed in and took their seats. A few jurors shot glances at LaCaze. Most pretended not to notice him. Ronnie Williams, Sr., and his son's widow, Mary Williams, sat in the front row of the gallery, directly behind LaCaze. Not surprisingly, LaCaze looked uncomfortable. He was on trial for his life, but maybe he felt the Williams's eyes searing the back of his neck.

Once the jury was seated and the bailiff had called the court to order, Woods stood before the panel of jurors. He told them that Rogers LaCaze was charged with first-degree murder, he explained the legal definition of first-degree murder, he explained to some degree what an off-duty security detail was, and he explained that Officer Ronnie Williams and Officer Antoinette Frank worked the same shift at the 7th District *and* both worked the detail at the Kim Anh restaurant.

The prosecutor went on to outline the case, giving the jury glimpses of the evidence the prosecution had amassed against this man who sat before them, the man they were being asked to judge. He wrapped up his brief summation by warning the jury that they would have to see some very gruesome pictures. He also said, "We are going to demonstrate to you that this was a brutal murder—brutal. It was brutal. You are going to see how Ha Vu was on her knees praying when she got shot. You are going to see her brother on the floor, shot in the head." Woods jabbed a finger at LaCaze, who seemed to sink into his chair. "The evidence will show, ladies and gentlemen, that that man is a cold-blooded killer. I mean cold blooded."

As Woods sat, Willie Turk lumbered to his feet. The defense lawyer looked like a man who'd spent the night staring up at the snowcapped peak of Mount Everest, knowing he had to try to climb it, but who'd realized he'd left his equipment at home.

Turk started out by thanking the jury for their patience and assuring them that his statement would be short and to the point. He agreed with Mr. Woods, he said, that the murders at the Kim Anh restaurant were brutal and had been committed by a cold-blooded killer, but that cold-blooded killer was not Rogers LaCaze. Mr. LaCaze, the lawyer asserted, was simply a patsy, a dupe in Antoinette Frank's plot to rob the restaurant and to lay the blame on someone else.

"Mr. LaCaze was at the restaurant," Turk admitted. "He got sodas, and they were going to go to a movie. She decided that it was too late. So she turns around, and they go back to get something to eat. They get food, they leave, and she takes Mr. LaCaze home.

"We're talking about an eighteen-year-old man swept up by a police officer. She set Mr. LaCaze up. We are not here to defend Ms. Frank. We are here to set the record straight that Mr. LaCaze was not a part of this brutal murder."

Assistant District Attorney Glen Woods called his first witness. Patrick Mazant, the manager of Mr. C's Pool Hall, took the stand. Mr. Mazant repeated to the jury what he'd told Detective Demma. He was positive that he'd seen Michael LaCaze wheeling around a pool table that night. Michael had been with a woman, but his brother, Rogers, had not been there.

On cross-examination, Turk tried to shake him. Was Mazant sure he could see the entire pool hall? Did he take a bathroom break that night? Did he keep a list of every customer who came in to shoot pool?

Turk played up the pool hall manager's assertion that the two brothers looked very similar. "Can you distinguish them from one another?"

Mazant nodded toward Rogers at the defense table. "His brother is in a wheelchair, and he is not."

Mazant was unshakable in his conviction that Michael was in the pool hall that night and Rogers wasn't.

Turk showed his desperation. "Do you sell alcoholic beverages in your place?"

"Yes, sir, I do."

"Do you drink, Mr. Mazant?"

At the prosecution table, Woods raised his hand. "Objection, Your Honor."

The judge cautioned Turk. "Objection sustained as to relevance."

Turk had no more questions. He slumped into his chair beside his client.

Woods next called officers and civilian employees from the police department Communications Division. The prosecutor played a tape for the jurors of Quoc Vu's frantic 911 call. They heard Quoc say that Antoinette and her nephew had robbed the place and shot everybody. Turk had no questions for cross-examination.

Sgt. Geraldine Prudhomme, assistant commander of Frank's platoon at the Seventh District, took the stand. Under Assistant District Attorney Elizabeth Teel's questioning, the sergeant told the jury that Frank had been one of the officers assigned to investigate the shooting death of Nemiah Miller and the wounding of Rogers LaCaze. Frank and LaCaze had met shortly after the shooting when she went to see him in the hospital.

Ex–sheriff 's deputy Irvin Briant said he'd helped Officer Frank when he thought she was fighting three male suspects. Turned out that one of them, Rogers LaCaze, was with her. LaCaze had been in Frank's police car when she'd pulled over two guys he'd gotten into a beef with at a party earlier that night.

NOPD officers Reginald Cryer and Darryl Watson testified that they saw LaCaze driving Frank's police car at the scene of a traffic accident.

Michael Morgani said that Frank and LaCaze had come into his body shop. Frank had tried to bully him into hiring LaCaze.

Elizabeth Teel questioned the two clerks from Wal-Mart. Each took the stand and told the members of the jury that Frank was in her police uniform when she and LaCaze had come into the sporting goods section and tried to buy 9 mm bullets. The day had been Friday, March 3. That night, three people would die in the Kim Anh restaurant after being shot with 9 mm bullets.

Ernest Smith, the New Orleans East resident who'd been having trouble with his daughter's ex-boyfriend—the boy had been lurking around, causing trouble—told the jury how he'd gotten so fed up with the boyfriend that he'd called the police. Officer Frank showed up with LaCaze in tow. She had introduced him as her "trainee."

Next up to take the stand was Wayne Farve, a fifteen-year police veteran. "Were you the first officer to arrive on the scene?" Woods asked.

"Yes, I was."

Farve told the jury what was going on when he and his partner arrived. As Chau Vu came barreling out the front door of the restaurant, he saw Frank chasing her. He had to grab Frank and ask her where the downed officer was. *"Behind the bar"* is all she said.

Only later, after Farve found the bodies of Ronnie Williams and Ha and Cuong Vu, did Frank claim that she'd seen three black males fleeing the scene in a dark car.

Yvonne Farve, Wayne's wife, took the stand. She was a beautiful woman with an ugly job. 1995 marked her eighteenth year as a New Orleans police officer. She told the jury how Chau had latched onto her and would not let her go. She had tried to comfort the poor girl. Yvonne Farve told the jury that she saw Frank inside the restaurant. Frank tried to rush past her. Yvonne grabbed her arm, demanding to know who she was. "She told me, *'I'm a twenty-six, I'm a twenty-six.'* I'm a police officer." Yvonne looked at the jury. "That's what twenty-six means."

"You didn't know that she was a police officer?" Woods asked.

"No, I didn't."

"Can you tell the ladies and gentlemen of the jury anything else about how she appeared to you?"

"She appeared trapped."

Yvonne Farve described how she first learned that Frank had been involved in the robbery and murders. She said that while she and Chau were in the kitchen checking her brother and sister for signs of life, Frank asked Chau what had happened to them. Chau got hysterical, and Yvonne moved her into the dining room, where she tried to get a description of the perpetrators. Yvonne told the jury that Chau described the person as a short black male with gold teeth. Yvonne added, "And she told me, *'He came in with Antoinette.'* "

"At this point," Woods said, "did you realize that the name of the police officer was Antoinette Frank?"

"She [Chau] nodded in that direction."

On cross, Turk tried to hammer away at the link with LaCaze. "Did Chau Vu tell you what happened?"

"No," Yvonne Farve said. "Basically, she said that they were just shooting. They were just shooting everybody. That's all she said."

"And her identification was of Antoinette Frank?"

"I asked her if she saw who did it, and she told me it was a short black male with gold teeth in front, and he had come into the restaurant with Antoinette Frank."

Several of the jurors glanced over at the man at the defense table, a short black man with gold teeth.

"Now let me ask you this, did she tell you that the short black male who did the shooting was the same person that she had seen earlier in the restaurant that she was introduced to?"

"Yes."

"She told you that?"

"Yes," came the emphatic answer.

"And did she tell you his name?"

Yvonne shook her head. "She didn't know his name."

Officer John Treadway took the stand. The senior firearms examiner for the police department testified that the bullets pulled out of the walls, the bullets pulled out of the bodies, and the expended cartridge cases at the scene were all fired from the same gun.

"And what kind of gun was that?" Woods asked.

"That's a nine-millimeter, semiautomatic pistol."

Marco Demma took the stand. Demma had supervised much of the collection of the evidence, and it was through him that Glen Woods wanted to introduce it into court. Plus, the wily prosecutor had a surprise. He was going to take the jury on a field trip, and he wanted Demma to be the tour guide.

# THIRTY-SIX

"**Sir**, would you please state your name and occupation for the record," Glen Woods said, as he stood in front of the witness stand.

"It's Marco Demma, Jr. I'm assigned to the Homicide Unit, New Orleans Police Department."

It was Tuesday, just after lunch. Prosecutors Glen Woods and Elizabeth Teel had spent the morning of the first real day of the trial painting a picture of Antoinette Frank and Rogers LaCaze's strange relationship. They'd let the jury listen to testimony from people who'd seen them together. They'd also fired a shot at what they knew was going to be LaCaze's main line of defense: his claim that he wasn't there when the murders happened, that he'd been shooting pool with his brother. Now the prosecutors wanted to give the jury a look at some physical evidence.

"Did you investigate a homicide that occurred on March the fourth, 1995, at the Kim Anh restaurant in New Orleans East?" Woods asked the veteran detective.

"Yes, sir, I did."

"And did you arrest a young police officer, a woman police officer, by the name of Antoinette Frank?"

"Yes, sir."

Woods turned to the bench. "Judge, I'd like the court to ask at this time that Antoinette Frank be brought out."

Sheriff's deputies threw open the courtroom doors and led Frank into the room. She shuffled down the aisle, leg irons around her ankles. She wore an orange jumpsuit, and her wrists were cuffed to a chain around her waist. As she stood before the packed courtroom, all eyes were on her. She smiled.

The judge ordered the deputies to take her away.

Woods turned back to Demma. "Did you recognize that woman?"

"That was police officer Antoinette Frank."

Under questioning from Woods, Marco Demma described the crime scene: the bodies of Ha and Cuong Vu in the kitchen, a pool of blood behind the bar where Ronnie Williams had fallen, a bloody smear on the floor at the end of the bar where paramedics had dragged the fallen officer in a vain attempt to save his life, spent 9 mm shell casings littering the floor, two 9 mm bullet holes in the wall behind the bar.

Woods showed the detective a series of crime scene photographs and asked him if he could identify them. Demma said they were pictures of the Kim Anh restaurant taken in the early morning hours of March 4. Woods asked him if they accurately reflected the condition of the crime scene.

"Yes, sir."

Woods looked at the bench. "Judge, at this time, the state would re-urge its motion to visit the scene."

Judge Marullo agreed. The jury did need to see the crime scene. He ordered a recess and told the sheriff 's deputies to load the jurors into vans. The courtroom moved to the Kim Anh restaurant.

There was a tense moment when they arrived. The sheriff's vans pulled into the parking lot about two-fifteen in the afternoon. A small crowd of spectators had gathered. Once the jurors piled out of the vans, a deputy led them toward the restaurant. Next it was LaCaze's turn. Deputies unloaded the chained-up prisoner from the back of a sheriff's car onto the parking lot. Suddenly, a Vietnamese man burst forth from the crowd. He rushed up to LaCaze. "Murderer, murderer," he screamed. LaCaze recoiled as sheriff's deputies pushed the man away.

Detective Demma led the jurors on an hour-long tour of the restaurant, pointing out where he and Rantz and the other detectives had recovered the evidence. He also showed the jury where the bodies had fallen.

Woods led the jurors into the cooler, into the dark, cramped space in which Chau and Quoc had hidden for their very lives. None of the jurors seemed to want to linger in there.

Back in the courtroom, Woods continued questioning Demma. The detective told the jury that when he and Sergeant Rantz arrested Frank, they found a loaded .38-caliber revolver hidden in the waistband of her jeans.

Woods started introducing evidence. The first thing he showed Demma was the revolver he and Rantz had taken from Frank. Then he showed the detective evidence envelopes containing spent bullets and shell cases recovered from the scene. He showed him a live 9 mm bullet recovered from Frank's Ford Torino that matched the kind used in the restaurant.

Woods handed the detective another envelope and asked him to identify its contents.

"This is a bullet that was removed from the left knee of Ha Vu during the autopsy by Dr. Tracy," the detective said in as dispassionate a voice as he could manage.

"And this?" Woods asked, handing him another evidence envelope.

"This bullet was also removed during the autopsy, from the right hip of Cuong Vu by Dr. Tracy."

During his testimony, Demma told the jury that when he showed a photo lineup to Quoc Vu, Vu had picked out the photograph of Rogers LaCaze as the person who was with Frank during the shooting.

Woods asked if Quoc had shown any hesitation in picking LaCaze out of the lineup.

"There was no hesitation whatsoever," the detective said.

Woods continued to ask Demma to identify the evidence they'd collected during the investigation. He handed Demma a brown paper bag. "I'll show you what I have marked as state's exhibit seventy-one. Can you identify that?"

Demma opened the bag and looked inside. He took a deep breath. "Yes, sir. This is the clothing that was worn by Officer Ronnie Williams that was taken from Charity Hospital."

"And what is contained in this bag?"

"One pair of jockey shorts, one pair of boxer shorts, one pair of police pants, one black belt, one pair of Flex Comfort shoes, and one pair of blue socks."

Across the courtroom, Mary Williams broke into sobs of pain.

Woods handed the detective a second brown paper bag and asked him to identify its contents.

"One blue, winter, bloodstained police shirt with badge number 1474, one blue tie with tie clip, and an insignia for the collar brass for the uniform shirt and the number seven, and one white, torn T-shirt, and one package of Marlboro cigarettes."

Willie Turk's cross-examination of Detective Demma was a jumbled mess. He asked the detective about the possibility of a *third* suspect, evidently forgetting that he was trying to show that his client wasn't the *second* suspect. Mentioning the possibility of a third suspect gave the impression that he was conceding that LaCaze was the second suspect and that he was only criticizing the police for not finding more suspects.

Turk repeatedly referred to the March 4 shootings as the "second shootings." He was implying that there had been an earlier shooting at the Kim Anh, but he'd introduced no evidence to support it. His questions were poorly worded, and Demma frequently had to ask the lawyer to restate them. Turk got completely mixed up on the two photo lineups the prosecution had introduced. He asked the detective why Quoc Vu's signature did not appear on the back of the photograph of Rogers LaCaze that John Ross, the night cashier at the Chevron on the west bank, had signed. Demma had to explain that he didn't reuse photo lineups. The photos he'd shown John Ross were not the same photos he'd shown to Quoc Vu.

Following up with a question about John Ross, the defense lawyer said, "Did he [Ross] at any time tell you that since he became friends with Michael and Rogers LaCaze that he furnished them with a gas card to purchase gas?"

Glen Woods spoke up before Demma could answer. Woods was having trouble understanding what Turk was talking about. It seemed to him that Turk was implying that John Ross, night cashier at the Chevron located mere blocks from Michael LaCaze's west bank apartment, had gone to work Friday night, March 3, 1995, at ten o'clock and had somehow gotten hold of Officer Williams's credit card—even though Williams hadn't been killed until nearly four hours later—and given it to the LaCaze brothers.

"I'm sorry," Woods said. He turned to Turk. "That John Ross furnished them with cards to purchase gas?"

"Yes," Turk said.

Glen Woods shrugged his shoulders and nodded for Demma to answer.

"No," the detective said.

"Detective Demma, did John Ross at any time indicate

to you that he and Rogers LaCaze had an altercation?" Turk was trying to float a theory that even though the Chevron cashier barely knew either of the LaCazes, he had concocted a story to try to convict Rogers of three counts of first-degree murder.

"No, sir."

The next witness was lead detective Sgt. Eddie Rantz. Woods began asking Rantz questions about the interviews with the witnesses and the suspects. He asked Rantz if he'd had occasion to interview Rogers LaCaze.

"Yes, I did."

"Prior to speaking with Mr. LaCaze, did you advise him of any rights?"

"Yes. I had Detective Demma read him his Miranda rights from a New Orleans Police Department form."

The prosecutor handed the sergeant a form and asked him if he could identify it. Rantz glanced at the form and told Woods that it was an NOPD Rights of Arrestee or Suspect form and that it spelled out each of the constitutional rights recognized under the U.S. Supreme Court decision known as *Miranda v. Arizona*. Those rights were the right to remain silent, the right to have an attorney present during questioning, the right to have a court-appointed attorney if the suspect could not afford to hire one himself, and the warning that anything the suspect said could be used against him in court.

Woods asked if the form that Rantz held in his hand was the form that Detective Demma had read and explained to Rogers LaCaze before they questioned him.

"Yes, sir, it is," the detective said. At the bottom of the form were the signatures of Sergeant Rantz, detectives Marco Demma and Patrick Young, and Rogers LaCaze.

"Now, Detective Rantz, did Mr. LaCaze seem to understand those rights?"

"Yes, he did."

"And did he, in fact, speak with you?"

"Yes, he did."

Woods handed a copy of the transcript of LaCaze's statement to each juror; then he played the taped interview.

The jury heard the disembodied voice of Rogers LaCaze spilling from a set of courtroom speakers as he described in chilling detail Antoinette's problems with Ronnie and Chau over her not getting enough hours at the restaurant, how Frank had told him, "I'm gonna get that motherfucker," about his understanding that "Ronnie always be fucking her over," about Frank filing a false police report and claiming that her 9 mm pistol had been stolen from her car, about LaCaze and Frank pulling up to the restaurant with guns in their hands, about her signal for him to come inside—a gunshot—about LaCaze's admission that he knew she was going there to shoot someone, about Frank telling him, "One of the bitches got away," about her plan to go to the Seventh District and report that two gunmen wearing ski masks had robbed the restaurant and shot everybody.

When the tape stopped, there was dead silence in the courtroom.

# THIRTY-SEVEN

**The** second day of testimony began with the medical evidence. Two pathologists described in gory detail the way that Ronnie Williams, Ha Vu, and Cuong Vu had been gunned down. The doctors tracked for the jury the exact path the bullets had taken and illustrated with words the tremendous damage they'd done to the bodies of those three young people. Dr. Richard Tracy also described what appeared to have been blunt trauma to Cuong Vu. "A laceration due to some kind of hard object banging on the eyebrow." Trauma delivered *before* Cuong was shot, trauma consistent with being pistol-whipped.

Elizabeth Teel pounced on the information, suggesting to the jury that LaCaze and Frank had beaten seventeen-year-old Cuong until he told them where his sister had hidden the money; then Frank shot him in the chest, the back, and the head.

Standing before the witness stand, Teel said, "Doctor, were you able to determine the cause of death of Cuong Vu?"

"Yes. He had been shot several times. He had four different potentially fatal bullet wounds. The death was caused by bullets passing through the head. They entered on the right side of the back of the head and exited the left side of the forehead."

Next, Ms. Teel introduced photographs of the victims and asked the doctors to identify them.

Turk tried to cross-examine the doctors as best he could, but he had little to work with. He questioned them about the distances the gun was fired from, blood spatter, and gunpowder stippling. He got nowhere.

The judge looked at Ms. Teel. "Call your next witness."

Teel stood. "The state calls Chau Vu."

A blanket of silence smothered the courtroom as a deputy escorted Chau to the witness stand.

The judge spoke more like a grandfather than a seasoned jurist. "Now, would you please state your name, ma'am, for the record."

"My name is Chau Vu."

Teel stepped close to the witness stand. "How old are you, Chau?"

"I'm twenty-three."

"Are you from New Orleans?"

"I'm from Vietnam. I have been living in the United States for five years."

Under the gentle probing of Elizabeth Teel, Chau recounted the night's events. The courtroom was transformed into a theater as witness and prosecutor took center stage and performed for the jury the Shakespearean tragedy of the Kim Anh restaurant.

Toward the end of Chau's testimony, Teel handed her a photograph and asked her if she could identify it.

"This is the kitchen, where my sister and my brother died."

Chau broke into tears.

"Do you want to take a few minutes?" Teel asked.

"No—just—no." Chau choked back her tears. "I'm all right."

Somehow, Chau managed to continue her story. She explained to the jury that when she saw the first police car cruise through the parking lot, she hesitated to leave the relative safety of the cooler. "I was a little bit happy, but I still don't want to go outside because I know Antoinette is police, too."

After more police cars arrived, Chau bolted from the cooler. When she reached the parking lot, she saw Antoinette Frank chasing her, but she also saw someone she instinctively knew would help her—Yvonne Farve. "I saw a lady with a uniform. I ran to her, and she hug me."

Frank approached both of them. Chau told the jury, "She run to me. She say, *'Chau, Chau, what happened with your brother and sister?'* And I say, 'You was there. You know everything. Why you ask me that question?' "

Chau said she saw the paramedics load Ronnie Williams onto a gurney and haul him away. She waited by the front door for the medics to bring out her brother and sister, but they didn't. "I was so mad," she told the jurors, "because why they don't try to save my sister and brother's life. I be waiting, waiting, and then finally they say my sister was dead. I can't—" Chau fell apart on the witness stand.

Glen Woods jumped to his feet. "Judge, we are going to ask for a ten-minute recess."

The judge sent the jury away and asked Chau to step down.

Fifteen minutes later, Chau was ready to continue. The jury returned. The trial resumed.

Chau described her initial conversation with Detective Yvonne Farve, about how she told Farve that it had been Antoinette and the man she said was her nephew who'd come into the restaurant and killed everyone.

"Chau, do you see in the court today the man that came

into the restaurant those two times with Antoinette Frank?" Teel asked.

Chau took a deep breath. "Yes, I see him."

"Would you please point him out and describe what he is wearing?"

Chau raised her thin right arm and aimed an accusing finger at Rogers LaCaze, the eighteen-year-old thug who was trying to melt into his chair. "He's right there. He's wearing a striped shirt with the white, black, red, and green."

"Are you positive?"

Chau's arm was straight as a rifle barrel as she laid the finger of death upon LaCaze. "Yes, he's right there."

Teel bent down and picked up three objects from a cardboard box resting on the floor beside the prosecutor's table. She walked back to Chau carrying the objects in her hand. She handed one of them—a framed photograph—to Chau and asked her if she could identify the person in the picture.

"That's my brother."

Teel handed her another framed photograph.

"And this is my sister, my lovely sister." Chau sobbed. "They took her away from my family. She scared to die. She don't want to die."

Teel handed her a third picture.

Sobs racked Chau Vu's small frame. "This is Ronnie, the person that be there with us every time we need him. He should not have died." A pitiful wail of grief and pain spewed from Chau's slender throat as she cried out, "They don't deserve to die—too young."

Some of the jurors bowed their heads and wept.

Defense attorney Willie Turk stood. It was time for him to cross-examine Chau.

Turk was in an unenviable and unwinnable situation. Chau had been the only witness so far who put his client inside the Kim Anh restaurant at the time of the murders. He needed to rip her apart and destroy her credibility, but he could not win one ounce of favor from the jury by tormenting this poor girl. For the mere appearance of going after Chau, the jury might well condemn both him and his client to death. He had to tread carefully.

Turk asked Chau why, when she had seen Frank coming back for the third time, she had shouted to Officer Williams not to open the door.

"It just a natural feeling inside that I felt when I saw she keep coming back. That's the third time, so I just feel something is not right."

Then he asked about Antoinette's brother. "Do you know an individual by the name of Adam Frank?"

"Yes, I know him."

"Did Adam Frank ever come around your restaurant?"

Chau explained to Turk that Antoinette used to drop her brother off at the restaurant while she was working.

Turk forced Chau to go over the story again of Frank bursting into the restaurant that third time, about Frank pushing Chau and her brother into the kitchen, about Chau hearing gunshots explode inside the dining room. The defense attorney pulled out photographs of the inside of the restaurant and asked Chau to trace her and Quoc's path into the cooler. Turk kept insisting that they had ducked into the cooler through the convenience store side, but Chau told him over and over again that he was wrong. They had entered the cooler from the kitchen side.

He asked her if she saw LaCaze inside the restaurant that third time.

"I saw him when we were in cooler," she said.

Turk tried to trip her up, tried to force her to be inconsistent, but Chau was adamant. She had seen LaCaze inside the restaurant *after* the first gunshots had gone off. She would not accept Turk's ludicrous suggestion that in her terror she had mistaken the six-foot, five-inch Adam Frank Jr.—whom she knew well—for the five-foot, two-inch LaCaze.

Turk's questions showed his desperation. "Did you by

any chance see a third party running through the restaurant?"

"No, I didn't."

Turk hammered her about the screen door in the kitchen. Did they keep it locked? Yes, Chau told him. They kept the door locked. What about at night when they took out the garbage; surely they unlocked it then? No, Chau said. They didn't take out the garbage at night. What about *that* night, was it locked?

"The door is always locked at night," Chau said.

Back to Adam Frank, Jr. Turk asked about the fight Adam got into at the restaurant. Chau told him that Adam hadn't gotten into a fight; he'd merely been trying to break up a fight between some customers.

Did Adam get angry after he was told not to come back to the restaurant?

"No, he didn't get angry with me," Chau said. "He very friendly."

"Did he call you back to threaten you in any way?" Turk asked.

"No, he didn't because I didn't tell him to leave. Ronnie told his sister."

Turk fought on. He asked if Antoinette Frank got mad that Ronnie Williams was working the detail that weekend.

"No, she just say, *'Okay. I see you later.'* "

Had there been another shooting at the restaurant before the one on March 4?

"No, sir," Chau said. There had been an occasional argument, a fight or two, she said, but there had never been a shooting.

Turk threw in the towel. He had probably alienated the entire jury and had gained nothing.

Elizabeth Teel stood up. Lest any of the jurors buy into Turk's implication, she asked if there had ever been a shooting at the restaurant before the one that took the lives of Ha and Cuong Vu and Ronnie Williams.

"No," Chau repeated.

Teel then asked Chau if she was positive it had been Rogers LaCaze and not Adam Frank whom she had seen eating dinner in the restaurant with Antoinette Frank and later running around inside the restaurant after the shooting started.

"Yes."

Turk had a follow-up question. It illustrated the absolute hopelessness of his situation. "Now, you testified that you were trying to see when you was in the cooler—that you was trying to see outside, and you were ducking and weaving. Could you, ducking and weaving, could you in fact see out the cooler, or was there a cloud over the cooler door?"

Chau had only been in the United States for five years. She probably thought that maybe it was her English that was bad. "What do you mean, a cloud?"

"Okay," the defense lawyer said, "when you open the freezer door, sometimes there is moisture that comes before the window and makes it kind of hard to see. Was the window in the cooler clear?" He was suggesting that the fog of condensation, or maybe the fog of war, had obscured Chau's vision enough so that she had mistaken Adam Frank for Rogers LaCaze.

"It was clear," Chau said.

"So when you were ducking and weaving, could you actually see through the door of the cooler?"

"Yes."

Turk's shoulders sagged. "No further questions, Your Honor."

# THIRTY-EIGHT

**Glen** Woods called Quoc Vu to the stand. Much of his testimony was a reiteration of what his sister had said. They had seen and heard the same thing. The only difference was perspective. Quoc had been in the dining room, standing next to the bar talking to Ronnie Williams, when Frank came back the third time.

"What was he [Williams] doing at that point?" Woods asked.

"He was standing behind the bar drinking a Coke."

After the initial shooting, what did Quoc see while he and his sister hid inside the cooler?

"I saw Antoinette digging in this little area where we always hide our money."

"Did you see anyone with Antoinette?"

Quoc nodded. "Yes, I saw her friend that she ate with."

"What was he doing?"

"He was running all around the store and banging. I heard banging."

Through the glass cooler doors, Quoc saw Frank and

LaCaze run into the kitchen where he'd last seen Ha and Cuong. "And then, after that, I heard shooting—more shooting."

Several minutes later, Quoc said, after things got quiet, his sister sneaked out and got her cell phone. She told him Ronnie Williams had been shot. "I told her I was going to run to my friend's house, and I ran out the cooler towards the kitchen, and as soon as I stepped out, I saw my brother and my sister lying there. I told my sister [Chau] they got shot."

After Quoc told the jury about his mad dash to his friend's house and his frantic call to 911, Woods took him through the story of the police questioning him and of Detectives Rantz and Demma showing him a photographic lineup. Quoc confirmed for the jury that he did not hesitate before picking out the photograph of the person he'd seen in the restaurant with Antoinette Frank during the shootings.

"Do you see that man in court today?" Woods asked.

"Yes, I do."

"Can you point him out and tell the jury what he is wearing?"

Quoc glared across the courtroom as he pointed at LaCaze. "He's sitting over there with the striped shirt."

"Your Honor," Glen Woods said, "let the record reflect that the witness, Quoc Vu, has identified the defendant, Rogers LaCaze."

Woods handed Quoc a pair of photographs. Quoc had trouble looking at them. They were crime scene shots taken in the kitchen of the Kim Anh. Ha and Cuong lay twisted up on the blood-slicked floor. After a minute, Quoc handed them back. "That's my brother and sister."

"Thank you, Quoc," Woods said. "Answer Mr. Turk's questions." The prosecutor took his seat. His job was to put murderers in prison, but he hated the pain he had to cause to do it.

At the defense table, Willie Turk struggled to his feet.

Turk launched an immediate attack on Quoc's consistency, asking him if he remembered testifying at a preliminary hearing back in March. "Yes," Quoc said.

Turk held a transcript of Quoc's testimony. "Let me read for you one of those questions taken from page fifty-six."

Woods rose to his feet. "Objection."

The judge glared at Turk. "Approach the bench, Mr. Turk."

Turk hesitated. Woods repeated his objection.

"Approach the bench, Mr. Turk," Judge Marullo said again.

At the bench, Turk tried to explain to the judge what he was doing. Judge Marullo didn't like surprises. "Step into my chambers for a second."

The judge, the attorneys, and Quoc Vu disappeared into the judge's office.

Turk argued to the judge that at the preliminary hearing, Quoc had told the court that he hadn't seen who fired the shots, nor had he seen who had come into the restaurant with Frank. Turk felt those statements were in direct conflict with what Quoc had just said in response to the prosecutor's questions.

Woods looked at the transcript of the hearing. Midway down one of the pages, he found the question Turk was referring to. A lawyer asked Quoc if he had seen the person who'd come into the restaurant with Antoinette Frank. Quoc said he had not. However, the judge at the hearing, concerned that Quoc had not fully understood the question, said, "Do you understand the question? Do you need an interpreter?" Quoc told the judge, "No. I don't understand."

Woods pointed to a line farther down the page; the lawyer again asked if Quoc had seen who fired the shots. Quoc answered no. Then, according to the transcript, the lawyer said, "Did you see the person who came in the restaurant at all with Ms. Frank?"

Quoc's answer had been "Yes."

The lawyer had asked who it was, and Quoc had pointed directly at Rogers LaCaze.

Quoc had apparently misunderstood the question the first time by thinking he was being asked if he'd seen LaCaze come into the restaurant with Frank, which he hadn't. By the time LaCaze sneaked into the restaurant, Frank was already shoving Quoc and Chau into the kitchen. He had only seen LaCaze *after* the first shots that killed Ronnie Williams.

Woods handed the transcript to the judge. "So, Judge, where is the contradiction?"

Judge Marullo scanned the transcript for himself. Then he peered across his desk through his thick glasses. "Where is the contradiction, Mr. Turk?"

Sagging, Turk said, "I guess there is no contradiction."

Back in the courtroom, Willie Turk continued his cross-examination, but apparently forgot the time-honored lawyer's rule of thumb that you shouldn't ask a question you don't already know the answer to.

"Mr. Vu, you have testified that you saw Mr. LaCaze running around in the restaurant. Do you wear glasses?"

"Yes, I do."

"Did you have your glasses on that night?"

"Yes, I did."

Turk pounced. "Well, you don't have them on right now!"

"Right now I have contact lenses on."

Turk floundered. He asked if Quoc had seen LaCaze get out of Frank's car the third time she showed up, had he ever met LaCaze before, did he see LaCaze at the police station. Desperation tinged Turk's questions as he tried to suggest some reason Quoc would have picked LaCaze out of that photo lineup, some reason other than that Quoc had seen LaCaze ransacking the restaurant during the shootings.

"No," Quoc said. He had only seen LaCaze at the restaurant.

Glen Woods asked how long LaCaze and Frank had been in the restaurant eating.

"About fifteen or twenty minutes," Quoc said.

"How is it that you so distinctly remember Mr. LaCaze?" Woods asked.

"He kept staring at me."

**The** next day, it was the defense's turn to put on witnesses and present evidence. First up was Sheri Gaterius, a hired crime scene and blood pattern analyst. She tried to discredit some of the prosecution's conclusions about the crime scene, particularly those about gunpowder stippling and blood back spatter. She described an experiment she had conducted for the defense in which she'd fired a bullet into a blood-soaked sponge.

Opening her cross-examination, Elizabeth Teel asked, "At what point did you visit the crime scene in this case?"

"I've never been to the crime scene."

"You told us, Ms. Gaterius, that your expertise is crime scene investigation and reconstruction."

"Yes, it is."

"Would it not have been helpful for you to go to the crime scene and observe where the victims' bodies were found?"

"Yes."

Ms. Teel asked when Gaterius had looked at the crime scene photographs.

She had not looked at the photographs.

When did she examine the bodies of the victims?

Gaterius said she had not examined the bodies.

When had she seen photos of the victims?

Gaterius said she had not seen photos of the victims.

When did she examine the defendant's clothing?

Gaterius had not examined LaCaze's clothing.

Teel glanced at the jury, then looked back at the witness. "Let me make sure that I have this correct, Ms. Gaterius. Your expertise is in reconstructing crime scenes, investigating scenes, and [examining] a perpetrator's clothes, and yet you have never examined any of this evidence?"

"That's correct."

Turk then called a couple of police officers to testify about Adam Frank, Jr. According to them, Adam Frank was a troublemaker and a fugitive, an all-around ne'er-do-well. Turk suggested that maybe Adam was mad enough at Ronnie Williams for putting him out of the restaurant that he wanted to kill the policeman.

Then came a series of alibi witnesses, including Rogers's girlfriend, Renee Braddy, and his brother, Michael. They dredged up the Mr. C's alibi. When asked about the statement he'd given to the police, the statement in which he'd told them that his brother had admitted to him that he and Frank had committed the murders, Michael shrugged it off. The police made him say that, he said. Michael claimed a detective had aimed a gun at his daughter and threatened to shoot her if he didn't implicate his brother in the murders.

Next up was Rogers LaCaze himself. Over Turk's objections, LaCaze decided to take the stand and tell his version of what happened.

On direct examination, Turk led his client through his meeting of Antoinette Frank and allowed LaCaze to discuss what he believed was Frank's obsession with him. LaCaze actually told the jurors that he had wanted to be a police officer since he was five years old. Yet he also confessed to the jurors that he used to sell drugs, mainly powdered cocaine, and that he used to make a fair amount of money from it.

He admitted that he had driven Frank's police car, that he'd been with her trying to buy 9 mm bullets, that he went to the restaurant with her to eat. He was with her, he said, when she called Chau from her cell phone and asked for a couple of hamburgers. But he noticed that Frank was acting weird at the restaurant. "Ms. Frank is very strange," LaCaze testified. "She got like three personalities."

He said Frank dropped him off at his Cindy Place apartment at 12:20 A.M. He called his brother, and his brother picked him up to go shoot pool at 12:35.

LaCaze said he and his brother left the pool hall at 1:50—the exact time Quoc's call reached 911. After that, LaCaze said he went to his brother's apartment and went to bed. He claimed that he did not buy gas at 2:29 A.M.

Turk asked about his contact with Eddie Rantz. "Did he ask you to give a confession?"

Yes, he did, but according to LaCaze, before that, Rantz left him with Detective Patrick Young.

"What did Officer Young do to you?"

"He handcuffed me, he beat me with a telephone book, and he kept punching me in my chest, and he made me get on my knees and face the wall."

"Before you gave your statement, were you given your Miranda warnings?"

"No, sir, I wasn't." Apparently, Turk and LaCaze forgot that the taped statement that Woods had already played for the jury included Detective Marco Demma reading LaCaze his rights and LaCaze acknowledging that he understood them. On the same tape, LaCaze also confirms that he had read and signed a rights acknowledgment and waiver form.

According to LaCaze, he only gave the taped confession because Detective Patrick Young held a gun to his head. His entire confession, LaCaze maintained, was a lie. "I would have to be a total idiot to participate in killing a white New Orleans police."

"Now, Roger," Turk said, his voice solemn even as he forgot the "S" at the tail end of his client's name, "you know what is at stake here?"

"Yes, sir. My life."

"I tender the witness," Turk said.

Glen Woods stood. He asked LaCaze if he was absolutely sure—positive beyond a doubt—that he had been with Antoinette Frank when she called the restaurant from her cellular telephone to order food for the two of them.

"Yes, sir."

"No doubt?" Woods asked.

"No doubt."

Abruptly, Woods then veered off the subject of the phone call and spent a long time going over the statement LaCaze gave the detectives about his involvement in the murders and the alleged beating he suffered at the hands of Detective Patrick Young.

Then Woods got back to the telephone call. He verified once more with LaCaze that he was with Frank when she made that call to Chau to order food. LaCaze patiently explained to Woods yet again how he'd gotten back to his apartment at about 12:20 and that his brother had picked him up to shoot pool at 12:35.

With the judge's permission, the prosecutor handed LaCaze a sheet of paper. It was a telephone company record of the calls made from Antoinette Frank's cellular telephone, the one detectives had seized from her Ford Torino. He pointed to a line indicating a call from Frank's cell phone to the Kim Anh restaurant.

"Now, I want you to read the time that phone call was made," Woods said.

"0051," LaCaze said.

"Is that fifty-one minutes after twelve?"

LaCaze nodded. "I guess it is."

"And Michael picked up at 12:35?"

"Yes," LaCaze mumbled.

Woods looked at the jury first, then at the judge. "No further questions."

In wrapping up the state's case, Glen Woods said, "We

have enough evidence to bury Rogers LaCaze from this room all the way down to the pits of hell."

That evening, the jury got the case. They took the evidence with them into the jury room. They were gone for less than an hour and a half. They returned with three unanimous verdicts, once for each of the victims. Judge Marullo read aloud the first verdict. "We, the jury, find the defendant, Rogers LaCaze, guilty as charged of first-degree murder."

He read the second and the third verdict aloud. Each time, he said the same thing.

**The** next day, the jury returned at noon to begin the penalty phase. They would decide if Rogers LaCaze was to be sentenced to life in prison or condemned to death for murdering Ha and Cuong Vu and Ronnie Williams.

Mrs. Vu took the stand, as did Ronnie Williams's mother and his widow. LaCaze's mother also testified; so did Renee Braddy and Renetta Marigany—two women who'd had children with LaCaze.

Then Rogers LaCaze mounted the witness stand to again try his hand at testifying. He pleaded with the jury, "I would like you all to please spare my life. Please. I did not pull no trigger and kill them people." He moaned again and again that he did not shoot anybody. "I don't even know them people. I didn't have no reason."

*Them people*. They had names: Ha Vu, Cuong Vu, Ronnie Williams.

Today, Glen Woods still mourns the victims. "They were people, they had a life, they had aspirations, they had dreams," he says.

Rogers LaCaze may not have known their names, but the jury did. And for his crimes, the jury, after just more than three hours of deliberation, returned to the courtroom with their decision. Judge Marullo read it into the record.

"The jury unanimously determines that the defendant, Rogers LaCaze, be sentenced to death."

Defense attorney Willie Turk maintains that he was dumbfounded by the outcome of the trial. In his opinion, the evidence was almost all circumstantial. "If Rogers had not used that credit card," Turk says, "he would have gotten off. That is the one thing that got him convicted."

# THIRTY-NINE

**The** trial of Antoinette Frank got under way on Tuesday, September 5, 1995, under the scrutiny of a full-fledged media circus. Reporters from across the country and around the world descended on New Orleans to monitor the trial, and since it was New Orleans—to party.

A week or so before the trial, Frank's defense attorneys, Robert Jenkins and Frank Larré, approached Colin Danos, Frank's former partner in the 7th District. They asked him if he would consider testifying on Frank's behalf. He turned them down.

Since Frank's arrest, Danos had gotten several letters from Prime Time Video, a video store he frequently rented movies from in New Orleans East. Prime Time claimed he'd rented several movies months before and hadn't returned them. "They were movies about drug dealers and gangster movies that I wouldn't even watch, like *King of New York* and *New Jack City*," Danos says. For the lost movies and late fees, the video store claimed Danos owed them a couple of hundred dollars. For an honest cop, it was a lot of money.

One day, Danos dropped by the store and took at look at the rental agreements. It was his name signed on the cards but not in his hand. The signature had a distinctive female flair to it. He talked to the clerk who'd rented out most of the movies. "Oh, that was your partner who signed for those," the clerk told him.

"Antoinette Frank!" Danos said.

"I guess so. It was that girl you used to ride with."

Danos made a reasonable settlement with the store, but it cost him his membership. He was disgusted.

"I didn't even go to the trial," he says.

Officer Ronnie Williams's widow, Mary, had been dreading the second trial. "I know it's important that I go," she told a news reporter as she sat at home with her two sons, Christopher, six years old, and Patrick, just six months old, "but, oh, I don't want to go through it. All through the last trial, on the way in, I was drinking Pepto-Bismol, and all I could eat was peppermints. It was so nerve-wracking. The only place I feel at ease is at the cemetery."

The jury pool of 150 filled the courtroom, which Judge Marullo sealed off from spectators. Two rows near the jury box were reserved for the press. Frank sat at the defense table, her hair pulled back in a tight braid, a pair of wire-rimmed glasses resting on her face. She scribbled notes on a legal pad.

An hour into the proceedings, Frank leaped to her feet. "Judge, I want a new attorney!"

Marullo pulled her and the lawyers into his chambers. He pointed a finger across his desk at Frank. "You watch your step in there. One more outburst like that, I can gag you and bind you and tape your mouth shut."

"I've been poor all my life," Frank said. "I'm not saying that to receive any sympathy; I'm saying it because the courts have denied me certain constitutional rights." She told the judge that Rantz and Demma had tricked her. "I was forced to give a statement under duress."

"That's for me to decide, not you," Judge Marullo said.

Frank pointed to lead counsel Robert Jenkins. "But he don't know what he's—"

The judge raised a hand and silenced her. "Believe me, I'll gag you if I have to."

The in-chambers meeting ended.

The defense tried for a change of venue. They wanted to get out of New Orleans. The judge denied the motion.

Assistant District Attorney Glen Woods's opening statement painted a picture of a cold-blooded, manipulative monster. Defense attorney Robert Jenkins's opening portrayed an innocent, big-hearted policewoman, out to try to change a troubled young man's life. Jenkins closed by telling the jury, "We are sure you'll find Antoinette Frank not guilty."

Prosecutors Glen Woods and Elizabeth Teel had an advantage in that they had already tested their case with a live jury, and it had worked. "I was relieved that the first jury had convicted Rogers," Woods says, "and I expected nothing less for Antoinette."

The defense had an advantage, too. The first trial had tipped the prosecution's hand. Jenkins and Larré knew exactly what to expect and had more than a month to prepare for it. They could jump on inconsistencies in any of the prosecution witnesses' testimony.

Inconsistencies are a fact of life. They happen—to everyone. Tell a true story once; better yet, write it down. Wait a month, then tell it or write it again from scratch. Compare the two versions, and you'll always find differences, sometimes slight, sometimes sizeable. Both versions are true. The reason for the differences is that the mind is a cauldron, a bubbling pot of gumbo, in which memories, like chunks of meat and gobs of seasoning, take turns churning to the surface.

*If it ain't broken, don't fix it.* With very few exceptions, Glen Woods and Elizabeth Teel presented the same case against Frank that they had presented against LaCaze.

Through their witnesses' testimony, they told this new jury about Frank and LaCaze's first meeting, about their burgeoning friendship, about LaCaze driving Frank's police car, about the pair's arrest of Anthony Wallis on bogus robbery charges, about trying to buy 9 mm bullets at Wal-Mart. The jury saw the grisly crime scene photographs, they heard the medical and ballistic evidence, they visited the crime scene, they saw Rogers LaCaze dragged into the courtroom so that John Ross, the Chevron gas station night cashier, could identify him as the man who had used Officer Williams's stolen credit card, they saw LaCaze flash his wicked gold teeth.

Then they heard the haunting ring of Antoinette Frank's own words as Glen Woods played her taped interview.

"He said shoot 'em, shoot 'em, shoot 'em," Frank said, "and it went off."

"You shot them," a detective asked.

"Yes," Frank answered.

Other than her outburst at her attorneys the first day, Frank showed no emotion during the trial. "She scared me," admits Elizabeth Teel. "She would stare at me and smile, and it would send the worst shivers up and down my back." No other defendant had ever had that effect on Teel. "I think she is just an evil person."

Late Saturday afternoon, the prosecution concluded its presentation. The judge handed the case to the defense, which had subpoenaed thirty-nine witnesses. The promise of a long weekend and an even longer week hung in the air.

Attorney Robert Jenkins rose to his feet. He had been contentious throughout the state's case, objecting to everything and everyone. On Thursday, Jenkins had made a dramatic motion for a mistrial, which the judge tossed out. Everyone in the room expected a vigorous defense. Glen Woods and Elizabeth Teel braced for the attack.

Jenkins looked across the bench at the judge. "At this time, on behalf of Antoinette Frank, the defense rests."

For just a second, a pin drop would have sounded like an explosion. Then the courtroom erupted in a clamor of surprise. Through it all, Frank maintained her seat, her face a blank.

Closing arguments began on Monday, September 11.

Jenkins tried to persuade the jurors that Frank hadn't killed anyone—despite what she'd told police—that she was an innocent patsy caught up in Rogers LaCaze's evil plan.

Elizabeth Teel fired back, mocking Frank's claim during her taped confession that she couldn't remember how many shots she fired at the Vus as they crouched on the kitchen floor. "What is it she can't remember?" Teel asked the jury. The prosecutor jabbed her finger at pictures of Ha and Cuong's wounds. "Was it this shot? This shot? This shot? . . ." She said it over and over again until she'd accounted for all nine gunshot wounds.

Standing before the jury, Teel held up the .38-caliber revolver Rantz and Demma had found tucked inside Frank's waistband when they arrested her. She also held up the police radio they'd later found inside her Ford Torino. "Even if you buy all the lies," Teel said, "she knew she could have done something about it and chose not to."

The prosecutor also reminded the jurors that Frank had gone to Wal-Mart the very day of the murders, in full police uniform with LaCaze tagging along with her, and tried to buy a box of cheap 9 mm bullets. And what kind of gun had she recently reported stolen from her car? A 9 mm. And what kind of gun had killed all three victims at the Kim Anh restaurant? A 9 mm.

The jury took twenty-two minutes to decide the case, less time than it takes to drink a cup of coffee.

Judge Marullo read the verdicts. They were all the same. "We, the jury, find the defendant, Antoinette Frank, guilty as charged as to first-degree murder."

Tuesday morning, court convened for the penalty phase.

As if in a mini-trial, both sides put on witnesses, this time arguing not guilt or innocence, but whether the defendant deserved to die. After testimony from a string of heart-wrenching witnesses from both sides that included Ronnie Williams's widow, Mrs. Vu, and Frank's mother and grandmother, the lawyers got one last chance to sway the jury.

None of it seemed to faze Frank. She sat impassively at the defense table.

Frank Larré stood and begged the jurors for mercy. "The question now is what is the correct punishment? It's whether she spends the rest of her natural life in jail or has poison pumped into her arm until she is dead, dead, dead."

Elizabeth Teel rose to her feet. It had been the most emotional case of her life. She pointed to Frank. "The woman before you for judgment today is responsible for taking not one, not two, but three precious human lives. She used her position as a police officer to kill these people. She swore to serve and protect these people, and instead she executed them. The only question is whether you are going to give her what she deserves."

Glen Woods was more direct when he spoke to the jury. "It took you all about twenty minutes to come back with a guilty verdict. It ought to take you about ten minutes to come back with a sentence of death."

It took the jury about forty minutes.

Once again, Judge Marullo read it into the record. "As to count one, the jury unanimously determines that the defendant, Antoinette Frank, be sentenced to death." He repeated the same thing for counts two and three.

Ann Williams, Ronnie's mother, held Mrs. Vu's hand as they left the courtroom. Mary Williams hugged Chau Vu. When prosecutors Glen Woods and Elizabeth Teel got to the bottom of the courthouse steps, members of the Vu and Williams families applauded. Woods told a reporter, "It would have been a mockery of justice if Antoinette Frank was to walk away without getting the death penalty."

Ronnie Williams's father, Ronald Sr., said, "You can never get even, but it's some consolation to see the system works."

As he had been throughout the entire case, Sgt. Eddie Rantz was there for the finale. Responding to a question about which of the defendants he thought was the most responsible, he said, "If it wasn't for Frank, LaCaze never goes to that restaurant." Arresting a police officer for murdering another police officer had been one of the most difficult tasks of Rantz's long and distinguished career. "She's not a cop," he said. "She's trash."

**The** murder convictions and jury recommendations for death sentences were not the end. In the weeks following the trials, the lawyers and the judge stayed busy with the case. Judge Marullo had to order the Department of Corrections to conduct pre-sentence investigations of both defendants. He ordered what in Louisiana is called a lunacy hearing for LaCaze, at which evidence of his IQ could be presented. Frank filed a motion for a new trial. The motion was denied. She refused to be interviewed by a court-appointed psychiatrist.

On September 15, 1995, just six months after he shot Officer Ronnie Williams in the back of the head, a couple of sheriff's deputies dragged Rogers LaCaze into court. He wore a prison orange jumpsuit and chains on his wrists and ankles. Standing before the bench, LaCaze stared up at Judge Marullo. "You've got the wrong guy," he whined.

The judge peered down at LaCaze and told him that the evidence had been overwhelming. Then he said, "I hereby sentence you to death by lethal injection, and may God have mercy on your soul."

In October, Frank stood before the judge, clad and manacled the same as her partner in crime had been. She stood silent before the bench. The Vu and Williams families watched from the gallery.

Judge Marullo repeated what he'd said to LaCaze: "I sentence you to death by lethal injection, and may God have mercy on your soul."

Outside the courtroom, Chau Vu told a reporter, "Now my brother and sister and Ronnie can rest in peace, now that they see the persons who killed them have the death sentence."

# FORTY

**On** November 6, 1995, eleven-year-old Dwayne Manning was playing in his backyard with his dogs. The Mannings lived on a quiet street in New Orleans East. It was a working-class neighborhood, it was peaceful, nothing much ever happened.

Dwayne sat on the back steps and watched his dogs. They were fighting over something. They gripped it with their teeth. It was something they'd pulled from under the house, some kind of bone. Not a ham bone or a steak bone or anything like that. Whatever it was, it was much bigger than that. Dwayne stepped toward the dogs to get a better look.

Then he recognized what it was they were fighting over. He'd seen something like it in school. It was a spine. A human spine.

Dwayne bolted into the house to tell his dad.

Officer Warren Fitzgerald was working an overtime shift out of the 7th District when he got a call to respond to 7524 Michigan street. Until her recent convictions for three counts of first-degree murder, Antoinette Frank had lived at 7524 Michigan Street. It had also been the temporary home of her brother, Adam Frank, Jr., until he got word the cops were looking for him; and of her father, Adam Frank, Sr., until he disappeared in September 1993.

Officer Fitzgerald met with Dwayne's dad, Oscar Manning, who escorted the policeman into the backyard. Officer Fitzgerald took one look at what the dogs had been fighting over and called the command desk. The dogs had found more than a spine, and what they had found was definitely human.

Homicide detectives, crime scene techs, coroner's investigators, the 7th District brass—all converged on the house on Michigan Street. They stretched crime scene tape around the backyard and started searching.

Under the house, the police found a shallow grave filled with lime. Like archaeologists digging through the rubble of Pompeii, homicide detectives and evidence technicians sifted through the dirt and lime. They pulled out more bones: an arm, part of a rib cage, and a human skull. The skull had a jagged hole punched through it, a hole about the size of a bullet.

As word spread throughout the police department, few of the officers had any doubt about whose bones the dogs had dug up under Antoinette Frank's old house. The almost unanimous consensus was that they belonged to Adam Frank, Sr., who had not been seen or heard from in the more than two years since his daughter had strolled into the 7th District station and reported him missing. There was also very little disagreement about who put the bullet hole in Adam Sr.'s head and who scraped out a hole under the house for his final resting place. Conventional wisdom said it had been the work of Antoinette Frank.

Sgt. Dave Slicho, Frank and Williams's squad sergeant, was there when the bones were hauled out. For him, the lime in the grave was a dead giveaway. He says people in the country use lime when they bury animals. It keeps the smell down and speeds up decomposition. He points out that Antoinette Frank was from the country.

"She killed him," says former prosecutor Elizabeth Teel.

As expected, Franks's defense attorneys disagreed. A few days after the bones were uncovered, Robert Jenkins said, "With the whole climate surrounding Antoinette, of course there's going to be speculation about the bones, but she denies any knowledge of the skeleton."

Because Adam Frank, Sr., was an Army veteran, the coroner's office requested copies of his military dental records, but after a lengthy wait, the Army notified them that Frank's records had been among those destroyed a few years before when fire struck the military records archives center in St. Louis.

That left only DNA as a means of positively identifying the skeleton, but Frank, sitting in her jail cell on death row at St. Gabriel Women's Prison, refused to provide investigators with a DNA sample for comparison to DNA extracted from the bones found under her house.

"She is not charged in this investigation," Attorney Robert Jenkins said, "and it violates her constitutional right against self-incrimination."

But according to Caddo Parish assistant district attorney Hugo Holland, who specializes in the prosecution of Louisiana death penalty homicide cases, the Fifth Amendment right against self-incrimination doesn't apply to the gathering of biological evidence such as hair samples, blood samples, fingernail clippings, or DNA. "Those are Fourth Amendment issues," Holland says, referring to the constitutionally guaranteed protection against unreasonable searches and seizures.

Holland explains that the district attorney's office could serve Frank with either a D.A.'s subpoena or a grand jury subpoena, or the police could obtain a search warrant for Frank's person and remove a DNA sample from her even if they have to restrain her to get it. But, Holland says, the easiest way to obtain a sample of Frank's DNA would be to "have a guard walk into her cell and take her damned toothbrush." There would be many times more DNA material on Frank's toothbrush than is needed for testing. The same could be done with her hairbrush or sanitary napkins.

According to Holland, prison officials have a right to search prisoners, their belongings, and their cells whenever they want. They don't need a reason, and the inmates have no recourse. "There is no Fourth Amendment in a jail cell," Holland says.

Despite the ease with which they could force a DNA sample from Frank, the New Orleans district attorney has yet to do it.

Early in the investigation, the Orleans Parish Coroner's Office sought help from the Louisiana State University Department of Anthropology, specifically from noted forensic anthropologist Mary H. Manhein, who specializes in the reconstruction of decomposed human remains. But to this day, neither the police department, nor the district attorney's office, nor the coroner's office will discuss the case. The body found under Frank's house remains unidentified.

A former New Orleans police sergeant speculates that the police department has no reason to identify the body. "If it's her dad, it's just going to reopen the whole thing," he says. According to the former sergeant, the police department wants everyone to just forget about Antoinette Frank.

One person who is sure about the identity of the body found under Frank's house is Rogers LaCaze. In a letter from prison, he said, "Antoinette is crazy. Hell, she killed her own dad and buried him under her house."

**Since** late 1995, Antoinette Frank has spent twenty-three hours every day in a six-by-nine-foot prison cell at the Louisiana Correctional Institute for Women at St. Gabriel, Louisiana. But she hasn't been idle.

In the years since her conviction for murdering Ha and Cuong Vu and Ronnie Williams, information has surfaced—mainly from Frank herself—about the very strange relationship that existed between her and her father, information that suggests a possible motive, or at least an excuse, for Frank if she is ever officially accused of killing her dad. The new information is also her excuse for the triple murder at the Kim Anh restaurant and formed the basis for one of her appeals to the Louisiana Supreme Court.

In 2000, Frank petitioned the court, asking that she be granted, if not a new trial, at least a new penalty phase, which would give her a chance to escape her death sentence. Her appeal asserted that the trial judge should have provided state-funded expert witnesses to testify about her troubled past at the penalty phase of her trial.

Through a new set of attorneys, Frank claims that her father started raping her when she was nine years old, that he got her pregnant several times, and that he forced her to have abortions. In 2001, the Louisiana Supreme Court ordered Judge Marullo to consider evidence of mitigating circumstances. They asked him to decide if any circumstances existed that should have been considered during the penalty phase of Frank's trial, and to determine if Frank should have received state-funded assistance in presenting evidence of abuse and the resulting psychological damage. If so, Frank could get a new sentence.

At a series of hearings in 2002, Frank's attorneys presented expert witnesses who tried to buttress Frank's position that she killed Officer Williams and the Vus because she was suffering from post-traumatic stress disorder (PTSD), a condition she maintained she *inherited* from her father, whom she said suffered from it after his service in Vietnam, and a condition she *developed* because of her father, after she suffered through years of his sexual, physical, and emotional abuse.

In response, the state put Dr. George Seiden, a court-recognized expert on forensic psychiatry, on the stand. Dr. Seiden testified that Frank presented no indicators, other than her own unsupported claims, of sexual abuse, such as a history of abusive relationships or relationship instability. He said that, rather than become hyper-aggressive, female victims of abuse tend to put themselves in situations in which they can be abused again.

Dr. Seiden told Judge Marullo that his evaluation of the reported relationship between Frank and LaCaze indicated to him that it was Frank who appeared to be the more forceful one. "There was nothing to indicate that he was dominating her."

The state presented evidence that during her first few years in prison, Frank denied several times that she had ever suffered any abuse. According to one mental health expert, "She [Frank] can't remember anything she's ever done that she feels guilty about."

On the stand, Dr. Seiden called that statement extraordinary, one that he admitted he couldn't make about himself. His conclusion on the issue of abuse was that it either didn't happen, or if it did, Frank was psychologically resilient enough that it didn't affect the rest of her life. "Not all victims of abuse are scarred by it," the psychiatrist said. But, he added, "Even if we accept that the abuse occurred, there's no reason to believe it had anything to do with the crime."

On the subject of Frank's post-traumatic stress, Dr. Seiden said that although Adam Frank, Sr.'s reported behavior was consistent with PTSD, Antoinette's behavior was not. Among the many symptoms of the disorder that she did not report suffering from were hyper-vigilance, trouble sleeping, and loss of appetite.

Seiden said he agreed with the diagnosis of a psychiatrist who examined Frank in 1995 and again in 1999, that she did show symptoms of "Narcissistic Personality Disorder with anti-social features," things such as a lack of empathy toward others, a feeling of entitlement, rage, and manipulation in relationships. He said that someone suffering from that disorder responds to even mild criticism with rage. It is the same diagnosis many have made of Hitler and Stalin.

The psychiatrist who examined Frank in 1995 and again in 1999 found that she exhibited no signs of PTSD, a conclusion with which Dr. Seiden told the judge he agreed. Other than narcissistic personality disorder, Dr. Seiden said, "I see no symptoms of any other mental illness."

The state also presented evidence that Frank had refused the assistance of a state-funded psychologist who had offered to help her try to avoid the death penalty.

In December 2002, as soon as the lawyers finished their oral arguments, Judge Marullo ruled from the bench that Frank did not deserve another penalty phase. "She has refused the help of experts throughout the whole case," he told Frank's lawyers. "It would be ludicrous now for me to grant your motion."

**Like** his one-time lover and partner in crime, Rogers LaCaze also spends twenty-three hours of his day in the solitude of a tiny cell tucked away on death row. His cell is at the Louisiana State Penitentiary at Angola. LaCaze sees himself as Antoinette Frank's ultimate victim. "She was the one with the plan the whole time," he says. "It was right under my nose, and I couldn't smell it."

Despite the overwhelming evidence, including eyewitness testimony from Chau and Quoc Vu that LaCaze was inside the restaurant at the time of the shootings, his own taped confession, his brother's statement to police that Rogers admitted to the crime, and an eyewitness who puts him using Ronnie Williams's credit card less than forty-five minutes after the murders and three blocks from his brother's apartment where he was arrested, Rogers LaCaze continues to protest his innocence. "I didn't do this crime," he said in a letter from prison.

The police, the district attorney, the judge, the night cashier at the Chevron station, the manager of Mr. C's Pool Hall, even the victims ("The Vu people lied a lot," he says)—all are part of a far-reaching conspiracy, LaCaze says, designed to put him in prison and put him to death. Everyone, Lacaze contends, lied at his trial except him and his brother. He claims to be the victim of a corrupt criminal justice system and the target of a corrupt police department. The NOPD, he says, had to put him away because he knew too much about their illegal activities. "One of those police," LaCaze says, "when they came and picked me up across the river, used that credit card."

The reality is that the police didn't even know Ronnie Williams's credit card was missing until three weeks later when his widow got the bill. LaCaze executed her husband, then stuck her with a $15 tab.

In 2002, the Louisiana Supreme Court upheld LaCaze's conviction and death sentence, so while his lawyers dream up new appeals, LaCaze waits for the chemical cocktail that will end his life. He spends his time complaining about how unfair the criminal justice system is. He also writes a little poetry. One of his poems ends:

*So live, love, and laugh today as if it were your last,*
*think not about the future and forget your bad past,*
*just live.*

Glen Woods left the D.A.'s office in 2000 and now works exclusively in his private practice. In his office, he keeps a crime scene photo of Ha and Cuong Vu. "It's shocking the way they died," he says. The picture reminds him of the evil that exists in the world.

Elizabeth Teel is also in private practice, specializing in

environmental law. The LaCaze and Frank trials were the most traumatic of her career. "I'd be lying if I said it wasn't personal," she says.

Marco Demma retired—to work homicides. He retired from the New Orleans Police Department in 2003 and got a job with a sheriff's office in a neighboring parish. He heads their homicide unit and is still putting killers in jail. "Marco Demma could disarm Satan," Glen Woods says.

Sgt. Eddie Rantz retired in December 1997, after twenty-seven years on the job. Rantz loves a challenge. When he suggested he might like to become a lawyer, someone told him he'd never make it through law school. He graduated from Loyola University Law School and is now in private practice. Recently, he decided that he might like to seek public office. Someone told him he could never get elected . . .

The Vu family still owns and operates the Kim Anh restaurant in New Orleans East. Chau is married and has two children. She and Quoc still help their parents at the family businesses, which now include a Laundromat and a reception hall.

Mary Williams lives just outside New Orleans with her two sons, Christopher, fifteen and Patrick, nine. Christopher sometimes works as a busboy at the Vus' reception hall. Mary, Chau, Quoc, and Mrs. Vu remain close friends. They work a booth together every year at the New Orleans Jazz Fest, selling Vietnamese food.

As with the Vus, Mary's pain never goes away. It ebbs and flows like the tide. Sometimes it's bearable, sometimes it's not. In her mind, the image of her husband remains frozen. He's a big, strapping twenty-five-year-old in a sharp police uniform, with just a trace of dirt under his nails from working around the house. He's laughing, because he always laughed. He was a joker. That's just the way Ronnie was. Mary Williams often wonders how her life would be different if . . .

In his closing argument at LaCaze's trial, prosecutor

Glen Woods pointed across the courtroom at Rogers LaCaze and told the jury, "If Ronnie Williams had seen it coming, he'd have put this man out of his misery."

That's what should have happened, but it didn't. Instead, three good lives were taken and dozens of others tragically altered. All because of one bad cop. All because of Antoinette Frank. All because of a killer with a badge.